David Ricardo, James Bonar

Letters of David Ricardo to Thomas Robert Malthus, 1810-1823

David Ricardo, James Bonar

Letters of David Ricardo to Thomas Robert Malthus, 1810-1823

ISBN/EAN: 9783337016340

Printed in Europe, USA, Canada, Australia, Japan

Cover: Foto ©ninafisch / pixelio.de

More available books at **www.hansebooks.com**

LETTERS

OF

DAVID RICARDO

TO

THOMAS ROBERT MALTHUS

1810—1823

EDITED BY

JAMES BONAR
M.A. OXFORD, LL.D. GLASGOW

Oxford

AT THE CLARENDON PRESS

1887

CONTENTS.

PREFACE.

THE following Letters are printed for the first time from the original manuscripts, kindly lent for the purpose by Colonel Malthus, C.B. The representatives of Ricardo have been good enough to make search for the corresponding letters of Malthus, but without success.

The Collection covers the whole period of the friendship of the two men. What is of purely private interest (a very small portion) has, as a rule, been omitted. There is seldom any obscurity in the text; the handwriting of Ricardo is clear and good. The earlier letters have no envelopes. The breaking of the seal has frequently torn a page, and destroyed a word or two. In two cases we have nothing but the fragment of a letter. But fortunately the bulk of the series has reached us in a complete state.

These Letters were evidently known to Empson and MacCulloch, whose references to them are quoted in their proper place. Other letters of Ricardo, as well as his speeches in Parliament, are quoted here and there when they illustrate the text or fill up a gap. The Correspondence with J. B. Say is given at some length, as it is probably little known to English readers.

The Outline of Subjects will be found to contain only a bare sketch of the main positions taken up by Ricardo against Malthus in these Letters. It could not fairly be expanded into an account of both sides of the argument, for, when we are within hearing of only one of the disputants, we cannot with fairness believe ourselves to have the whole case before us. We cannot accept his statement of the terms of the discussion, for, though he had every desire to be just to his opponent, his cast of mind was so different that he can hardly be thought to have entered into his opponent's views with perfect sympathy [1].

[1] Cf. Letter LXXX, p. 200, cf. 236, etc.

These Letters indeed show on almost every page how completely the two economists differed in their point of view. Beginning in a deep mutual respect, their acquaintance with each other grew into a very close intimacy ; but it was the friendship of two men entirely unlike in mental character. Ricardo admits that he had been deeply impressed by the Essay on Population (p. 107), but thinks that Malthus is apt to miss the true subject of political economy, the inquiry into the distribution of wealth, and to confine himself to production, of which nothing can be made (pp. 111, 175); Malthus seems to his friend to have too strong a practical bias (p. 96); instead of reflecting on the general principles that determine (for example) the Foreign Exchanges, he tries to get light from Jamaica merchants and City bullion dealers (p. 3, cf. 12); he buries himself in temporary causes and effects instead of looking to permanent ones (p. 127); he gains his point by a definition instead of an argument (p. 237), and, perhaps through the same practical bias, he is too much absorbed in questions of his own College (p. 125), and not eager enough for political reform (pp. 151, 152). Malthus, Cambridge Wrangler and Haileybury Professor, was free from any academical bias in favour of abstract thinking ; he had in fact little of the typical University man except his love of boating (p. 158). Ricardo, a self-made and largely a self-educated man[1] (though he had neither the pride of the first nor the vanity of the second), had no traditions that were not mercantile, and made a large fortune on the Stock Exchange[2]. But, in his thinking, he was under no slavery to details ; he was even conscious of a strong theoretical bias (p. 96). He was fonder of 'imagining strong cases' to elucidate a principle, than of adducing actual incidents to establish it (pp. 164, 167). The very narrowness of his programme enabled him (as later it enabled Cobden and his school) to seem to exhaust all the

[1] See the obituary notice in Annual Register 1823, which appears (on comparison with MacCulloch's Preface to Ricardo's Works, p. xxxii) to have been written by James Mill. See also Prof. Bain's Life of James Mill, p. 210.
[2] He left £700,000. Gent. Mag. 1823.

difficulties of the subject, and dispose of them by plain straightforward proofs. Malthus, who had a less acute logical understanding, but saw more clearly the real breadth and complexity of the subject, seemed often more faltering, and less consistent with himself.

Ricardo agreed with his friend in looking, on the whole, at the bright side of things, and forecasting prosperity for England even in the dark days of Luddites and Six Acts (pp. 139, 141). They were, both of them, unready writers, partly from deference to each other's criticism (pp. 20, 23, 117, 125, 155, 159, 207),—partly, in Ricardo's case, from awkwardness in composition, where he was always, in his own opinion, the worse man of the two (pp. 104, 108, 145, 208),—partly because the obscurity of the subject was felt by them to be inconsistent with dogmatic certainty (pp. 111, 176, 181). But they are free in their criticism; they never dream of allowing it to affect their good temper (pp. 175, 240), and they are never afraid to confess mistakes (pp. 20, 184, 207, 231, etc.).

Personally, they agreed in enjoying society and travel, in loving 'law and order' and hating 'a row' (pp. 64, 208), and in being nowhere so happy as in their family circle, in Ricardo's case a patriarchally large one (p. 146). The robust health of Malthus was not shared by his friend (p. 140), but the latter had more of the qualities of a public man, and in the House of Commons he was by no means a silent member. Their range of interests was perhaps equally wide, though Ricardo's bent was to natural science as Malthus' to mathematics. In politics they were both in favour of Parliamentary Reform. Francis Place[1], writing in 1832 to a correspondent who had reproached Political Economists with hostility to reform, says that the study tends almost necessarily to political enlightenment, and points to Malthus, Mill, Ricardo, and others in confirmation. 'Mr. Malthus' (he says) 'was an aristocratic parson when he first published his Essay on Population . . . but in going

[1] Letter to George Rogers, 11th Jan. 1832, in the 'Place' Collection, British Museum.

on with his work and being obliged to study political
economy, his prejudices gave way before principles, and he
became the advocate so far as he dared of good government.
His work contains irrefragable arguments for universal
suffrage, which cannot be overlooked, but must be applied
by every reader who understands the subject; and there
are also in his work other indications of what you and
I should call liberal principles[1].' For myself, Place adds,
I have been 'a plain Republican for forty years;' James
Mill is 'as bad as myself.' As to Ricardo: 'He was one of
the most enlightened of reformers I ever knew; he was a man
who never concealed his opinions.' There is no doubt,
from all the evidence, what these opinions were. Ricardo
advocated a widely extended suffrage, frequent parliaments,
and especially secret voting. In his speeches in the House
of Commons, which are more than a hundred in number,
from the first on the 25th March, 1819, to the last on the
4th July, 1823, he speaks his mind plainly not only on the
Bank, the. Sinking Fund, the currency, agriculture, the
Poor Law, and the tariff, but on the reform of Parliament,
retrenchment, freedom of the press and right of public
meeting. His oratory seems in many respects to have
resembled that of Cobden. The arguments were given
with plain directness without elegance of diction; and they
were brought home by matter-of-fact similes from every-day
life or commercial experience. We know from Brougham
that his manner of speaking was earnest, modest, genial,
frank, and unaffected; and, as he only spoke on what he
knew, he was always heard with attention[2], though his
sentiments were unpalatable and he was usually in a
hopeless minority.

---

[1] The political philosophy of Malthus is described by the present editor at
some length in ' Malthus and his Work,' Book III.

[2] Brougham's testimony is the more valuable because he is by no means
a disciple or admirer of Ricardo as an Economist. ' Statesmen of the Time of
George III,' vol. ii. pp. 166 seq. For other authorities on the subject see
Joseph Garnier's life of Ricardo in Dict. de l'Écon. Polit., and Bain's Life of
Jas. Mill.

Bentham claimed to be the spiritual grandfather of
Ricardo[1], and Ricardo may have got his first thoughts on
Politics from him and Mill, as on Economics from Adam
Smith ; he may also have caught from Bentham his habit of
reasoning abstractly. But the arguments he uses on behalf
of his political opinions are such as to leave the impression
that he reached his politics through his political economy,
the former being only the latter from a different point of
view. He seems to construct his notion of a free government
on the lines of his notion of a free trade. When he takes
the unpopular side in the case of the Carliles[2], imprisoned for
blasphemous libel, he is not unfairly described by Wilberforce as simply 'carrying into more weighty matters those
principles of free trade which he has so successfully ex-
pounded' in other cases. His interest in popular education
seems to spring from the desire that our people may be
rightly equipped for industrial competition. He attends
a City dinner to the Spanish Minister at a time when the
European Powers are threatening Spain, and appeals to
the principle of Non-Intervention[3], thus anticipating the
Manchester School and applying *laissez faire* on the large
scale. He applies the same principles perhaps too abstractly
in the case of the Spitalfield Acts[4], which made the wages
of the silkweavers to be fixed by the Justices instead of
by the 'higgling of the market,' and in the case of the
Truck System[5], or payment of wages in kind ; but there was
much to justify his hostility to the first, and there was
Robert Owen's successful use of something very like the
Truck system in New Lanark to excuse his defence of the
second. He had a statesman's willingness to accept part
where he could not get the whole, and to welcome a
compromise rather than no progress at all. He would
not abolish the Corn Laws at a stroke, but would prepare
our agriculturists for the change by lessening the duty
on imports year by year till nothing was left but 10*s.*

---

[1] See note to Letter XXI. [2] March 26, 1823.
[3] Speech of March 18, 1823. [4] May 21, 1823, etc. [5] June 17, 1822.

a quarter, to remain as a 'countervailing duty' roughly equal in amount to the peculiar burdens of the British agriculturist[1]. Some of his opponents called him a 'mere theorist'; but this is a common taunt of men who cannot render a reason against men who can. Even his disciple MacCulloch thinks that his investigations were 'too abstract to be of much practical utility[2].' But in his own hands they were not so abstract that they were divorced from practice, or unmodified by the needs of each case. Such measures as he recommended in the House were of great practical utility, and have nearly all been embodied in subsequent legislation; yet he founded them all on certain general principles which in the order of his thinking were economical first and political afterwards. As far as politics are concerned, we find the principles abstract simply because they are not in our own day the principles most needed in legislation.

In short, Ricardo's thinking was abstract only in the sense in which Bentham's was so. They had arrived, by a different road, at the same political philosophy. Ricardo had a fixed idea of the individual as being logically prior to society; and the interest of the community only meant to him the interest of a large number of individuals, the collection as a whole having no qualities not possessed by each of the parts, and there being no spiritual bond. Nature (which means in this case theory instead of history) begins and ends with individuals; Nature made the individuals, and Man made the groups. Ricardo agreed with Bentham that 'the community is a fictitious Body, composed of individual persons who are considered as constituting, as it were, its Members. The interest of the community then is what? The sum of the interests of the several members who compose it[3].' We find Ricardo arguing: 'Let me know what the state of men's interests is, and I will tell you what measures they will recommend;' and 'that State

---

[1] April 29, cf. May 7, 1822.

[2] MacCulloch's 'Funding and Taxation,' Preface to 1st Ed. (1845).

[3] Bentham, 'Princ. of Morals and Legislation,' I, IV.

is most perfect in which all sanctions concur to make it the interest of all men to be virtuous,' in other words, to promote the general happiness [1]. Now, to consider human beings as first and chiefly separate from one another and having a separate self-interest which rules their action, is certainly to reason abstractly. But this abstract reasoning of the Philosophical Radicals is due, in the case of the Economists among them, more to Adam Smith than to Bentham. Most of them, like Ricardo, had got not only their first economics but their first lessons in thinking, from the 'Wealth of Nations.' The 'Wealth of Nations' bore the stamp of that Individualism which we usually associate with Rousseau. Its author had written, seventeen years before, a book in which he gave almost exclusive consideration to the common bond that unites man to man, the power one man has of putting himself by thought in the place of another, or (in a wide sense of the word) to sympathy. There is no need to suppose that Adam Smith had forgotten or recanted the 'Moral Sentiments;' but it is certainly the case that in the later and greater work, which became the text-book of Political Economy, he deliberately takes up another point of view, and presents men as dominated by private interest. With every allowance for his frequent qualifications ('upon the whole,' 'in many respects,' etc.), there is no doubt that he there considers ' the natural effort which every man is continually making to better his own condition' as a principle of growth and health which owes little or nothing to State or Society, but is continually transforming them and bringing good out of their evil. He is fully aware how industry in all its forms has been affected by the government and civilization of a people; but he regards industry itself, or the commercial ambition of the industrious classes, as more potent still. As far as industrial progress is concerned, he would have said with Bentham that Nature begins and ends with individuals; in matters of trade he has no confidence in associations of men, even when they are

[1] Ricardo's Wks. p. 554 (from ' Observations on Parliamentary Reform ').

voluntary. To him, the really beneficent association is that unintended and unpreventible organization resulting from the division of labour, the separation of trades, and the uncontrolled movements of commercial ambition on the part of individual men. He is careful to say that Political Economy is not Politics[1]; but he insists that all political restraints and preferences must be taken away from industry, and 'the obvious and simple system of natural liberty' will 'establish itself of its own accord.' It is not surprising that this lesson in individualism was learned by his successors without the cautions with which the teacher would have surrounded it. The pupils unconsciously argued as if political individualism was part and parcel of economical principles, for it certainly seemed so in the one book of their teacher that they had been led to study; and, when Bentham made self-interest a leading principle of politics, Ricardo, to follow him, needed only to make clear to himself the underlying political basis of his economical ideas. In Malthus, economical individualism is held in check by a strong devotion to the principle of nationality, as well as by a wide range of philosophical and general interests. But to Ricardo political economy is all in all; the ruling principles of all his thinking are determined for him by the economical; and the result is individualism in politics as well as in political economy. The animosity of his critics is perhaps as often due to their strong dislike of this political philosophy underlying his doctrines, and derived through Adam Smith from Rousseau, as to any real or supposed abstractness of the doctrines themselves.

Ricardo's political work has therefore the merits and the defects of the theory of individualism and policy of *laissez faire*, which crowned its achievements with the Repeal of the Corn Laws and Navigation Acts. John Stuart Mill, who was bred an individualist, has left us in his writings a faithful reflection of the change which has passed over English politics and English economics in the course of his

---

[1] B. IV, ch. IX, middle, p. 307. I (McCulloch's ed.).

lifetime, and which he himself welcomed with some misgivings. We have ceased to believe that the removal of
obstacles is enough to secure the highest good either in
government or in industry. But we must not deny that
the Manchester School and its predecessors were indis-
pensable in their own day.

It is sometimes said that in addition to the faults of
his school, Ricardo had flaws of his own which were due
to a certain strong bias of self-interest[1]. We might answer
that his arguments must none the less stand or fall by their
own logic. But there is no reason to suppose any bias in
Ricardo except his peculiar character of mind and cast of
thought. He had the intellectual interest of a reasonable
man in getting the right instead of the wrong answer to
a difficult question; and his selfish interest as a member
of the 'propertied' classes was not clear enough to be
a snare to him. 'It would puzzle a good accountant' (he
says in the House[2]) 'to make out on which side my interest
predominated; I should find it difficult myself from the
different kinds of property which I possess (no part funded
property) to determine the question.' He could be chivalrous
and even Quixotic on occasion. His best political friends[3]
thought he was Quixotic when he proposed to levy a
high property tax to pay off the National Debt: 'I should
contribute any portion of my own property for the
attainment of this great end if others would do the same[4].'
There was chivalry in his praise of Cobbett's Letter to
the Luddites[5]; Cobbett had given him abuse unmixed
with any drop of generosity. We may therefore look in
vain in Ricardo for any feeling of antipathy to landlords or
any other body of men, though he spoke, as in duty bound,

---

[1] E. g. by Held, 'Sociale Geschichte Englands,' article Ricardo, and by
Western in the House June 11, 1823, more coarsely by Cobbett in passages
quoted in Note to Letter LXIX, and many others.

[2] June 11, 1823, in reply to Western.

[3] E. g. Grenfell, March 11, 1823.

[4] Feb. 21, 1823, etc.

[5] May 30, 1823. He adds a crumb of criticism: Cobbett underestimated
the effect of machinery in throwing men out of work.

against landlords, bank directors, and all classes of mono-
polists, whenever they stood in the way of urgent reforms.
Like other men, he not improbably had a lurking partiality
for what had been the main business of his working life.
But in his writings and speeches he gives us not feelings
but arguments, and arguments that cannot be dismissed
as feelings in disguise.

In the purely economical works there is more of abstract
theory than the author is ever fully aware. Not only did
he as an individualist habitually regard men as separate
competing atoms, and the desire of wealth as the permanent
and dominant motive of men [1]; but he made his general
statements too absolute. He sometimes guarded himself by
saying (as he does in these Letters): What I am layig
down is true over any considerable period of time ; the
causes to which I point are permanent ; I allow that other
causes may prevail for short intervals ; temporary causes
may seem to overrule the permanent ones ; but I look to the
final settlement. Nevertheless, he admitted more than once
in the course of his career that he had stated the permanent
causes too absolutely. The doctrine of Value is first presented
by him as extremely simple,—the value of a thing depends
on the labour employed in producing it. Then, as we go
on, we find this is only true of 'the early stages of society
before much machinery or durable capital is used,' while it
is not meant to be true, even there, of objects that have
a 'fancy' value, due purely to their scarcity. Next, we are
told that in modern times the relative value of two things
is affected by the proportions in which fixed capital and
circulating enter into their production ; if fixed capital enters
more into one than into another, then a rise of wages will
lower the value of the first, for it will lower the rate of profits,
and, as there are more profits concerned in the first, the value
of the first will fall in relation to the other. This is not all ;
—if two things are produced with a like amount of fixed

---

[1] E. g. 'The greatest advantage will be sought and obtained at all times
by the employer of capital.' Evidence before Lords' Resumption Committee,
1819, Ques. and Answ. 75.

capital, yet, if the durability of the capital is different, there will be more labour where there is less durability, and more profits where there is more durability; the things produced by the more durable fixed capital will be lowered in value by a rise in wages, which lowers the rate of profit; and so on, *mutatis mutandis.* In short, value is affected not only by labour, but by the wages of labour. To these concessions we may add the important change of view, which (as we know from these Letters) made MacCulloch tremble for the Ark of his Covenant[1]; we had heard nothing at first but the praise of machinery as lowering prices and increasing the general wealth; now we are reminded that the invention of it may for the time cause serious injury to the working classes[2].

It is not difficult for men living two generations after Ricardo, and having (as he himself expressed it[3]) 'all the wisdom of their ancestors and a little more into the bargain,' to point out many unjustified assumptions, many ambiguous terms, and even many wavering utterances, in Ricardo's 'Principles,' in spite of their appearance of severe logic. The author's detached practical pamphlets were in those respects far more powerful than this volume of imperfectly connected essays on general theory. The flattering importunities of friends had induced an unsystematic writer to attempt a systematic treatise[4]. The cardinal doctrine, that of Value, is applied to only one class of cases, and, even to that, with serious modifications. It was left for later economists, like Jevons in this country, and Menger and Böhm Bawerk in Germany, to take up the task of giving a theory of value that will embrace all cases of it, not excluding those objects that possess a value 'wholly independent of the quantity of labour originally necessary to produce them, and varying with the varying wealth and inclinations of those who are desirous to possess them[5].'

---

[1] Letter LXXVI.

[2] Ch. xxxi. of Pol. Ec. and Tax. ; a chapter added in the 3rd ed., 1821.

[3] Speech of 9th May, 1822.

[4] This had been acutely observed (without aid from these Letters) by a writer in the Harvard 'Journal of Economics,' July, 1887.

[5] Ricardo, Pol. Ec. and Tax. Sect. I.

Malthus has left a clear statement of the points at issue between Ricardo and himself in the Quarterly Review for January, 1824. He contended against Ricardo that (1) Quantity of Labour is not the chief cause of Value, but (2) 'Supply and Demand' are more truly so described, while (3) Competition of Capital, and not fertility of the soil, determines the rate of profits. But, in regard to the first, he hardly gives Ricardo sufficient credit for his large concessions. In regard to the second, he does not realize that supply and demand are vague terms which can only be made definite by a theory of value itself. In regard to the third position, if fertility of soil be translated productiveness of the staple industry, Ricardo's view seems nearer the truth than his own. The inadequacy of the whole discussion on this third head is largely due to the fact that economists had not then been pushed by Socialism into a thorough investigation of Profits and Interest. They were content to borrow these ideas from every-day commercial life, and treat them as given ultimate facts needing no explanation. They therefore never fully accomplished the very first task of Political Economy, to state the facts as they are, and analyse into its fundamental laws the existing industrial system of modern nations. Still less did they fulfil its second task, to estimate the relation of the industrial system to the larger social and political body in which it lives and moves and has its being. The peculiar wants and motives of an individual people, changing, as they do, with the growth of civilization, must be viewed in their effects upon the production and distribution of the national wealth, if the truth about the latter is to be fully known. It is because the older economists did not attempt this that their discussions, carried on even by their most eminent representative men, seem to later readers superficial and unreal. But in their Economics, as in their Politics, they had their own work and not ours to do ; and we must not blame them for not answering questions that have only very recently occurred to ourselves.

OUTLINE OF SUBJECTS.

In only two cases do the letters of this collection form groups that have a subject of their own not discussed at any length in the other letters. Letters I to XIV are the only ones that discuss at any length the influence of the Depreciation of the Currency on the Foreign Exchanges. Letters LXXVIII to LXXXVIII are the only ones that so discuss the Measure of Value. After these the nearest approach to continuity is perhaps in Letters LXXI to LXXVII, when Over-production is the chief subject. But the discussion of Rent, Wages and Profits is not conducted by chapters as in a book ; it follows the course of conversations which were not recorded, and obeys suggestions that are given in replies lost to us. We cannot hope to make the propositions on these three heads fall into a consecutive logical series.

The following analysis of the letters is not meant to be exhaustive. Ricardo's opinions on the Bank of England (XXXV, etc.) and on the East India College (XL, etc.), for example, will not be found in it. It is simply a statement of the chief economical arguments.

In the early letters the correspondence turns chiefly on matters made prominent at the time (1810 seq.) by the Bullion Committee and Ricardo's own pamphlet, 'The High Price of Gold Bullion.' Though this pamphlet did not appear in its separate form till early in 1810, the matter of it had been published by Ricardo in a series of letters to the 'Morning Chronicle' beginning in September, 1809. These letters brought their author into public notice, and they seem to have led Malthus to seek his acquaintance. The earliest letters (of which Letter I in this collection was clearly not the first of the whole correspondence) were naturally on the subjects that first brought the two men together.

Ricardo's main positions as against Malthus are as follows :—

1. The amount of the currency of a nation is determined for it not simply by its size and population but by the

nature and extent of its trading transactions; and yet, when these elements are given, the currency of one nation will stand to the currency of another in some ascertainable normal proportion, to alter which is to alter the relative value of the currencies affected (VI, VII, X).

2. Such events as a bad harvest, a change in articles of consumption or the transmission of a subsidy abroad, will, by altering the relative value of our currency, produce effects on the exchanges which, apart from their own specific remedy, are permanent, not transitory (I, VII, X).

3. An increase in the amount of gold and silver in a country will lead to an increased use of these metals for general purposes rather than to a proportionate fall in their value, there (II, III).

4. An increase in the value of a nation's exports and imports may involve no increase of its wealth or its capital, but may be due to a mere change from one set of articles of consumption to another, or to a carrying trade with foreign capital (IV).

5. In any case, such an increase is not the cause, but the effect of a change in the currency; it is a sign that money is going from where it is cheap to where it is dear (IV, VI, IX, cf. XII and XVII), and the Exchanges are an accurate measure of the difference (VII).

6. There has certainly been an increase of wealth in our own country in recent years, but it has not necessarily been accompanied with an increased rate of profits (V, cf. XX).

In Letters XV to XXI the following are the chief propositions :—

1. Restrictions on the importation of corn by keeping up the price of necessaries have a tendency to lower profits (XV), unless, indeed, they are followed by a great reduction of capital (XVI, XVII).

2. The only cause of permanently high or low profits is the facility of procuring necessaries, for on that mainly depends the rate of wages (XVI, XVIII, XIX, XX, XXI, cf. V, and for qualification LXXIX, LXXX).

3. Other causes, such as bad harvests, new taxation, changes in demand, or excessive accumulation, are merely temporary (XX, XXI. Cf. Ricardo's Pol. Econ. and Tax., ch. vi. ' On Profits ').

4. Improvements in agriculture or machinery by increasing productiveness permanently increase profits (XX, cf. V and XXIII).

To these may be added—

5. Consumption and accumulation equally promote demand, and are both of them ineradicable tendencies of our nature, the one adding to our enjoyments, the other to our power (XIX).

6. Accumulation increases not only production, but consumption (XXI).

7. It is worth while to establish the truth of a principle, even if we cannot establish its utility (XXI).

In Letters XXIII to LXVIII, and in LXXVIII to LXXX, the positions are as follows:—

1. By importing cheap foreign corn the public saves the whole difference in price (XXIII, XXIV).

2. It must be allowed that the prices of articles, besides varying with the amount of necessary labour bestowed on them, vary with the value of their raw material (XXV).

3. Apart from changes in the currency, a rise in the price of corn and a fall in the corn wages of labour, would be a contradiction (XXVI).

4. It follows from the principle of Population that the rate, as distinguished from the amount, of agricultural production, grows not greater, but less, when the increase of population drives agriculture to the cultivation of poorer soils (XXVII, XXVIII, cf. XLIX).

5. This means that the whole cost in corn will be greater in proportion to the whole produce of corn, and, though the whole cost in money may be less in proportion to the whole produce in money, the rate of profits from farming will fall (XXIX).

6. A tax on home corn raises prices twice over, and should be accompanied by a countervailing duty, not necessary in other cases (XXIX).

7. In order of time, the increased price of corn comes first, and the costly cultivation second, but this increase of farmers' profits may be due to a fall in general profits that is itself caused by the increased price of corn (XXIX).

8. The progress of wealth has a tendency to lower profits and increase rent (XXIX).

9. Mere increase in quantity of corn will not prevent

increase in price if the numbers of consumers have increased in equal or greater proportion. So it will be one day in America (XXX).

10. A rise in the price of corn will not be followed by a rise in the price of other commodities, but by a fall in profits (XXXI, XXXIV, XXXV).

11. An addition of rich land to our island would reduce the price of corn by reducing the cost of raising the total supply of corn; and it would not raise the value of manufactured goods (XXXII).

12. High prices, whether caused by depreciation of money or by difficulty of production, are not a public benefit; in the first case, they are a cause of distress, especially to the working classes; in the second, they are a sign but not a cause of prosperity (XXXIII, XXXIV).

13. Facility of production includes skill and appliances as well as fertility of soil, and in that sense, when suddenly introduced in a fertile country, it would for some time extinguish rent (XXXVI).

14. There is no real distinction between productiveness of industry and productiveness of capital; and in the progress of society both of them will diminish, and rents will increase (XXXVI).

15. Wages do not rise when labour is productive unless the productiveness of the labour gives rise to a new capital that demands new labour (XXXVII).

16. There can be no such demand for new labour unless there is a reduction in the value of food (XXXVII).

17. The only permanent cause of diminished demand for capital is the increased price of food (XXXVIII).

18. Low prices are not necessarily a discouragement to production (XXXIX).

19. The need of cultivating less productive soils is the cause of higher nominal and lower real wages (XLII), and it is the only cause in constant and permanent operation (XLVIII, cf. LXIX).

20. Profits depend on wages; wages on the supply and demand of labour, and on the cost of the labourers' necessaries (XLIX).

21. Profits will therefore rise if the last are easily produced, unless through stationariness of population demand for labour has increased (L).

22. In two lands with equal capital and equal population, but with different fertility of soil, profits would differ in favour of the more fertile (L).

23. The rate of interest is no sure indication of the rate of profits; and a low rate of interest may co-exist with a low rate of wages and a high rate of profits (LXIII).

24. Profits cannot be said to depend on ' the proportion which capital bears to labour,' for, where profits were lowest, most capital would be needed to produce a given return, and, where highest, least, in proportion (LI).

25. By a rise in the value of money it is possible (though not probable) that a reduced cost of labour, materials, and machinery might be followed by an increase instead of a reduction, in their money value (LXIII).

26. A dearth may increase profits and wealth by making labour cheap (LXIII).

27. Free trade in corn may increase the amount of profits more than a policy of Restriction may increase the amount of Rents (LXVII, cf. LXX).

28. Rent is always a transfer, and never a creation of wealth (LIII, LXVIII).

29. There cannot be two rates of profit at the same time in the same country (LXXVIII), nor under free trade could there be a very different rate in different countries, the cost of necessaries and therefore the rate of wages being brought nearly to a level, allowance being made for differences between one country and another in regard to the standard of living (LXXIX). It seems impossible that under free trade a fertile country, unless agriculture were its sole and only industry, and its capital were small, would long continue to sell its corn at the high prices of its less favoured rivals; the prices would fall to cost price (LXXX).

In Letter LXV, and in Letters LXIX to LXXVII, the positions are as follows :—

1. Natural Price should not be described as depending, like Market Price, on Supply and Demand, for it can never permanently fall below or rise above the expenses of production (LXV).

2. A universal over-production is impossible (LXXII, LXXVII), and a glut of particular articles may be cured by a cessation in the production of those articles (LXXII); a ' superior genius ' might so lay out our capital even now, that all might be prosperous (LXXIII).

3. It is not demand, but supply, which regulates value, and supply is itself determined by comparative cost of production (LXXIII, LXXIV).

4. If all labour and capital were devoted to production of necessaries, there might then be an over-supply or general glut, of them; but in no other case is such a glut possible (LXXIV, LXXVII).

5. Over-production tends to cure itself by destroying profits, and thereby removing the producer's motive for production. But production could not go on when this point had been reached, and therefore the over-production could not last (LXXVI).

6. The remedy would be not the greater consumption of non-producers, but the payment of lower wages, which means the securing of higher profits by the producers. When wages are excessive, the labourers are the unproductive consumers, and the employers who pay them are thereby causing instead of curing the over-production (LXXVI, LXXVII).

7. A diminished demand for labour may mean, not the employment of fewer men, but the payment of lower wages (LXXVII).

In Letters LXXVIII to LXXXVIII the positions are:—

1. It is better to take, as a Measure of Value, some foreign commodity [like gold], the cost of producing which is nearly invariable, than to estimate either by the amount of labour or by the amount of corn or of other goods generally that will be purchased by the article measured (LXXVII, LXXVIII).

2. There is nothing in the said labour which fits it to be a better measure of value than anything else; but, on the contrary, to use it as a measure is to involve ourselves in paradoxes (LXXXIII, LXXXV to LXXXVIII).

3. There cannot be an absolute or universal measure of value, for there is no uniformity in the conditions under which commodities are produced, the time taken and the proportion and durability of the capital employed being, for example, very different (LXXXIV).

LETTERS OF DAVID RICARDO

TO

THOMAS ROBERT MALTHUS.

I.

MY DEAR SIR,   STOCK EXCHANGE, 25th Feb., 1810.

I HAVE just time, after a very busy day, to tell you that I will endeavour to get Mr. Mushet[1] to meet you at my house at breakfast on Sunday morning. At any rate I shall expect you, and, if Mushet is engaged, I shall be able to tell you whether he will meet us on Monday or Tuesday in the City. He is exceedingly obliging, and would I am sure not mind trouble if he could contribute to throw light on the subject of exchanges, yet I think he will not be inclined to publish anything under his own name as he gave great offence to the higher powers on a former occasion.

You have clearly stated the point of difference now between us; I think we never so well understood each other before. There are some causes which operate on the exchange which are in their nature of transitory duration; there are others which have a more permanent character. If we agree that a change of taste in one country for the commodities of the other,—and the transmission of a subsidy will produce certain effects on the exchange,—the only question between us is as to their

---

[1] Robert Mushet of the Mint. He published 'An Enquiry into the Effects produced on the National Currency and Rates of Exchange by the Bank Restriction Bill' in this very year 1810.

B

duration. I am of opinion that they will operate for a very considerable time and that in fact recourse is not had to bullion but as a last resort.

I cannot believe that you give a correct account of your habits of application any more than you did of your memory when I last saw you. From all my observations I should have been led to the very opposite conclusions from those which you have formed; and I believe most of your friends would be of my opinion. When you have once fairly begun, I expect that you will advance at a giant's pace.

I beg you to remember me kindly to Mrs. Malthus.

I am, my dear Sir,

Yours very truly,

DAVID RICARDO.

II.

MY DEAR SIR,   STOCK EXCHANGE, 22 *March*, 1810.

Mrs. Ricardo is expecting Mrs. Malthus to accompany her on Friday next to Knyvett's concert, and will, I am sure, be very much disappointed at the information which I am to give her that she will not be able to accompany you to town. I will not however quite give up all hopes of seeing her.

You must positively not think of leaving us before Tuesday. I have engaged several of your friends to meet you at dinner on Monday, and I not only advance my own claims but those of Mr. Wishaw[1], Mr. Sharp[2], Mr. Tennant[3], and Mr. Dumont[4].

---

[1] John Whishaw, of Lincoln's Inn, the editor of Mungo Park's 'Life and Travels' (1815, etc.): see Edin. Rev., Feb. 1815; Brougham's 'Statesmen in Time of George III,' ed. 1855, i. 369.

[2] Richard Sharp, called 'Conversation Sharp,' author of 'Letters and Essays in Prose and Verse' (1834), member of the Bullion Committee.

[3] Probably Smithson Tennant, the chemist.

[4] P. E. L. Dumont of Geneva, the friend of Mirabeau and Romilly, best known as the admirer of Bentham, whose works he brought out in French as

I have been making enquiries concerning a bullion merchant. I find that the trade is mostly carried on by a class of people not particularly scrupulous in their modes of getting money, and I am told that they would not be very communicative, particularly on the subject of their *exports*. There are however some well-informed merchants who know a great deal of the trade without themselves being actively engaged in it, to whom I hope I shall be able to introduce you.

I do not admit that if you were to double the medium of exchange it would fall to half its former value, not even if you were also to double the quantity of metal which was the standard of such medium. The consumption would increase in consequence of its diminished value, and the fall of its value would be regulated precisely by the same law as the fall in the value of indigo, sugar, or coffee.

Mr. Mushet will dine with us on Sunday. What do you think of Mr. Vansittart's financial talents?

Yours very truly,

DAVID RICARDO.

NOTE.—Speaking in the House of Commons on Agricultural Distress, on May 7, 1822, Ricardo gives an illustration which bears on some points in the foregoing and following letters : ' Suppose my own case. I am possessed of a considerable quantity of land, the whole unburthened with a single debt. Now according to the honourable member (Mr. Attwood) I and the tenants on that land would have only been injured to the amount of the increase which the change in the value of money has made in the burthen of taxation; but we are in point of fact injured much more.' ' The superabundant supply' has caused a sinking in the value of corn greater than in proportion to the additional quantity itself. To understand why, take the case of a commodity introduced for the first time, say a particular kind of superfine cloth : ' If 10,000 yards of this cloth

a labour of love. See Bentham's Works, ed. Bowring, vol. x. pp. 184-5. Like Whishaw, Sharp, and Tennant, he was a member of the ' King of Clubs.' See following letter.

were imported, under such circumstances, many persons would be
desirous of purchasing it, and the price consequently would be
enormously high. Suppose this quantity of cloth to be doubled;
the aggregate value of the 20,000 yards would be much. more
considerable than the aggregate value of the 10,000 yards, for the
article would still be scarce and therefore in great demand. If
the quantity of cloth were to be again doubled, the effect would
still be the same, for, although each particular yard of the 40,000
would fall in price, the value of the whole would be greater than
that of the 20,000. But, if they went on in this way increasing
the quantity of the cloth until it came within the reach of the
purchase [*sic*] of every class in the country, from that time any
addition to its quantity would diminish the aggregate value. This
argument would apply to corn. Corn is an article which is
necessarily limited in its consumption, and, if you went on increasing it in quantity, its aggregate value would be diminished
beyond that of a smaller quantity. I make an exception in favour
of money. If there were only £100,000 in this country, it would
answer all the purposes of a more extended circulation; but, if the
quantity were increased, the value of commodities would alter
only in proportion to the increase, because there is no necessary
limitation of the quantity of money [wanted].' (Cf. Letter III,
p. 3.) So on June 12th he says: ' Quantity regulates the value
of everything,' though it is also true (he says in a speech of
May 9, 1822) ' that the price of every commodity is constituted
by the wages of labour and the produce [*sic*] of stock.'

III.

                              STOCK EXCHANGE, 24 *March*, 1810.

MY DEAR SIR,

I have left you quite free for Friday, but I regret
that your engagements will not conveniently allow you
to come to us on that day. We shall expect you on
Saturday morning. I hope Mrs. Malthus' visit will not be
deferred longer than the next meeting of the King of Clubs [1].

It appears to me that you ascribe the difference in the

---

[1] See note at the end of this letter.

variations of price which would probably be the effect of doubling the quantity of coffee, sugar, or indigo, on [the] one hand, or of doubling the quantity of the precious metals on the other, to a wrong cause. Coffee, sugar, and indigo are·commodities for which, although there would be an increased use if they were to sink much in value, still, as they are not applicable to a great variety of new purposes, the demand would necessarily be limited; not so with gold and silver. These metals exist in a degree of scarcity, and are applicable to a great variety of *new* uses; the fall of their price, in consequence of augmented quantity, would always be checked, not only by an increased demand for those purposes to which they had before been applied, but to the want of them for entirely new employments. If they were in sufficient abundance, we might even make our tea-kettles and saucepans of them. It is to this essential difference between these commodities, and not to the circumstance of one of them being employed as a circulating medium, that I should attribute the different effects which would follow from the augmentation of their quantity. In any point of view however I do not see how it bears materially on the question between us, namely whether the precious metals are frequently resorted to for the payment of debts between countries when no disturbance has taken place in the amount or proportion of the currency.

I wonder as you do that the stocks have not felt the effects of Mr. Vansittart's vigorous system. The delay which has taken place in creating new stock, the good news from abroad, and, above all, the want of refléction in the mass of stockholders may be considered as the cause.

Ever truly yours,
DAVID RICARDO.

NOTE.—' The King of Clubs' is described in the Life of Sir James Mackintosh, (by his son,—2nd ed. 1836), vol. i. p. 137

(under date 1800) : 'As an agreeable rallying point in addition
to the ordinary meetings of a social circle, a dinner-club
(christened " The King of Clubs " by Mr. Robert Smith
[Bobus, brother of Sydney Smith]), was founded by a party at
his [Mackintosh's] house, consisting of himself [Mackintosh]
and the five following gentlemen, all of whom still survive :
—Mr. Rogers, Mr. Sharp, Mr. Robert Smith, Mr. Scarlett, and
Mr. John Allen.   To these original members were afterwards
added the names of many of the most distinguished men of the
time ; and it was with parental pride and satisfaction that he
received intelligence some time after of their " being compelled to
exclude strangers and to limit their numbers, so that in what way
' The King of Clubs ' eats, by what secret rites and institutions
it is conducted, must be matter of conjecture to the ingenious
antiquary, but can never be regularly transmitted to posterity by
the faithful historian." '—The biographer adds in a note that the
Club was suddenly dissolved in the year 1824.   Some of the most
distinguished members are enumerated, among them Ricardo (l. c.
p. 138 n.).   To judge by a letter of Mackintosh to Sharp on 29th
June, 1804, the Club at that date included (besides the writer and
his correspondent) only Sydney Smith, Scarlett, Boddington, the
poet Rogers, Whishaw, and Horner (Mack. Life, vol. i. 209).   The
time of meeting seems to have been the first Saturday of every
month.   See below Letter XLIV, but cf. XLIII.   Add Memoirs
of Horner, i. 193, under date April 1802, and Holland's Memoir
of Sydney Smith i. 91, &c.

IV.

MY DEAR SIR,   LONDON, 10 *Aug.*, 1810.

On my return to London, after a short excursion to
Tunbridge Wells, I found your obliging letter. . . . On
further reflection I am confirmed in the opinion which I
gave with regard to the effect of opening new markets
or extending the old.   I most readily allow that since the
war not only the nominal but the real value of our
exports and imports has increased ; but I do not see how

this admission will favour the view which you take of the subject.

England may have extended its carrying trade with the capital of other countries. Instead of exporting sugar and coffee direct from Guadaloupe and Martinique to the continent of Europe, the planters in those colonies may first export them to England, and from England to the continent. In this case the list of our exports and imports will be swelled without any increase of British capital. The taste for some foreign commodity may have increased in England at the expense of the consumption of some home commodity. This would again swell the value of our exports and imports, but does not prove a general increase of profits nor any material growth of prosperity.

I am of opinion that the increased value of commodities is always the effect of an increase either in the quantity of the circulating medium or in its power, by the improvements in economy [in] its use [*sic*][1],—and is never the cause[2]. It is the diminished value, I mean nominal value, of commodities, which is the great cause of the increased production of the mines; but the increased nominal value of commodities can never call money into circulation. It is certainly an effect and not a cause. I am writing in a noisy place; you must therefore excuse all blunders. I must offer the same apology for my two half sheets[3]. I did not like to copy the first half over again.

With best compliments to Mrs. Malthus, I remain,

Yours very sincerely,

DAVID RICARDO.

---

[1] The same phrase occurs in Appendix to ' High Price of Bullion ' (Ricardo's Works, p. 297) etc.

[2] Malthus regarded the change in the currency as in some cases the effect (and not the cause) of a change in trade. See references under Letters VI, XII.

[3] Fastened with wax at one corner.

V.

MY DEAR SIR,   STOCK EXCHANGE, 17 *Aug.*, 1810.

... I cannot deny myself the pleasure of accepting your kind invitation for Saturday next. I will be with you at the usual hour.

That we have experienced a great increase of wealth and prosperity since the commencement of the war, I am amongst the foremost to believe; but it is not certain that such increase must have been attended by increased profits, or rather an increased rate of profits, for that is the question between us. I have little doubt however that for a long period, during the interval you mention[1], there has been an increased rate of profits, but it has been accompanied with such decided improvements of agriculture both here and abroad, for the French Revolution was exceedingly favourable to the increased production of food, that it is perfectly reconcileable to my theory. My conclusion is that there has been a rapid increase of capital, which has been prevented from showing itself in a low rate of interest by new facilities in the production of food. I quite agree that an increased value of particular commodities occasioned by demand has a tendency to occasion an increased circulation, but always in consequence of the cheapness of some other commodities. It is therefore their cheapness which is the immediate cause of the introduction of additional money.

I have not been home since I received your letter. I will look at the passage you refer me to in Adam Smith[2], and will consider of the other matters in your letter, so as to be prepared to give you my theory when we meet.

---

[1] Probably 1793 to 1810. See Malthus' Pol. Econ. (1820), p. 324, etc.

[2] Probably Wealth of Nations (McCulloch's ed., 1863) I. xi. 95. 1, where the precious metals are said to be especially useful in the case of a roundabout trade of consumption. Cf. Edinb. Rev. Feb. 1811, p. 362.

The facts you have extracted from Wetenhall's tables are curious [1], and are hardly reconcileable to any theory. I attribute many of them to the state of confusion into which Europe has been plunged by the extent and nature of the war; and it would be quite impossible to reason correctly from them without calculating what the state was of the real as well as the computed exchange during the periods referred to. Pray make my best respects to Mrs. Malthus, and believe me,

Truly yours,

DAVID RICARDO.

VI.

DEAR SIR,

I lose no time in answering your obliging letter and endeavouring as far as lies in my power to remove the very few objections which prevent us from being precisely of the same opinion on the subject of money and the laws which regulate its value in the countries which have constant commercial intercourse with each other. I have no view in this discussion but that which you have avowed, the circulation of truth; if therefore I should fail to convince you, and you should express your opinions in print, it is immaterial to me whether you mention my name or not. I trust you will do that which shall most fully tend to establish the just principles of the science.

There does not appear to me to be any substantial difference between bullion and any other commodity as far as regards the regulation of its value and the laws which determine its exportation or importation. It is true that bullion, besides being a commodity useful in the arts, has been adopted universally as a measure of value and a medium of exchange; but it has not on that account been taken out of the list of commodities. A new use has been found for a

---

[1] Wetenhall's 'Course of Exchange.' See note to Letter XI.

particular article; consequently there has been an increased
demand for it and an augmented supply. This new use
has made every man a dealer in bullion; he buys it to sell
it again, and the general competition of all these dealers
will as surely, and as strictly, regulate its value in every
country, as the competition of the same or other dealers
will regulate the value of all other commodities. I have
your sanction for calling every purchaser of commodities a
dealer in bullion; and, though in the language of commercial men the sellers of money are in all cases called purchasers, it is not on that account less true that they are
sellers of one commodity and purchasers of another. The
nature of corn was not changed by the discovery that a new
use might be made of it by fermentation and distillation;
and, if we should hereafter discover that it might be used
for a hundred other purposes, contributing to the comforts
and enjoyments of mankind, the demand for it would increase, and its price would in the first instance be considerably augmented; but this would be the only change it
would undergo; it would continue to be imported and exported by the same rules as every other commodity. I
have no doubt that on this point we should not differ; it
remains therefore for you to show why the new uses, to
which gold has been applied in consequence of its being
adopted as the money of the world, should exempt it from
the general law of competition, and why it should not certainly and invariably (invariably only as that term is applied
to other commodities) seek the most advantageous market.

It is probable that the word 'redundancy' has not been
happily chosen by me to express the impression made on
my mind of the cause of an unfavourable balance of trade;
but on looking over the article in the Review[1] I find that
you use it precisely in the sense in which I wish to convey
my meaning, for you admit that a relatively redundant

[1] Edinb. Review, Feb. 1811. See 'Malthus and his Work,' p. 285.

currency may be, and frequently is, a cause of an unfavourable balance of trade; but you contend that it is not the only cause. Now I, so understanding the word, contend that it is the invariable cause. This relative redundancy may be produced as well by diminution of goods as by an actual increase of money (or which is the same thing by an increased economy in the use of it) in one country; or by an increased quantity of goods or by a diminished amount of money in another. In either of these cases a redundancy of money is produced as effectually as if the mines had become more productive. I do not deny that temporary fluctuations do occur in the value of the precious metals; on the contrary I maintain that those fluctuations never cease; but I attribute them all to one cause, namely a redundancy of the currency produced in one of the ways above mentioned, and not to the demand for particular commodities. These demands are in my opinion regulated by the relative state of the currency; they are not causes but effects. You appear to me not sufficiently to consider the circumstances [which] induce one country to contract a debt to another. [In] all the cases you bring forward you always suppose the [deb]t already contracted, forgetting that I uniformly contend that it is the relative state of the currency which is the motive to the contract itself. The corn, I say, will not be bought unless money be relatively redundant; you answer me by supposing it already bought and the question to be only concerning the payment. A merchant will not contract a debt for corn to a foreign country unless he is fully convinced that he shall obtain for that corn more money than he contracts to pay for it, and, if the commerce of the two countries were limited to these transactions, it would as satisfactorily prove to me that money was redundant in one country as that corn was redundant in the other. It would prove too that nothing but money was redundant. If indeed sugar were exported

by some other merchant, the debt for corn would be paid
without the exportation of money, and I should say that
sugar was the redundant commodity; and the exportation
of sugar, the more redundant commodity, by diminishing
the aggregate amount of commodities, would raise the
value of money, so that in a short time money would, if corn
continued to be imported and sugar exported, no longer be
redundant even as compared with corn. Your observation
is just, concerning the extra expenses attending the exportation of bulky commodities; but in all these discussions
we must suppose these expenses to make part of the price
of the commodity; our comparison is made on the prices at
which the importer, could afford to sell them, and those
prices necessarily include expenses of every sort. I do not
think that the knowledge of the computed ˉexchange of
Jamaica would throw any light on the subject in dispute [1].
I will, however, endeavour to learn every particular concerning it, and hope to be able on Saturday next to pay
you a visit in Hertfordshire, when we will further discuss
these seeming difficulties.

I am, dear Sir, with great respect,

Your obedient Servant,

DAVID RICARDO.

THROGMORTON STREET, 18*th June*, 1811.

VII.[2]

DEAR SIR,

I have been so much engaged since I had the
pleasure of receiving your letter that I have not had an
opportunity of answering it till this evening.

The information which you are desirous of obtaining
respecting the premium on bills in Jamaica from the year

---

[1] Some information on that point had been given by Mr. Thomas Hughan,
a West Indian merchant, before the Bullion Committee (Evidence, pp. 55-61).

[2] Franked by Richard Sharp.

1808 to the present period, I will endeavour to procure, but, as these transactions all take place in Jamaica, and as the merchants here are frequently not acquainted with the prices at which the bills remitted to them are negociated, I am not sure that I shall be successful.

I very much regret that there is so little probability of our finally agreeing on the subject which has lately engaged our attention. The definition which you give of the word 'redundant,' as applied to the currency, is not satisfactory to me. Though it should be allowed that the rise in the price of one commodity, in the case of a scarcity of corn, should be accompanied with a fall in the prices of all others, why should a redundancy of currency be impossible under such circumstances? The currency must, I apprehend, be considered as a whole, and as such must be compared with the whole of the commodities which it circulates. If then it be in a greater proportion to commodities after than before the scarce harvest, whilst no such alteration has taken place in the proportions between money and commodities abroad, it appears to me that no expression can more correctly describe such a state of things than a 'relative redundancy of currency.' Under these circumstances not only money but every other commodity would become comparatively cheap as compared with corn, and would therefore be exported in return for the corn which would be in demand in this country. By relative redundance then I mean, relative cheapness, and the exportation of the commodity I deem, in all ordinary cases, the proof of such cheapness. Indeed, from one who allows that the amount of money employed in any country is regulated by its value, and might therefore be comparatively redundant though it consisted only of a million, or deficient though it amounted to a hundred millions, I should not have expected any difference of opinion on the comparative cheapness of money being the only satisfactory proof of its redundance. If however I thought that the difference between us was as to the correct use of a word, I should immediately yield the point in dispute, but I am persuaded that we do not agree in the principle. You are of opinion that a bad harvest will raise the price of corn, but will lower in some degree the prices of other commodities. Whether it would or would not do so is not material; but, if your opinion is correct, then I say there would be no exportation of money, because money would not be the cheapest exportable commodity. If, before the deficient harvest, money was at the same value in any two countries, that is to say all their exportable commodities without exception were at the same prices in both, then, according to your view of the question, after the scarcity the prices of all commodities would fall in the country where such scarcity occurred. Whilst then the prices were unequal in the two countries, commodities only would be exported in exchange for corn, and there would be no question between us, because we differ as to the cause of the exportation of money. You have indeed said that there may be a glut of commodities in the foreign market. What! a glut of commodities with a dearer price! impossible,—these two circumstances are incompatible. If the price of any commodity had been £20 in both countries and in consequence of the bad harvest it had been lowered to £15 in one of them, there could not be a glut of that commodity in the other country till it had there also fallen to £15. Not only must the price of one commodity fall in the foreign market, but the prices of all (because you suppose them all to have fallen in England) before money could be exported in exchange for corn, and then I would allow that money would be exported, but even then it would be so only because it was more cheap on the whole, as compared with commodities in the exporting country, and this I contend is the proof of its relative redundance. You maintain that money is rendered cheap by a bad harvest as compared with corn only, but with all other commodities it is dearer than before,—and then, what appears to me very inconsistent, you insist that this commodity thus rendered scarce and dear will be exported, though, before it had increased in value, it had no tendency to leave us, whilst too there are commodities which have undergone an opposite change, which from being dearer have become cheaper, and which will nevertheless be obstinately retained by us. This is a mode of reasoning which I cannot reconcile.

With respect to the other point, namely, that the exchange accurately measures the depreciation of the currency [1], I cannot but humbly retain that opinion notwithstanding the high authorities against me. I do not mean to contend that a convulsed state of the exchange, such as would be caused by a subsidy granted to a foreign power, would accurately measure the value of the currency, because a demand for bills arising from such a cause would not be in consequence of the natural commerce of the country. Such a demand would therefore have the effect of forcing the exports of commodities by means of the bounty which the exchange would afford. After the subsidy was paid the exchange would again accurately express the value of the currency. The same effects would follow, as in the case of a subsidy, from the foreign expenditure of Government. These have a natural tendency to create an unfavourable exchange, yet if the demand for bills is regular it is surprising how this bounty on exportation will be reduced by the competition amongst the exporters of commodities. I am of opinion that in the ordinary course of affairs, if, from any of the circumstances so often mentioned, there should be a slight alteration in the value of the currencies of any two countries, it

[1] See note to Letter XII.

will speedily be communicated to the exchange; and, if such a state of things should permanently continue, the exchange has no tendency to correct itself. The fact however appears to be that there is no degree of permanence in the proportions between the currencies and the commodities of nations,—they are subject to constant fluctuations always approaching an absolute level but never really finding it. I hope I have not wearied you with the defence which I have endeavoured to make for the opinions which I have imbibed. I assure you that I am not obstinately attached to any system, but am ready to relinquish any views I may have taken as soon as I am satisfied that they are incorrect. I shall not fail attentively to consider the chapters in Sir J. Steuart's work which you have mentioned[1]. I hope before the summer is over to pay you a visit at Hertford.

I am, dear Sir,

Yours very sincerely,

DAVID RICARDO.

NEW GROVE, MILE END, 17 *July*, 1811.

VIII.

DEAR SIR,

I hoped long ere this to have had the pleasure of seeing you in London. I am anxious for an opportunity of introducing Mrs. Malthus and Mrs. Ricardo to each other, and I shall certainly claim the half promise which Mrs. Malthus made me on that subject when I experienced your hospitality at Hertford. We have few engagements, and have a bed always at your disposal, so that I shall hope on your very first visit to London you will favour me by occupying it.

---

[1] The passages were probably the first three or four chapters of the third book of Sir Jas. Steuart's ' Inquiry into the Principles of Political Economy' (1st ed. 1767), more especially ch. iii, ' Is the loss which the course of exchange marks upon the trade of Great Britain with France real or apparent ? '

A friend of mine has been writing on the subject of bullion. I take the liberty of sending you the MS[1]. If you could look over it and give me your opinion of it you will much oblige me. He would be induced to prepare it for the press if he thought that the mode in which the argument is put is more likely to silence our adversaries and convince those who are not our adversaries than the mode in which it has been put by any other person. Should you be so engaged that you cannot devote your attention to it at the present time, use no ceremony with me, but return the MS. by the coach, directed to me at No. 16 Throgmorton Street. With best respects to Mrs. Malthus,

I am, dear Sir,

Yours very truly,

DAVID RICARDO.

STOCK EXCHANGE, *17th Oct.*, 1811.

IX.

DEAR SIR,   THROGMORTON STREET, *22nd Oct.*, 1811.

I am exceedingly obliged to you for the trouble which you have taken in looking over the papers which I sent you, and for the remarks which you have made upon them. Notwithstanding your flattering encouragement I think I shall not have sufficient confidence again to address the public;—the object which I had in view is completely attained,—the public attention has been awakened, and the discussion is now in the most able hands. I regret, however, that you cannot bring yourself to subscribe to my doctrine respecting the exchange being influenced by no other causes but by the relation which the amount of currency bears to the uses for which it is required in the

---

[1] Ricardo's 'Appendix' to the fourth edition of his tract on the 'High Price of Gold Bullion.' This Appendix embodies most of the opinions set forth in these early letters. See his Works (ed. McCulloch) pp. 291 seq. Cf. 'Malthus and his Work,' p. 287.

C

different nations of the earth. This may proceed from
your interpreting my proposition somewhat too rigidly.
I wish to prove that if nations truly understood their own
interest they would never export money from one country
to another but on account of comparative redundancy. I
assume indeed that nations in their commercial transactions are so alive to their advantage and profit, particularly
in the present improved state of the division of employments and abundance of capital, that in point of fact money
never does move but when it is advantageous both to the
country which sends and the country that receives that it
should do so. The first point to be considered is, what is
the interest of countries in the case supposed? The second
what is their practice? Now it is obvious that I need not
be greatly solicitous about this latter point; it is sufficient
for my purpose if I can clearly demonstrate that the interest
of the public is as I have stated it [1]. It would be no answer
to me to say that men were ignorant of the best and
cheapest mode of conducting their business and paying
their debts, because that is a question of fact not of science,
and might be urged against almost every proposition in
Political Economy. It rests with you therefore to prove
that a case can exist where it may become the *interest* of a
nation to pay a debt by the transmission of money rather
than in any other mode, when money is not the cheapest
exportable commodity,—when money (taking into account
all expenses which may attend the exportation of different
commodities as well as money) will not purchase more
goods abroad than it will at home. You appear to me to
have repeatedly admitted that it is the relative prices of
commodities which regulates their exportation. Is it not

---

[1] ' It is self-interest which regulates all the speculations of trade; and, where
that can be clearly and satisfactorily ascertained, we should not know where
to stop if we admitted any other rule of action.' Appendix to ' High Price of
Bullion ' (Works, p. 292).

then as certain that money will go to that country where the major part of goods are cheap, as that goods will go to any other country where the major part are dear? I say the major part, because if the cheapness of one half of the exportable commodities be balanced by the dearness of the other half, in both countries, it is obvious that the commerce of such countries will be confined to the exchange of goods only. When you say that money will go abroad to pay a debt or a subsidy, or to buy corn, although it be not superabundant, but at the same time admit that [it] will speedily return and be exchanged for goods, you ap[pear to me] to concede all for which I contend, namely, that [it will] be the *interest* of both countries, when money is not superabundant in the one owing the debt, that the expense of exporting the money should be spared, because it will be followed by another useless expense,—sending it back again.

If in any country there exists a dearness of importable commodities and no corresponding cheapness of exportable commodities, money in such country is above its natural level and must infallibly be exported in payment of the dear commodities,—but what does this state of things indicate but an excess of currency, and it may surely be correctly said that money is exported to restore the level not to destroy it. I ought to apologise for again troubling you with my opinions, but you have drawn me into it. I shall be happy to renew our conversation on these disputed points as soon as you can make it convenient to visit us in London, and I trust it will not be long before Mrs. Malthus and you will favour us with your company. On some future day I shall have great pleasure in again visiting you at Hertford.

I am, dear Sir,

Yours very truly,

DAVID RICARDO.

X.

My dear Sir,   New Grove, Mile End, 22*nd Dec.,* 1811.

I write to you, in the first place, to remind you that Mrs. Ricardo and I fully depend on having the pleasure of Mrs. Malthus' and your company at Mile-end in the next month, when we hope that our endeavours to make your visit comfortable will induce you to make a long stay with us. In the second place, I am desirous of correcting some of the errors in the papers which I left with you and which I have been enabled to discover, as I have many others, by the ingenious arguments with which you have opposed my conclusions. In my endeavours to trace the effects of a subsidy[1] in forcing the exportation of commodities, I stated, if I recollect rightly, that it would occasion, first, a demand for bills; secondly, an exportation of all those commodities the prices of which already differed so much, in the two countries, as to require only the trifling stimulus which the first fall in the exchange would afford; thirdly, a real alteration in the relative state of prices, viz. a rise in the exporting and a fall in the importing country,—in a degree too to counterbalance the advantage from the unfavourable exchange; and lastly, a further fall of the exchange and a consequent exportation of an additional quantity of goods and then of money till the subsidy were paid. It appears, then, that if the subsidy were small it would be wholly paid by the exportation of commodities, as the fall in the exchange would be sufficient to encourage *their* exportation, but not sufficient to encourage the exportation of money. If the exportation of money were in the same proportion as the exportation of commodities, that is to say, supposing the commodities of a country to be equal to 100, and its money equal to two, then if not less than one fiftieth of the

[1] See above, p. 15.

exports in payment of the subsidy consisted of money, prices would after such payment be the same as before in both countries, and, although the exchange must have fallen to that limit at which the exportation of money became profitable, it would immediately have a tendency to recover, and would shortly rise to par; but it is precisely because less than this proportion of money will be exported that the exchange will continue permanently unfavourable and will have no tendency to rise, more than it will have to fall.

I believe you admit, that in the case of an augmentation of 2 per cent. to our currency, although it were wholly metallic, the prices of commodities would rise in this country 2 per cent. above their former level, and that such rise being confined to this country alone it would check exportation and encourage importation ; the consequence of which would be a demand for bills and a fall in the exchange. This rise of prices and fall of the exchange, proceeding from what you do not object to call a redundant currency, would not be temporary but permanent, unless it were corrected by a reduction of the amount of the currency here, or by some change in the relative amount of the currencies of other countries. That these would be the effects of a direct augmentation of currency, I believe, you, with very few qualifications, admit. Now, as a bad harvest or the vote of a subsidy tend [*sic*] to produce the very same effects, namely, a relative state of high prices at home, accompanied by an unfavourable exchange, they admit only of the same cure,—and, as in the case of an augmentation of currency the exchange would have no tendency to rise, neither would it in the case of a subsidy, the unfavourable exchange being in both instances produced by a redundant currency, or in more popular language by a relative state of prices which renders the exportation of money most profitable[1]. I have

---

[1] See 'High Price of Gold Bullion,' Ricardo's Works (McCulloch's edition), pp. 264, 282.

uniformly maintained that the money of the world is distributed amongst the different countries according to their commerce and payments, and that, if in any country it should from any cause happen to exceed that proportion, the excess would infallibly be exported to be divided amongst the other countries. I have, however, always supposed that my readers would understand me to mean that this would be strictly the fact only if money could be exported free from all expense. If the expenses of exporting money to France be 3 per cent., to Vienna 5 per cent., to Russia 6 per cent., and to the East Indies 8 per cent., the currency of England may exceed its natural level as compared with those countries by 3, 5, 6, and 8 per cent. respectively, and consequently the exchange may permanently continue depressed in th[ose pr]oportions. If an excess of currency once occurs, [the unfa]vourable exchange must continue till some alterati[on in] the relative amount of currency. The circumstances which [may] occasion such an alteration are numerous, and are fully detailed in the papers which I left with you. To the precise agreement between the effects of an augmented currency and the effects of a subsidy I most particularly request your attention, as on such agreement depends the whole success of the argument which I am advancing in favour of my opinion that an unfavourable exchange has no tendency to correct itself. It may be urged that the relative state of high prices at home occasioned by an augmentation of currency is the natural effect of such a cause, but that this is not the case in a subsidy; that the exportation of commodities in payment of a subsidy is forced, and that it will produce a glut in the foreign market, but that after the subsidy is paid and the necessity for exportation shall cease prices will rise in the foreign market to their former rate. This however will not be true. Commodities may rise in a trifling degree abroad, but cannot regain their former rate unless the exchange should also rise to par, but this it can never do whilst the demand for bills do[es] not exceed the supply. Now, as the prices of foreign commodities in the home market, which could not have been supplied in the usual abundance during the operation of the subsidy when we had a large balance to pay, would fall, and would be in greater demand from the moment that our commodities would be received in exchange, the exportation of our goods would be balanced by the importation of foreign goods, and the sellers of bills would neither exceed nor fall short of the purchasers. These are the substance of the amendments which I wish to make to my paper, which is now so faulty that I shall be glad to have it returned to me. Have the goodness to bring it with you when you come to town.

I am, my dear Sir,

Yours with great esteem,

DAVID RICARDO.

XI[1].

MY DEAR SIR,   LONDON, *29th August*, 1812.

I intend leaving town this evening for Ramsgate, where I think I shall stay about a fortnight, so that I cannot accept your kind invitation for Saturday next; but I hope it will not be long before I bend my steps towards your hospitable roof. If on Saturday the 19th of September you should be quite disengaged and it should be every way convenient to you and Mrs. Malthus, I shall be glad to take tea with you on the evening of that day. I shall be obliged to quit you on the Monday morning. I hope I need not say that I shall be exceedingly sorry if I put you to the least inconvenience and that it will

[1] The Fragment on p. 105 should perhaps come here.

be equally agreeable to me to visit you on any Saturday after the 19th if I am not engaged to go to Ramsgate.

Perhaps you will be so good as to write a few lines directed to the Stock Exchange a few days previously to the 19th as I shall certainly be in town at that time. I am obliged to you for the interest you take in the price of Omnium. It appears to be in a very thriving condition. Mr. Goldsmid[1] informs me that at the period of the improvement in the exchange about Christmas last there were no importations, as far as he knows, of gold from France. A small quantity was imported from Lisbon. I have consulted Wetenhall's list[2], and the following appear to be the variations in the exchange and the price of gold about Christmas last.

	Exchange with Hamburgh.	Doubloons, per oz.			Portuguese gold, [per oz.]		
1811.		£	*s.*	*d.*	£	*s.*	*d.*
Nov. 29	24	4	15	0		......	
Dec. 3	24·6		......		4	18	6
,, 6	24·6	4	14	6	4	18	6
,, 13	25	4	15	6		......	
,, 20	25		......		4	19	0
,, 31	27 6		......			......	
1812.							
Jan. 3	27·6	4	14	0	4	18	6
,, 31	27·6		......		4	18	6
Feb. 21	28		......		4	17	0
Mar. 20	29		......		4	15	6
,, 31	29·4	4	14	6	4	13	6
April 21	29·4	4	17	6	4	17	6
June 5	28·6		......		4	18	6
July 31	28·9	4	19	0	5	0	0
Aug. 28	28·9	5	0	0		......	

The price of dollars yesterday was 6/3½ per oz., higher

---

[1] Aaron A. Goldsmid, of Mocatta and Goldsmid, bullion brokers. See Report of Bullion Committee, Evidence of Witnesses, pp. 1-18, 61. He was nephew of Abraham and Benjamin Goldsmid, who died by their own hand in 1810.

[2] Wetenhall got his information from Mocatta and Goldsmid. See Bullion Report, Evid. p. 2.

by one penny than any price ever yet quoted. I should think that a very trifling rise more will send the tokens out of circulation. We will speak on our old subject when we meet. I am now in great haste and must therefore conclude. Pray make my kind compliments to Mrs. Malthus,

And believe me, my dear Sir,

Yours very truly,

DAVID RICARDO.

[At the end is written in pencil in Malthus's handwriting, 'Was any bullion imported from Hamburg in March?']

XII.

MY DEAR SIR, LONDON, 17 *Dec.*, 1812.

I have written to Mr. Thornton[1] to request him to meet you at dinner, at my house, on any day most convenient to him, after Saturday and before Thursday, but I have not had his answer in time for this day's post. I will send you a line at the King of Clubs. I shall only ask Mr. Sharp to meet us. Will you not stay with us whilst you are in town? I assure you it would be quite convenient, and it would afford me great pleasure. If Mrs. Malthus accompany you it will be still more agreeable, and I am desired by Mrs. Ricardo to add her solicitations to my own.

On many points connected with our old question we are I believe agreed,—though there is yet some difference between us. I have not lately given it so much consideration as you have,—and I always regret that I do not put down in writing, for I have a very treacherous memory, the chief points of difference that occur in our discussions. I cannot help thinking that there is no un-

[1] Henry Thornton, M.P., member of the Bullion Committee, author of 'An Enquiry into the Nature and Effects of the Paper Credit of Great Britain,' 1802. See J. S. Mill, Political Economy III. xi. § 4.

favourable exchange which may not be corrected by a diminution in the amount of the currency, and I consider this to afford a proof that the currency must be redundant for a time at least. Whilst the exchange is unfavourable it is always accompanied, though not always caused, by an excess of currency. With best respects to Mrs. Malthus,

I am, my dear Sir,

Yours most truly,

DAVID RICARDO.

. . . . As I was about leaving the city I received Mr. Thornton's answer. He is engaged on Wednesday and Thursday, and has fixed on Monday for our meeting, but he wishes us to meet at his house as there is to be a debate in the House of Lords on the Bullion question, and he is not sure that his presence may not be necessary in the Commons. I will settle this point with him, and if you do not hear from me I shall expect you at my house on Monday, if you do not agree to come on Saturday evening.

NOTE.—Thomas Tooke, in his 'History of Prices and of the State of the Circulation from 1839 to 1847' (publ. 1848)[1], refers to this dispute between Ricardo and Malthus, on the relation of the currency to the balance of trade, and quotes long extracts from the article of Malthus in the Edinburgh Review, where (as in this correspondence [2]) Malthus maintains that the precious metals are continually used in payments made by one country to another even if, till that moment, the currencies of both have been at their usual level. The view of Ricardo is that nothing but the state of the currency can influence the foreign exchanges. As late as 1840 statesmen clung to the idea that the Directors of the Bank of England could only operate on the exchanges by increasing or diminishing the circulation [3]. Tooke (followed later by Newmarch, hardly a less authority) sides with Malthus, and thinks that

[1] Part III. ch. i. § 5 : 'On the Opinions of the Bullion Committee on the Phenomena of the Circulation in 1809–1811,' pp. 100–110.

[2] See especially Letters IV and VI.   [3] Tooke, Hist. of Prices, p. 359.

Ricardo's reply to him, in the Appendix to the Tract on Bullion, is 'little more than a repetition in varied forms of expression, according to the phraseology peculiar to the theory in question, of the axiom that gold will not be exported unless it is cheaper than another commodity, assuming consequently the fact to have been that all commodities were at that time dearer in this country than they were abroad, and relatively to gold;'—whereas it appears[1] that between 1809 and 1811 the bulk of commodities were at a far higher price (measured in gold) on the Continent than in England; the 'continental system' had forced vast stores of goods to lie unsaleable in England for want of physical ability, on the part of the merchants of them, to land them on the Continent, though they did their best to smuggle them by way of Heligoland or Turkey into Germany and the door of Portugal was ajar. Coffee was unsaleable in England at 6d. the pound, and at the same time it was fetching 4s. or 5s. on the Continent. Napoleon used to look at the English price current, and, if he found gold dear and coffee cheap in England, he was satisfied that his Berlin and Milan decrees were well carried out, while the English saw only another proof that the Bank was extending its issues overmuch. Tooke and Malthus agreed that the difference between the market price and the mint price of gold bullion was the full measure of the depreciation of the currency; but the 'ultra-bullionists' would not stop there. Tooke, like Ricardo on another occasion (see Letter XLII), had to 'write a book to convince' them, namely his 'Thoughts and Details on the High and Low Prices of the last Thirty years,' (1823).

XIII.

LONDON, 30*th Dec.*, 1813.

MY DEAR SIR,

I have been amusing myself for one or two evenings in calculating the exchanges, price of gold, etc., at Amsterdam, and I enclose the result of my labour. I have every reason to believe that my calculations are correct,—though

---

[1] As was shown also in ' Letters on the Corn Laws,' by H. B. T. (J. Deacon Hume.) London, 1834.

I am somewhat puzzled at the profit which there appears
to be on the importation of gold from Amsterdam, if the
prices there be quoted correct [*sic*].   If the difference were
the other way, we might ascribe it to the money of
Holland not being so good as it ought to be by the mint
regulations; but in the present instance for guilders, as
good as they are coined, gold can be bought 9½ per cent.
cheaper than in London.   I am told that gold which
cannot be exported has sunk considerably in price although
gold that may be exported keeps its price.   I fully expect
that foreign gold will be lower.

We have had a continuance of foggy weather ever since
Monday.   We are obliged to burn candles during the day,
and at night it is with the greatest difficulty we can find
our way to our homes.   I hope you are more fortunate
and breathe a clearer atmosphere.   We shall expect you
in Brook Street on your next visit to London.   Have the
goodness to write the day before you come.   With best
wishes to Mrs. Malthus,

I am, dear Sir,

Yours very truly,

DAVID RICARDO.

[TABLES ENCLOSED IN LETTER XII.]

Columns 11 and 12 will show on inspection whether
silver be passing from London to Amsterdam or from
Amsterdam to London.   Suppose the price of silver in
London to be *6s. 7d.* and the exchange with Amsterdam
28*s*.   Against *6s. 7d.* in column 11 the par of exchange
is 29.41 in column 12; consequently being at 28 it is
unfavourable to Amsterdam, and silver can be exported
from Amsterdam to London with a profit of 5 per cent.

If under the same circumstances the exchange had been
31, silver could have been exported to Amsterdam with
a profit of 5 per cent.

Columns 8, 9 and 10 will show from which country gold
may be profitably exported.   Suppose the price of gold in
Amsterdam to be 16 per cent. premium, the agio 3 per cent.,
the exchange with London 31, and the price of gold in
London £5 10*s.*, from which country would gold be exported and with what profit?

Against 16 per cent. in column 1 the par of exchange in
column 8 is 39·64, and against £5 10*s.* the price of gold in
London in column 9 the multiplier ·708 stands in column 10.
39·64 multiplied by ·708 gives 28·06 as the par for bank
notes; therefore, when the exchange is at 31, it is unfavourable to Holland, and gold may be exported from
thence with a profit of 10½ per cent. nearly.   Or thus:
an oz. of standard gold, when the marc could be bought
at 16 per cent. premium at Amsterdam, would cost 154·3
Flemish shillings banco, when the agio was 3 per cent.,
which reduced into English money at 31 [Flemish] shillings
per £ sterling will give £4 19*s.* 6¾*d.*   But it will sell in
London for £5 10*s.* which is a profit of 10½ per cent.
nearly.

1	2	3 [1]	4	5	6 [2]
Price of gold at Amsterdam, Premium on ƒ. 355 per marc.	Value of a marc in current guilders.	Corresponding price of an oz. of standard gold in London.	Corresponding price of an oz. of standard silver in London.	Value of an oz. of standard gold in Flemish current shillings.	Value of an oz. of standard gold in Flemish Banco shillings. Agio 3 p. c.
Par ƒ. 355	ƒ335	...... *£ s. d.*	68·00 *pence*	137	133
1 p.c. prem.	358·55	......	67·32	138·4	134·3
2 „	362·10	......	66·67	139·8	135·7
3 „	365·65	......	66·02	141·3	137·2
4 „	369·20	......	65·38	142·5	138·6
5 „	372·75	......	64·76	143·9	139·8
6 „	376·30	......	64·15	145·3	141·1
7 „	379·85	......	63·55	146·6	142·5
8 „	383·40	......	62·96	148	143·9
9 „	386·95	......	62·39	149·3	145·3
	389·37	3 17 10½	62	150·3	146·0
10 „	390·50	3 18 1	......	150·7	146·3
11 „	394·05	3 18 10	......	152·1	147·6
12 „	397·60	3 19 6½	......	153·5	149·0
13 „	401·15	4 0 3	......	154·8	150·3
14 „	404·70	4 0 11½	......	156·2	151·7
15 „	408·25	4 1 8	......	157·5	152·9
16 „	411·80	4 2 4½	......	158·9	154·3
17 „	415·35	4 3 0½	......	160·3	155·6
18 „	418·90	4 3 9	......	161·7	157·0
19 „	422·45	4 4 5½	......	163·1	158·3
20 „	426	4 5 2	......	164·5	159·6
21 „	429·55	4 5 10½	......	165·8	161·0

[1] When the price of gold in Holland is above 10 p.c. premium, and the mint in England is open to the public, silver will be the standard in London. Consequently its market and mint prices will agree, and gold will be above the mint price. When under 10 p.c., silver will be above the mint price, and gold will be the standard.

When the price of gold in Holland was above 9 p.c. premium, the English £ sterling would be estimated in silver and therefore the par of exchange would invariably continue 38.61 currency ; and 37.48 Banco if the agio were 3 p.c.

[2] The agio is variable, but is supposed to be constant in this table for the purpose of calculation.

A marc weight = 3798 grains troy. A marc is divided into 5120 onsen [a], 200 onsen [a] of pure silver in a guilder. Gold and silver are sold by the marc in Holland perfectly pure [b].

British standard—gold 11 fine, 1 alloy; silver 11·2 fine, 18 dwts. alloy.

---

[a] The word is indistinct.
[b] The gold mark is meant. See Adam Smith's account of the Bank of Amsterdam in 'Wealth of Nations,' IV. iii. p. 212 n. (McCulloch's ed.).

7	8	9	10	11	12
Real par of exchange in Flemish current shillings per £ sterling in gold.	Real par of exchange in Flemish Banco shillings per £ sterling in gold. Agio 3 p. c.	When the price of gold in London in bank notes is	The bullion par must be multiplied by	Price of standard silver in London in bank notes per oz.	Par of exchange with Amsterdam in Banco. Agio 3 p. c.
		£ s. d.		s. d.	
35·20	34·17	......	......	......	......
(1.) 35·55	34·51	4 0 0	·973	5 2	37·48
(2.) 35·90	34·85	4 1 0	·961	5 3	36·88
(3.) 36·25	35·19	4 2 0	·949	5 4	36·60
(4.) 36·61	35·54	4 3 0	·938	5 5	35·75
(5.) 36·95	35·87	4 4 0	·927	5 6	35·21
(6.) 37·31	36·22	4 5 0	·916	5 7	34·68
(7.) 37·66	36·56	4 6 0	·905	5 8	34·17
(8.) 38·01	36·90	4 7 0	·895	5 9	33·67
(9.) 38·36	37·24	4 8 0	·885	5 10	33·19
... 38·61	37·48	......	......	......	......
(10.) 38·71	37·58	4 9 0	·875	5 11	32·72
(11.) 39·06	37·92	4 10 0	·865	6 0	32·27
(12.) 39·62	33·27	4 11 0	·856	6 1	31·84
(13.) 39·77	38·62	4 13 0	·838	6 2	31·42
(14.) 40·12	38·96	4 15 0	·820	6 3	30·98
(15.) 40·48	39·30	4 17 0	·803	6 4	30·58
(16.) 40·83	39·64	4 19 0	·786	6 5	30·17
(17.) 41·18	39·98	5 0 0	·779	6 6	29·79
(18.) 41·54	40·32	5 2 0	·764	6 7	29·41
(19.) 41·89	40·67	5 4 0	·749	6 8	29·04
(20.) 42·24	41·02	5 6 0	·735	6 9	28·69
(21.) 42·59	41·36	5 8 0	·721	6 10	28·33
......	......	5 10 0	·708	6 11	27·99
......	......	......	......	7 0	27·66
......	......	......	......	7 1	27·32
......	......	......	......	7 2	27·02
......	......	......	......	7 3	26·71
......	......	......	......	7 4	26·40
......	......	......	......	7 5	26·11
......	......	......	......	7 6	25·82

XIV.

LONDON, 1 *Jan.*, 1814.

My DEAR SIR,

Having finished a table for the Hamburgh exchanges, similar to that which I have already sent you for Holland, I thought you might like to have a copy of it[1]. In this as well as in the other the result is not quite satisfactory; for example, at the present time I believe the exchange with Hamburgh is quoted 28*s.* and the price of dollars 6*s.* 11½*d.* By the table it appears that with [such] a price of dollars the exchange at par would be 25*s.*; consequently it is now unfavourable to Hamburgh 12 per cent., which appears to me to be excessively high. In fact, under the present circumstances, there can be no intercourse with Hamburgh, and the quotation must be only nominal. Mrs. Ricardo and I leave London to-morrow early for Bradford; from thence we intend going to Gatcomb[2], and expect to be in town again on Thursday. I hope we shall soon see you. With best wishes to Mrs. Malthus,

I am, dear Sir,

Yours very truly,

DAVID RICARDO.

---

[1] A good commentary on these Tables and on the whole of these early letters will be found in the Evidences of the Witnesses examined before the Bullion Committee (1810).

[2] His favourite country-seat, in Gloucestershire.

Price of a ducat or 53 grains of fine gold in marks banco.	Price of an oz. of standard gold in Flemish shillings banco.	Par of exchange with London in Flemish shillings banco per £ sterling of gold.	Corresponding price of an oz. of standard silver in London in pence.	Corresponding price of an oz. of standard gold in London in £, etc.	When the price of gold in London in bank-notes is per oz. (£ s. d.)	The bullion par of exchange must be multiplied by	When the price of dollars in London is per oz. (s. d.)	The par of exchange in silver is
5·39	119·33	30·60	70·97	......	4 0 0	·973	4 11½	35·08
5·45	120·66	30·94	70·19	......	4 1 0	·961	5 1	34·22
5·51	121·99	31·28	69·43	......	4 2 0	·949	5 2¼	33·39
5·57	123·32	31·63	68·68	......	4 3 0	·938	5 4	32·61
5·63	124·65	31·97	67·95	......	4 4 0	·927	5 5½	31·87
5·69	125·98	32·33	67·23	......	4 5 0	·916	5 7	31·15
5·75	127·31	32·68	66·53	......	4 6 0	·905	5 8½	30·47
5·81	128·64	33·03	65·84	......	4 7 0	·895	5 10	29·82
5·87	129·96	33·37	65·17	......	4 8 0	·885	5 11½	29·19
5·93	131·29	33·72	64·51	......	4 9 0	·875	6 1	28·59
5·99	132·62	34·07	63·86	......	4 10 0	·865	6 2½	28·02
6·05	133·95	34·42	63·23	......	4 11 0	·856	6 4	27·46
6·11	135·28	34·76	62·61	......	4 13 0	·838	6 5½	26·93
6·17	136·61	35·08	62	3·893	4 15 0	·820	6 7	26·42
6·23	137·92	35·42	......	3·931	4 17 0	·803	6 8½	25·93
6·29	139·25	35·76	......	3·968	4 19 0	·796	6 10	25·46
6·35	140·57	36·11	......	4·005	5 0 0	·779	6 11½	25
6·41	141·89	36·45	......	4·043	5 2 0	·764	7 1	24·55
6·47	143·21	36·79	......	4·081	5 4 0	·749	7 2	24·13
6·53	144·54	37·14	......	4·119	5 6 0	·735	......	......
6·59	145·86	37·48	......	4·157	5 8 0	·721	......	......
6·65	147·19	37·83	......	4·195	5 10 0	·708	......	......
6·71	148·51	38·18	......	4·233	......	......	......	......
6·77	149·84	38·52	......	4·270	......	......	......	......
6·83	151·17	38·87	......	4·308	......	......	......	......
6·89	152·50	39·22	......	4·346	......	......	......	......

N.B.—3 marks are equal to 8 Flemish shillings banco. When dollars are 4s. 11½d., standard is 2½d. more. When 6s. 1d., 3d. more. When 7s., 3½d. more.

XV.

My dear Sir,   LONDON, 26 *June*, 1814.

.... I cannot partake of your doubts respecting the effects of restrictions on the importation of corn in tending to lower the rate of interest. The rise of the price or rather the value of corn without any augmentation of capital must necessarily diminish the demand for other things even if the prices of those commodities did not rise with the price of corn, which they would (tho' slowly) certainly do. With the same capital there would be less production and less demand. Demand has no other limits but the want of power of paying for the commodities demanded. Everything which tends to diminish production tends to diminish this power. The rate of profits and of interest must depend on the proportion of production to the consumption necessary to such production,—this again essentially depends upon the cheapness of provisions, which is after all, whatever intervals we may be willing to allow, the great regulator of the wages of labour. Nothing can tend more effectually to diminish the demand abroad for our manufactures than to refuse to import corn and other commodities which we [had] usually taken in exchange for such manufactures. If we rigorously refused to import any [foreign] commodity whatever, I firmly believe that we should soon cease to export any commodity, even if we made gold an exception to the general rule. Our money would stand at a higher level than in other countries, but there are limits beyond which it could not go. All trade is at last a trade of barter, and no nation will long buy unless it can also sell,—nor will it long sell if it will not also buy. If by adopting such policy [*sic*] a country were to enhance the value of the raw materials which it consumed, of which corn is the principal, it would thereby lower the rate of interest. If otherwise, it might be deprived of many luxuries and many comforts, or might enjoy them in less abundance, but the rate of interest would not fall. This is a repetition, you will say, of the old story, and I might have spared you the trouble of reading at 200 miles distance what I had so often stated to you as my opinion before; but you have set me off, and must now abide the consequences. I never was more convinced of any proposition in Political Economy than that restrictions on importation of corn in an importing country have a tendency to lower profits. Remember me kindly to Mrs. Malthus.

Yours very truly,

DAVID RICARDO.

XVI.

GATCOMB PARK, NEAR MINCHIN HAMPTON, GLOUCESTERSHIRE,
25th July, 1814.

MY DEAR SIR,

I am writing to you from Gatcomb, where I arrived with S—— as my companion yesterday afternoon. To enable me to quit London at the time I did I was obliged to bestow an unusual degree of attention to business of all sorts, and, though I had written a letter to you in answer to your last before I left Brook Street, I was so dissatisfied with it that I could not resolve to send it. I shall, I fear, succeed no better now, but you shall have it whatever it may be, as, if I defer writing any longer, you may have quitted Bangor before my letter arrives there [1]. It appears to me that you have changed the proposition on which we first appeared to differ. The proposition advanced by you, if I recollect right, was that restrictions on the importation of corn would not lower the rate of profits and interest,—

---

[1] This actually happened; and the letter is re-addressed first to 'Aylesbury' and then to 'Hayleybury'.

but now you add—or rather your argument leads to that conclusion,—'if the consequence of such restriction be a great reduction of capital.' So amended I should not object to the proposition,—but I think it material that causes should be kept distinct, and their due effects ascribed to each. Restrictions on the trade of corn, if capital suffers no diminution, will occasion a fall in the rate of profits and interest. A reduction of capital independently of restrictions on importation of corn will have a tendency to raise profits and interest,—but there is no necessary connection between these two operating causes, as they may at the same time be acting together or entirely in opposite directions. Effective demand, it appears to me, cannot augment or long continue stationary with a diminishing capital; and your question why if this were true profits rise at the commencement of a war? does not, I think, bear any connection with the argument, because profits will augment under a diminution of capital and produce, if demand though diminished does not diminish so rapidly as capital and produce. For the opposite reason profits will diminish when capital and produce increase. This is totally independent of the rate of production, and often, I think, may counteract the effects which usually follow, and in the long run will almost always follow, from increasing or diminishing capital. You say that 'the proportion of production to the consumption necessary to such production seems to be determined by the quantity of accumulated capital compared with the demand for the products of capital, and not by the mere difficulty and expense of procuring corn.' It appears to me that the difficulty and expense[1] of procuring corn will necessarily regulate the demand for the products of capital, for the demand must essentially depend on the price at which they can be afforded, and the prices of all com-

---

[1] Here and elsewhere written 'expence'.

modities must increase if the price of corn be increased. The capitalist 'who may find it necessary to employ a hundred days' labour instead of fifty in order to produce a certain quantity of corn' cannot retain the same share for himself unless the labourers who are employed for a hundred days will be satisfied with the same quantity of corn for their subsistence that the labourers employed for fifty had before. If you suppose the price of corn doubled, the capital to be employed, estimated in money, will probably be also nearly doubled,—or at any rate will be greatly augmented; and, if his monied income is to arise from the sale of the corn which remains to him after defraying the charges of production, how is it possible to conceive that the rate of his profits will not be diminished? I hope you continue to enjoy yourself amidst the wild scenery with which you are encompassed.—The weather here is delightful, and I am as happy as I can be, separated from the whole family (except S——) and surrounded by upholsterers, carpenters, etc. . . . .

Yours very truly,

DAVID RICARDO.

I believe that in this sweet place I shall not sigh after the Stock Exchange and its enjoyments.

XVII.

MY DEAR SIR,   GATCOMB PARK, 11 *Aug.*, 1814.

I received your letter last Sunday, and in the evening of that day Mrs. Ricardo and the rest of my family arrived here. I have been showing them all the beauties of this place, and my time has been pretty well engrossed by them these three last days. . . . . The fall in Omnium is I believe to be attributed to our continued

expenses, and the expectation of another loan before the
payments on the present are completed. The present
state of the Exchanges seem[s] to indicate a real fall in
the value of foreign currencies; it cannot be attributed
to any change of taste for particular commodities, or any
other caprice. I expected that Peace would lower the
value of foreign currency, but I confess not in the degree
which has taken place. It leaves the question between us
undecided—namely, whether the exchange is not operated
upon solely by the relative preponderance of currency.
Peace has rendered the currency of the continent much
more efficacious to the business to be done.

With regard to our present question, we differ as to
effects which must *necessarily* follow from restrictions on
the importation of foreign corn. I do not think that a
diminution of capital is a *necessary*, but a probable effect.
We agree as to the consequences which will attend a
diminution of capital, but I should say that a real diminution of capital will diminish the work to be done, and
consequently will affect the wages of labour, and the
demand for food. In the case supposed, restrictions on
importation of corn, encouragement is given to the further
cultivation of our own land,—but *if* accompanied by a
diminution of capital a discouragement is also given to
the cultivation of the land, and whether profits rise or fall
must in my opinion depend upon the degree of these
contra-operating causes. It is true that the woollen or
cotton manufacturer will not be able to work up the same
quantity of goods with the same capital if he is obliged to
pay more for the labour which he employs, but his profits
will depend on the price at which his goods when manufactured will sell. If every person is determined to live
on his revenue or income, without infringing on his
capital, the rise of his goods will not be in the same proportion as the rise of labour, and consequently his per-

centage of profit will be diminished if he values his capital, which he must do, in money at the increased value to which all goods would rise in consequence of the rise of the wages of labour. In such case I should say that the effective demand had diminished, because the same quantity of commodities could not be annually consumed. If the same quantity of commodities continued to be consumed, then it must be evident that it would be at the expense of capital. In such case capital would diminish faster than demand, which would tend to keep up profits. But how long will [people] continue to indulge in luxuries at the expense of a continual diminution of capital? It is the road to ruin, and, though frequently persisted in by a few individuals, it is not often found to be the folly of nations. On the contrary, if any causes interrupt the progress of nations, if restrictions on their trade, or expensive wars, tend to diminish their capital, at such times more economy is practised, and, as Adam Smith has observed, the profusion of governments is counteracted by the frugality of individuals. If so, I cannot be incorrect in saying that, though for a short period capital and produce may diminish faster than demand,—yet in the long run effective demand cannot augment or continue stationary with a diminishing capital. You say, what I did not before understand you to admit, 'that the whole amount of demand will from advanced prices diminish of course, but the proportion of demand to supply, which is always the main point in question, as determining prices and profits, may continue to increase, *as it does in all countries the capital of which is retrograde;*' but I do not agree even to this explanation, and it appears to me to be at variance with an opinion which I have often heard you express, viz. The temptation to save from revenue to augment capital is always in proportion to the rate of profits, and, if from accumulation of capital profits and interest should fall very low indeed, at that point accumulation would nearly stop, because it would be almost without an object. In this opinion I most cordially agree, and I cannot help thinking that it is at variance with the above sentence which I have quoted from your letter. I maintain, as I think you have done, that consumption as compared with production is always greatest where capital is most accumulated. Diminish the capital of England one half, and you undoubtedly augment profits, but it will not be in consequence of a greater proportion of demand but of a greater proportion of production; demand as compared with production could hardly fail to diminish. Individuals do not estimate their profits by the material production, but nations invariably do. If we had precisely the same amount of commodities of all descriptions in the year 1815 that we now have in 1814, as a nation we should be no richer; but, if money had sunk in value, they would be represented by a greater quantity of money, and individuals would be apt to *think* themselves richer. I shall be in town either next week or the week after. I wish you would return here with me. We would discuss these important points in our shady groves. With kind regards to Mrs. Malthus,

I am, yours truly,

DAVID RICARDO.

XVIII.

GATCOMB PARK, MINCHIN HAMPTON,
30th Aug., 1814.

MY DEAR SIR,

I left London on the 19th, the day before your letter arrived there, having dispatched all my business in four days. The appearance of the Omnium was not sufficiently inviting to induce me to protract my stay longer than was absolutely necessary. David[1], who is come to pass his holidays with us, brought me your letter. I regret that I shall not see you for some time, as you cannot come here, and I shall not have it in my power at present to visit Hail[e]ybury. I expected to have a great deal of leisure time in the country, but as yet I have not had any. Walking and riding with my family, and friends who have visited us, have entirely occupied me; besides which, the only room in my house which is not finished is the library, owing to the tedious time which they have taken to fix my bookcases.

I think if we could talk together we should not *very* much differ on the question which has lately engaged us ; our principal difference is about the permanence of the effects. It will often happen that the scarcity of a commodity or the increasing demand for it will for a time increase profits ; but it is not therefore correct to say that, where profits are high, they are so because the demand for produce is great compared with supply. There are many other causes which will occasion profits to be permanently high. There may be two countries, in one of which, from bad government and the consequent insecurity of property, or from the little disposition to saving in the people, profits may be permanently high and interest at 12 per cent., whilst in the other, where these causes do not operate, profits may be permanently low and interest at 5 per cent. It would surely be incorrect to say that the cause of the high profits was the greater proportion of demand for produce, when in both countries the supply would be or might be precisely equal to the demand and no more. In America profits are higher than in England, and yet I can have no doubt that the proportion of supply

[1] Ricardo's second son. The eldest was Osman, the third Mortimer. Ricardo had five daughters, three of whom were married, one to Mr. Clutterbuck, mentioned later in the correspondence. (See Gentl. Mag. 1823, pt. ii. 376.)

to demand is greater in the former country. I think it must necessarily be so in all countries which are most rapidly increasing in riches, for from whence do riches come but from production preponderating over consumption? Profits are sometimes high when corn is scarce and dear; but this arises from the stimulus which the high prices give to industry. If the population could immediately accommodate itself to the scanty supply, no such effects would follow; and in fact they only continue till time has gradually equalised them.

I sometimes suspect that we do not attach the same meaning to the word 'demánd.' If corn rises in price, [you] perhaps attribute it to a greater demand. I should [attribute it to] a greater competition. The demand cannot, I think, be said to increase if the quantity consumed be diminished, although much more money may be required to purchase the smaller than the larger quantity. If it were to be asked what the demand was for port-wine in England in the years 1813 and 1814, and it were to be answered that in the first year she had imported 5000 pipes, and in the next 4500, should we not all agree that the demand was greater in 1813? Yet it might be true that double the quantity of money was paid for the 4500 pipes.

Have you read the report of the Lord[s'] Committee on the Corn question? It discloses some important facts; but how ignorant the persons giving evidence appear to be of the subject as a matter of science! The Editor's remarks too are very unworthy of his paper.

.   .   .   With best compliments to Mrs. Malthus,

I am, yours truly,

DAVID RICARDO.

NOTE.—The 'Editor' was Lord Hardwicke, who moved for the Committee 10th June, 1814, and presented its report to the House on 23rd Nov. 1814. See Hansard, under date Feb. 17, 1815, p. 796;

Ann. Register 1815, Gen. Hist. p. 130. The reports were 'ordered to be printed' 25th July, 1814. The first was on a single sheet, and was simply a complaint that the Committee could not take evidence; the second reported that they had heard evidence, but thought that before any certain conclusions could be reached the inquiry must go on further. There is a copiously annotated copy of them in the ' Place' Collection in the British Museum.

XIX.

My dear Sir, Gatcomb Park, 16 *Sept.*, 1814.

. . . I agree with you that, when capital is scanty compared with the means of employing it, from whatever cause arising, profits will be high. Whether temporarily or permanently must of course depend upon whether the cause be temporary or permanent. It is, however, very important to ascertain what the causes are which make capital scanty compared with the means of employing it, and how far, when ascertained, they may be considered temporary or permanent.

It is in this inquiry that I am led to believe that the state of the cultivation of the land is almost the only great permanent cause. There are other circumstances which are attended with temporary effects of more or less duration and frequently operate partially on particular trades. The state of production from the land, compared with the means necessary to make it produce, operates on all, and is alone lasting in its effects.

We agree too that effectual demand consists of two elements, the *power* and the *will* to purchase; but I think the will is very seldom wanting where the power exists, for the desire of accumulation will occasion demand just as effectually as a desire to consume; it will only change the objects on which the demand will exercise itself. If you

think that, with an increase of capital, men will become
indifferent both to consumption and accumulation, then
you are correct in opposing Mr. Mill's idea[1], that in reference to a nation supply can never exceed demand; but does
not an increase of capital beget an increased inclination for
luxuries of all descriptions? and, though it appears natural
that the desire of accumulation should decrease with an
increase of capital and diminished profits, it appears equally
probable that consumption will increase in the same ratio.
Exchanges will be as active as ever; the objects only will
be altered. If demand *appears* more active where capital
is scarce, it is only because the *power* to purchase is comparatively greater. Wherever capital is scanty, the necessaries of life are cheap, if the country is commonly fertile ;
and, as capital and population increase, the necessaries of
life rise in price, and thus is the power of purchasing, though
really greater, comparatively less. In a country with little
comparative capital, the value of the yearly produce may
very rapidly increase ; and, if it be said to be in consequence of the greatness of demand, I should contend that in
such country the demand would not be limited in the same
degree by a want of power as in a country abounding in
capital, and merely because provisions would not rise in the
same proportion in the two countries. If half as much corn
[again] as usual were produced next year, a great part of it
would undoubtedly be wasted ; and the same might be said
of any commodities which we might be ingenious enough

---

[1] Announced as early as 1807 in the reply to Spence ('Commerce Defended'). Ricardo's friendship with James Mill seems to have begun about the
year 1811: 'With an estimate of his [Ricardo's] value in the cause of mankind,
which to most men would appear to be mere extravagance, I have the
recollection of a dozen years of the most delightful intercourse, during the
greater part of which time he had hardly a thought or purpose, respecting
either public or his private affairs, in which I was not his confidant and
adviser.' Letter of Jas. Mill to MacCulloch, 19th Sept. 1823 (Bain's Life of
Jas. Mill, p. 209).

to name: but the real question is this—If money should retain the same value next year, would any man (if he had it) want the will to spend half as much again as he now does? and, if he did want the will, would he feel no inclination to add the increase of his revenue to his capital and employ it as such? In short, I consider the wants and tastes of mankind as unlimited. We all wish to add to our enjoyments or to our power. Consumption adds to our enjoyments, accumulation to our power, and they equally promote demand.

Mrs. Ricardo and I are going this morning to Cheltenham, which is eighteen miles distant from us; we shall return to-morrow.

Mr. Smith[1], whom I met at your house, lives about nine miles from here.

. . . I hope you recollect that we are not quite twenty-eight miles from Bath. You and Mrs. Malthus might, I think, give us the pleasure of your company for a few days during your Christmas vacation[2], and might at the same time visit your friends; but as you have seen them so lately you would give us great pleasure if you would give us the whole of your time. Mrs. Ricardo, who is standing by me, has made me express myself in a more than usually bungling manner. She unites with me in kind regards to Mrs. Malthus.

Yours very sincerely,

DAVID RICARDO.

XX.

MY DEAR SIR, GATCOMB PARK, 23rd *Oct.*, 1814.

On the day that you were writing your last letter to me, I was travelling to London with Mrs. Ricardo,

[1] Thomas Smith of Easton Grey. His name is on the list of subscribers to Hone's Testimonial, 1818.

[2] Malthus was in the habit of spending his Christmas with his wife's relations at St. Catherine's near Bath, and it was in one of these visits that he died there, 1834. See *Malthus and his Work*, p. 415.

where my business detained me a little more than a week. On my return your letter was delivered to me. I am sorry that you cannot make it convenient to pay us a visit at Christmas. I shall however depend on your not allowing any common occurrence to prevent you and Mrs. Malthus from favouring[1] us with your company during your next summer vacation. I hope you will not repent having set me the example of using a larger sized paper. If you are tired with my long letter, you only will be to blame for it.

It does not appear to me that we very materially differ in our ideas of the effects of the facility or difficulty of procuring food on the profits of stock. You say that I 'seem to think that the state of production from the land compared with the means necessary to make it produce is almost the sole cause which regulates the profit of stock and the means of advantageously employing capital.' This is a correct statement of my opinion, and not, as you have said in another part of your letter and which essentially differs from it, 'that it is the *quantity* of produce compared with the expense of production that determines profits.' You, instead of allowing the facility of obtaining food to be almost the sole cause of high profits, think it may be safely said to be the main cause, and also a difficulty of acquiring food the main cause of low profits. There appears to me to be very little difference in these statements. You infer that my doctrine is not correct because improvements may take place in agriculture or manufactures, because new leases may not be granted precisely at the time of the rise in the price of raw produce, and because the price of labour may not rise without delay in the same proportion. But improvements in agriculture or in machinery which shall facilitate or augment production will according to my proposition increase profits because 'it will augment production compared with the means

---

[1] Here and elsewhere spelt ' favoring '.

necessary to that production.' The same may be said of
the wages of labour not rising in the same proportion as
the price of produce. As for old leases affecting the
question, you will observe that in calculating the profits
made by agriculture we must estimate leases at the value
which they bear at the time of the calculation and not at
the value agreed upon at an antecedent period. If the
question were concerning the profits of a manufactory or
distillery for example, we should calculate such profits
according to the then value of barley, although a few
individual distillers might have been so fortunate as to
purchase their barley when it was 25 per cent cheaper.
These points then are expressly allowed for in my proposition, and are by no means at variance with it. You
add to your statement ['] that in the interval between the
two extremes (of high profits and low profits caused by
facility or difficulty of procuring food) considerable variations may take place, and that practically no country
was ever in such a state as not to admit of increase of
profits on the land for a period of some duration, from the
advanced price of raw produce.' I agree that variations
will take place because the means of obtaining produce
are not always equally expensive; and, if they should be,
the produce itself may become more valuable, and in
either case profits will vary. But even during these
temporary variations the great cause, namely the accumulation of capital, may be paving the way for permanently
diminished profits. It appears to me important to ascertain what the causes are which may occasion a rise in the
price of raw produce, because the effects of a rise, on
profits, may be diametrically opposite. A rise in the price
of raw produce may be occasioned by a gradual accumulation of capital, which by creating new demands for labour
may give a stimulus to population and consequently promote the cultivation or improvement of inferior lands ;

but this will not cause profits to rise but to fall, because not only will the rate of wages rise, but more labourers will be employed without affording a proportional return of raw produce. The whole value of the wages paid will be greater compared with the whole value of the raw produce obtained. A rise of raw produce may proceed from one or more bad seasons, which will undoubtedly increase profits because the price of produce would rise considerably more than in the proportion of the deficient quantity, and would therefore be much ahead of the price [*sic*] of production. An advanced price of raw produce may also proceed from a fall in the value of currency, which would raise the price of produce, for a time, more than it would wages, and would therefore raise profits. Both these you will allow are temporary causes, no way affecting the principle itself but merely disturbing it in its progress. Restrictions on importation of raw produce may cause a rise in its price which will be permanent or temporary according as the bad policy which dictated the restrictive law may be permanent or temporary. In the first instance profits will be raised; but they will ultimately fall below their former level. From what I have said it will appear that I am of opinion that a permanent rise in the rate of profits on land is never preceded by a rise but by a fall in the price of raw produce; and, though profits may be raised by a rise of the price of produce, they will generally ultimately settle at a rate lower than that from which they started. The converse of this, as it regards low prices of produce, I hold to be equally true. I should be glad to have your sentiments on this point. There may be other causes of high price, which do not at present occur to me.

I allow that no country ever was or can be in such a situation as not to admit of increase of profits on the land, because there is no country which is not liable to lose or waste part of its capital; there is no country which is not liable to bad seasons, to depreciated currency, to a real fall in the value of the precious metals, and to other accidents which will, some permanently and some temporarily, raise profits. You observe that in rich countries profits are often much higher, and in poor countries much lower than according to my theory, to which I reply that profits are very much reduced in the poor country by enormous wages; the wages themselves may be considered as part of the profits of stock, and are frequently the foundation of new capital. In rich countries wages are low, too low for the comforts of the labourers; too large a portion of the gross produce is retained by the owner of stock and is reckoned as profit.

I am not aware that I have underrated the effect of the wants and tastes of mankind on profits; they frequently occasion large profits on particular commodities for short periods, but they do not, I think, often operate on general profits, because they do not often influence the growth of raw produce. Adam Smith, in Book V, ch. i, p. 134 [1], concisely expresses what appears to me correct, of the effects of demand on the price of commodities. I go much further than you in ascribing effects to the wants and tastes of mankind; I believe them to be unlimited. Give men but the means of purchasing, and their wants are insatiable. Mr. Mill's theory is built on this assumption. It does not attempt to say what the proportions will be to one another of the commodities which will be produced in consequence of the accumulation of capital, but presumes that those commodities only will be produced which will be suited to the wants and tastes of mankind, because none other will be demanded.

The very term 'accumulation of capital' supposes a power somewhere to employ more labour; it supposes the total

---

[1] Ed. 5th (1789). In McCulloch's ed. (1863), pp. 336, 337. See quotation at end of letter.

income of the society to be increased, and therefore to create a demand for more food and more commodities. You ask 'whether we can furnish to persons of the same incomes a great additional quantity of commodities without lowering the price so much compared with the price of production as to destroy the effective demand for such a supply, and consequently to check its continuance to the same extent.' We answer this is not our case; we are speaking of larger incomes, not of the same incomes; and instead of anticipating a fall in the price of commodities we should expect a rise, because the fall of profits which generally follows accumulation is in consequence of the increase in the price of production, compared with the price of produce, although they would both undoubtedly rise. You appear to think, indeed you say, 'that you know no other cause for the fall of profits which generally takes place from accumulation than that the price of produce falls compared with the expense of production, or in other words, that the *effective* demand is diminished;' and by what follows you seem to infer that commodities will not only be relatively lower but really lower; and this is in fact the foundation of our difference with regard to the theory of Mr. Mill.

You will by this time feel that you have enough if not too much.

Yours truly,

DAVID RICARDO.

NOTE.—The passage of the Wealth of Nations is as follows:—
'The East India Company represented in very strong terms what had been at this time [1730] the miserable effects, as they thought them, of this competition [between themselves and the Old East India Company and private traders]. In India, they said, it raised the price of goods so high that they were not worth buying; and in England, by overstocking the market, it sunk their price so low that no profit could be made by them. That by a more

plentiful supply, to the great advantage and conveniency of the public, it must have reduced very much the price of India goods in the English market cannot well be doubted; but that it should have raised very much their price in the Indian market seems not very probable, as all the extraordinary demand which that competition could occasion must have been but as a drop of water in the immense ocean of Indian commerce. The increase of demand, besides, though in the beginning it may sometimes raise the price of goods, never fails to lower it in the long run. It encourages production, and thereby increases the competition of the producers, who, in order to undersell one another, have recourse to new divisions of labour and new improvements of art, which might never otherwise have been thought of. The miserable effects of which the company complained were the cheapness of consumption and the encouragement given to production: precisely the two effects which it is the great business of political economy to promote.'

XXI.

MY DEAR SIR, GATCOMB PARK, 18 *Dec.*, 1814.

Since I received your last letter I have been unexpectedly called from home, besides having had friends staying with me, which have prevented me from writing sooner. I have been twice to Bath and once to Cheltenham, and have also been as far as Devonshire, to the old Abbey which Mr. Bentham[1] at present inhabits. I accompanied M. Say, the author of Économie Politique, on a visit to him and Mr. Mill[2];—and, had it not been for the incessant rain, we should have had a very pleasant excursion. M. Say came to me here from London at the request of Mr. Mill, who wished us to be acquainted with each other. He intends seeing you before he quits this

---

[1] See note at end of this letter.
[2] Mill had permanently taken up his abode with Bentham there in the summer of this year (1814). His biographer gives a long description of the house (*Life of Jas. Mill*, pp. 129 seq). It is in the valley of the Axe, four miles from Chard, on the borders of Devonshire and Somerset.

country. He does not appear to me to be ready in conversation on the subject on which he has very ably written, —and indeed in his book there are many points which I think are very far from being satisfactorily established,— yet he is an unaffected agreeable man, and I found him an instructive companion.

We intend to be in London in the middle of January, and have little doubt that we shall return here quite time enough to receive a visit from Mrs. Malthus and you next summer vacation, so I trust you will not project an excursion to any other quarter.

I perceive that we are not nearly agreed on the subject which we have been lately discussing. I have been endeavouring to get you to admit that the profits on stock employed in manufactures and commerce are seldom permanently lowered or raised by any other cause than by the cheapness or dearness of necessaries, or of those objects on which the wages of labour are expended. Accumulation of capital has a tendency to lower profits. Why? because every accumulation is attended with increased difficulty in obtaining food, unless it is accompanied with improvements in agriculture; in which case it has no tendency to diminish profits. If there were no increased difficulty, profits would never fall, because there are no other limits to the profitable production of manufactures but the rise of wages. If with every accumulation of capital we could tack a piece of fresh fertile land to our Island, profits would never fall. I admit at the same time that commerce, or machinery, may produce an abundance and cheapness of commodities, and if they affect the prices of those commodities on which the wages of labour are expended they will so far raise profits:—but then it will be true that less capital will be employed on the land, for the wages paid for labour form a part of that capital. A diminution of the proportion of produce, in consequence of the accumulation of capital, does not fall wholly on the owner of stock, but is shared with him by the labourers. The whole amount of wages paid will be greater, but the portion paid to each man will in all probability be somewhat diminished.

I do not recollect ever having allowed that an extension of foreign commerce will take capital from the land, unless we were an exporting country as far as regards corn, in which case my proposition would be true, namely that the rate of profits can never permanently rise unless capital be withdrawn from the land. I am not sanguine about the principle, if true, being of any use; but that is another consideration;—its utility has nothing to do with its truth, and it is the latter only which I am at present anxious to establish. I cannot agree with you when you say that 'without supposing capital to be taken from the land the throwing of new objects of desire into the market will increase the value of the whole mass of commodities in the country, estimated either in money, or in corn and labour,' —and it is because I think that there will not be a greater value of commodities to be exchanged for the raw produce, or for money, that I conclude no increased profits will anywhere be made. If the mass of commodities be increased we diminish their exchangeable value as compared with those things whose quantity is not augmented. If we double the quantity, or rather double the facility of making stockings, we diminish their value one half, as compared with *all* other commodities. If we do the same with regard to hats and shoes, we restore the accustomed relations between stockings, hats, and shoes, but not with respect to other things. It is here, I think, that our difference rests, and I hope soon to hear all that you have to advance in favour of your view of the question.

M. Say, in the new edition of his book, p. 99, vol. i, supports, I think, the very [same] doctrine that demand is regulated by production. Demand [is] always an exchange of one commodity for another. The shoemaker when he exchanges his shoes for bread has an effective demand for bread, as well as the baker has an effective demand for shoes,—and, although it is clear that the shoemaker's demand for bread must be limited by his wants, yet whilst he has shoes to offer in exchange he will have an effective demand for other things,—and if his shoes are not in demand it shows that he has not been governed by the just principles of trade, and that he has not used his capital and his labour in the manufacture of the commodity required by the society,—more caution will enable him to correct his error in his future production. Accumulation necessarily increases production and as necessarily increases consumption. Accumulation of *produce*, if properly selected, *may* always be accumulation of *capital*, and it cannot fail to be worth more than it cost, estimated in corn or labour,— and this I think would be true although all our soldiers, sailors, and menial servants were employed in productive labour. It appears to me that the consideration of money value may be the foundation of our difference on this point.

I must leave room for a request which I hope you will not refuse. I dined a little while ago at Mr. Smith's, whom I first met at your house. Mrs. Smith told me that she had a collection of the handwriting of a great number of men who had distinguished themselves by their writings, and she wished that I would give her a letter of yours to add to her collection. Knowing that I had many which would not discredit you, I assented; but after I came home I thought I had no right to do it without your consent— which I hope you will not refuse. I should be sorry to disappoint her, and should really cut a poor figure in making my apologies if I did; yet, as my opinion, that I should not do it without your consent, is confirmed by

Mrs. Ricardo, I must falter out my excuses if you are inexorable. With kind regards to Mrs. Malthus,

I am, ever yours truly,

DAVID RICARDO.

NOTE.—Of Ricardo, Bentham used to say: 'I was the spiritual father of Mill, and Mill was the spiritual father of Ricardo; so that Ricardo was my spiritual grandson. I was often *tête à tête* with Ricardo. He would borrow a sixpenny book instead of buying it. There was an *épanchement* between us. We used to walk together in Hyde Park, and he reported to me what passed in 'the House of Commons. He had several times intended to quote the 'Fragment'; but his courage failed him as he told me. In Ricardo's book on rent there is a want of logic. I wanted him to correct it on these principles; but he was not conscious of it, and Mill was not desirous. He confounded *cost* with *value*. Considering our intercourse it was natural he should give me a copy of his book;—the devil a bit!' (Life by Bowring in Works, vol. x. p. 498.) Then follows a letter to Ricardo, in which Bentham compliments him on his political progress: 'I told Burdett you had got down to *trienniality*, and were wavering between that and annuality, where I could not help flattering myself you would fix,—also, in respect of extent, down to *householders*, for which, though I should prefer universality on account of its simplicity and unexclusiveness, I myself should be glad to compound.' The suggestion of stinginess made by Bentham in the passage quoted is sufficiently rebutted by Bentham's own biographer, who tells us Ricardo was one of those who guaranteed the funds for Bentham's Chrestomathic School (Bentham, Works, x. p. 484), and by James Mill (Biography, p. 191), when he speaks of Ricardo's unwillingness to accept payment for his article (Sinking Fund) in the Encyclopædia Britannica on the grounds that, first, it was not worth payment, second, payment was no part of his inducement to write it.

The influence of Bentham on Ricardo's general ways of thinking is discussed elsewhere. In economical theory (if we judge Bentham by his 'Manual of Political Economy,' which was written some years before this time, though not published in England till long afterwards) there was no more than a general agreement between the two men.

XXII.[1]

MY DEAR SIR,   GATCOMB PARK, 13 *Jan.*, 1815.

I am pleased to learn that you are busy writing
with a view to immediate publication[2]. The public pay a
most flattering attention to anything from your pen, and
you are not fulfilling your duty to society if you do not
avail yourself of this disposition to endeavour[3] to remove
the cloud of ignorance and prejudice, which everywhere
exists on the subjects which have particularly engaged
your time and reflection. I hope your notes on Adam
Smith are in great forwardness, and that they will soon
follow the smaller publications which you are now preparing. I expect that they will not only be very useful
in giving correct notions to the public, but also in calling
the attention of those who are well informed in the science
of political economy to many points which have hitherto
escaped their consideration.

I cannot help thinking that Lord Lauderdale was mistaken (and I believe you hold the same opinion as him),
in supposing the farmer to lie under any particular disadvantage from not having the monopoly of the home
market, whilst so many other trades were enjoying that
benefit. You will agree that the monopoly of the home
market is eventually of no great advantage to the trade
on which it is conferred. It is true that it raises the price
of the commodity by shutting out foreign competition, but
this is equally injurious to all consumers, and presses no
more on the farmer than on other trades. If. monopolies

---

[1] The first sentences of this letter are quoted by Empson, Edinb. Review,
Jan. 1837, p. 498.

[2] He was writing the tract entitled : ' Grounds of an Opinion on the
Policy of Restricting the Importation of Foreign Corn, intended as an Appendix
to " Observations on the Corn Laws." ' It might however have been the tract
on Rent to which Ricardo is here alluding. See Letter XXIII.

[3] Here as elsewhere spelt ' endeavor.'

tend to raise the price of labour, the inconvenience must be suffered by all who employ labour, and will therefore not be particularly injurious to the farmer or landlord. If all the monopolies of the home market were immediately abolished, there would be at least as much disposition to import corn:—if so they do not interfere with the natural course of the corn trade. Lord Lauderdale, with his opinion of the effect of monopolies, is, I think, quite consistent in recommending a duty on the importation of corn.

I thought you maintained that the high or low profits on commerce were totally independent of the amount of capital which might be employed on the land, consequently that high profits might continue as long as commerce was prosperous, whether that was for twenty or for a hundred years. I now understand you to say, that the profits of commerce may take the lead, and may regulate the profits of agriculture for a period of some duration, possibly for twenty years.

I have always allowed that under certain circumstances profits on agriculture might be diverted from their regular course for short periods, so that we only appear to differ with respect to the duration of such profits; instead of twenty years I should limit it to about four or five.

If with the same labour we could obtain double the quantity of tin from the mines in Cornwall, after prices had found the[ir l]evel, would the value of the whole mass of commodities be increased in England? Should we obtain the same quantity of deals from Norway in exchange for a given quantity of tin as we now do? Although the mass of commodities both in the markets of Norway and in those of England would increase by the greater abundance of tin, or of some other commodity, if the labour employed in procuring tin were diverted to other objects, yet the estimated value of all their commodities in corn, money, or any article but tin, would, it appears to me, continue unaltered. It is sufficient that deals can be purchased cheaper in Norway than elsewhere to determine a portion of foreign trade to that quarter, although it should yield no more profits than those of other trades.

On the supposition which you have made of a great foreign demand for our raw produce, there can be no question that more capital would be employed on the land, and I think profits would fall. Such a demand cannot exist in the present situation of the world. Raw produce is always imported into the relatively rich country, and never exported from it, but on occasions of dearth or famine. I have no doubt that, if the free importation of corn is allowed into this country, inasmuch as it will direct foreign capital to foreign land, it will tend to lower foreign profits, and if all the earth were cultivated *with equal skill* up to the same standard, the rate of profits would be everywhere the same, though the superior industry and ingenuity of particular countries might secure to them a greater abundance of other commodities. . .

Your club meets, I think, on the 28th. . . Pray take a bed at our house. . .

Truly yours,

DAVID RICARDO.

XXIII.

[Headed by Malthus in pencil, *Feb.* 1815. Post Office mark, *Feb.* 6.]

MY DEAR SIR,

I have now read with great attention your essay on the rise and progress of Rent[1], with a view of selecting every passage which might afford us subject for future discussion. It is no praise to say that all the leading principles in it meet with my perfect assent, and that I consider it as containing many original views which are not only important

[1] 'An Inquiry into the Nature and Progress of Rent and the principles by which it is regulated.' 1815.

as connected with rent, but with many other difficult points, such as taxation, etc., etc.

I cannot, however, help regretting that you did not consider separately the relations of rent with the profits of stock and the wages of labour. By treating of the joint effect of the two latter on rent you have, I think, not made the subject so clear as it might have been made.

There are some parts in the essay with which I cannot agree. One of these is the effects of improvements, whether in the practice of agriculture or in the implements of husbandry, on rent. They appear to me in their immediate effects to be beneficial to the farmer only and not to the landlord. All the augmented produce obtained, or the saving in obtaining the same quantity of produce is, I think, wholly to the advantage of the farmer, and that the landlord only benefits remotely from it, as it may encourage accumulation and the cultivation of poorer lands. I think too that rents are in no case a creation of wealth ; they are always a part of the wealth already created, and are enjoyed necessarily, but not on that account less beneficially to the public interest, at the expense of the profits of stock [1].

Viewing rents in this light, it follows that I must withdraw the concession which I was inclined to make when you first started the question 'whether, in importing corn at a cheaper price than we could grow it, the whole difference of price was saved, or whether some abatement should not be made from the advantage for the loss of rent?' as I now decide[d]ly think that the whole difference of price would be gained without any deduction whatever. The arguments then of those who contend for a free trade in corn remain in their original full force, as rents are always withdrawn from the profits of stock. I will try, if I have

[1] In the original, 'trade' has been written first and then struck out in favour of ' stock.'

a little leisure, to put my thoughts on this subject on paper, and shall attempt to show that the effects of a tax and of rent are very different as far as regards importation. It may be economical to grow corn if its price is raised merely by taxation, as by importing it a part of the tax would be wholly lost to the country [import]ing it. No such consideration should influence us [with regar]d to rent being lost.

I differ, as you know, as to the effects of taxation on the growth of produce. You appear to me not quite consistent in admitting, as you unequivocally do, that the last portion of land cultivated yields nothing more than the profits of stock, no rent, and yet to maintain that taxes on necessaries or on raw produce fall on the landlord and not on the consumer.

. . I have paid Wettenhall £2 8s. for two years' lists, but it has since occurred to me that I paid him and you paid me for one year, and therefore that only one year can be due to him. If so, let me know, that I may get back £1 4s.

Ever yours,

DAVID RICARDO.

XXIV.

MY DEAR SIR,   *10th Feb.*, 1815.

I shall accept your kind invitation, and intend being with you on Saturday evening at the usual time. We can then talk over the points on which we differ. I will bring with me the papers on which I have been busy since you left London, and in which my objections are more fully stated than can be done in the compass of a letter[1].

---

[1] 'An Essay on the Influence of a Low Price of Corn on the Profits of Stock, shewing the inexpediency of Restrictions on Importation, with Remarks on Mr. Malthus's two last Publications,' 1815. Ricardo's Works (McCulloch), pp. 367-390.

In the case of the Scotch farmers who made such large profits on their capital during the latter part of their leases[1], they appear to me to have been enjoying rent, arising not from improvements in agriculture, but from poorer land being taken into cultivation. If their leases had expired sooner, rent would have been increased long before on those farmers. It would be desirable to know what the rent on those farms was when the lease was originally granted, or rather what proportion it bore to the capital then employed and what the proportion of rent is to the capital now employed.

The effects of monopoly cannot, I think, be felt till no more land can be advantageously cultivated. You have yourself said, and I very much admire the passage[2], that the last portion of capital employed on the land yields only the common profits of stock, and does not afford any rent. If so, corn, like everything else, is regulated in its price by the cost of production, and every other portion of capital employed on the land is reduced to the same level of profits only because no more capital can be employed with more advantage, and all which it anywhere yields more is rent and not profit.

I have read the Appendix[3] also with great attention, and cannot help thinking that you have quite thrown off the character of impartiality to which, in the Observations, I thought you fairly entitled. You are avowedly for restrictions on importation; of that I do not complain. It is not easy to estimate justly the dangers to which we may be exposed. Those who are for an open trade in corn may underrate them, and it is possible that you may overrate them. It is a most difficult point to calculate these dangers

---

[1] Cf. ' Nature and Progress of Rent,' p. 30, note.

[2] 'Rent,' pp. 21, 34. In the latter, Malthus says 'it would return only the common profits of stock with little or no rent.' Cf. ib. p. 36.

[3] ' Grounds of an Opinion.' See note on Letter XXII, p. 56.

at their fair value ; but in an economical view, although
you have here and there allowed that we might be benefited by importing cheap rather than by growing dear, you
point out many inconveniences which we should suffer
from the loss of agricultural capital and from other causes,
which would make it appear as if even economically you
thought we ought to import corn,—such is the approbation
with which you quote from Adam Smith of [*sic*] the benefits
of agriculture over commerce in increasing production [1],
and which I cannot help thinking is at variance with all
your general doctrines.

Your observations on the advantages (and therefore on
the injustice to other classes) which the stockholder would
reap from a low price of corn are, I think, very correct; but
I do not think these objections should stand in the way of
the general good.   They, the stockholders, have at different
periods suffered much, and, if the sinking fund be now
appropriated to other services [2], another striking injustice
will be added to the long list.   I meant to write only a few
lines and have filled a long letter. . . .

Yours very truly,

DAVID RICARDO.

XXV.

MY DEAR SIR,   LONDON, *9th March*, 1815.

My acquaintance lies so little amongst political
economists that I have very few opportunities of knowing

---

[1] Probably the passage in Book II, ch. v, quoted by Ricardo in Pol. Econ.
ch. ii (on Rent), p. 39 foot (McCulloch's ed. of Works).   It contains the
Physiocratic paradox that in manufactures nature does nothing, man does all ;
in agriculture nature does nearly all and man very little.

[2] Ricardo's opinion, expressed frequently and emphatically afterwards in
the House of Commons, and most fully on paper in his article on the Sinking
Fund written for the Encycl. Brit., was that no safeguards could prevent the
Sinking Fund from being appropriated by a needy government, and that it
was therefore from the point of view of the public interest a mere snare
and delusion.

whether what you consider as my peculiar opinions have any supporters, or indeed are read or attended to. As for my own judgment on the subject, it is perhaps too partial to merit attention; but after my best efforts not to be biassed in favour of my own opinions, I continue to think them correct.

I would indeed rather modify what I said concerning the stationary state of the prices of commodities under all the variations of the price of corn, either from wealth on the one hand or the importation from foreign countries or improvements in agriculture on the other. I made no allowance for the altered value of the raw material in all manufactured goods[1]. They would, I think, be subject to a variation in price not on account of increased or diminished wages, but on account of the rise or fall in the price of the raw produce which enters into their composition, and which in some commodities cannot be inconsiderable. It is a matter of mortification to me that my execution has been so faulty; I was too much in a hurry, and have not made my meaning intelligible even to those who are familiar with such subjects, much less to those who skim over these matters.

Since I have seen you I received a note from Mr. Edward West, who is the author writing under the title of a Fellow of University College; he speaks in favour of my opinions of course, because they are very similar to his own. I have read his book with attention, and I find that his views agree very much with my own. He is a barrister, a young man, and appears very fond of the study of political economy. Mr. Brougham has, I think he said, promised to introduce him to you. Mr. Jacob[2] has handled both him

---

[1] Cf. Ricardo's Pol. Econ., ch. vi. 65 (ed. McCulloch).

[2] In his 'Letter to Samuel Whitbread, Esq., M.P.; being a Sequel to Considerations on Protection of Brit. Agriculture, with Remarks on the Publications of a Fellow of University College, and Mr. Ricardo, and Mr. Torrens.'

and me rather roughly; but he will not condescend to argue with us. I shall be very easy if he is the most formidable opponent that is to attack me, for he seems totally ignorant of the scientific part of the subject.

The opposition to the bill [1] is more formidable than I expected, but they appear so determined in the House of Commons, that I suppose it will finally pass. I regret that the people should have proceeded to acts of riots and outrage. I am too much a friend to good order to wish to succeed through such means, besides that I am persuaded that they hurt rather than promote the object which they and I have in view.

I wish you could have dined with me on Saturday. I expect Mr. Phillips [2] and Mr. Dumont; it would be a very agreeable surprise to me if you should join our party. Perhaps you may be inclined to come to London and wil[l] take a bed in Brook Street. Do if you can [and] do not think it necessary to write on purpose to say you cannot. I shall fully depend on your staying with us when you come to the next club.

Sir F. Burdett and some others think that the high price of our corn is owing to enormous taxation, and that it ought not nor cannot fall without oppression to the landholders till our debt is diminished. If I could convince myself that any part of the price of corn was owing to taxation, I should be in favour of a protecting duty to that amount.

Dated 25th Feb. 1815. He discusses West in a long ' Note,' and the two others in a longer ' Appendix.' Ricardo (whose tract on ' The Influence of a Low Price of Corn on the profits of Stock ' he has just read) has, he says, ' little practical knowledge,' but brings forward ' truisms mixed with vagaries, clothed in the technical cant of political economy.' Torrens does not escape much more easily.

[1] The New Corn Law, prohibiting importation when the home price of wheat should be under 80s. a quarter.

[2] Possibly William Phillips, F.R.S., F.G.S., the Quaker and eminent mineralogist and geologist, member of the Geological Society. Born 1773, died 1828. Ricardo in early life was himself devoted to geological study.

But, if he were right, the high price would not be accompanied by high rents or by the cultivation of inferior lands. These I consider as unequivocal marks of the high price being caused by wealth and a scarcity of fertile land. Indeed my theory leads me to think that no taxes but those directly on the land or on its produce would raise the price of corn, and even such taxes would have no effect if all exportable commodities were taxed in the same degree, for a tax on exportable commodities in a country which imports corn does not act very differently from a duty on the importation of corn. Kind regards to Mrs. Malthus.

Ever yours,

DAVID RICARDO.

XXVI.[1]

MY DEAR SIR,UPPER BROOK STREET, 14 *March*, 1815.

I have read Mr. Torrens' pamphlet [2] and think it on the whole a very able performance. I differ with him in most of his views in chap. 2, part 2, with many of the 3rd chap., and with a few in the remainder of the work. I am glad to hear that you are going to make some observations on it [3]. I think he is an adversary worthy of your pen,

---

[1] Part of this letter (5th sentence to 8th) is quoted by Empson, Edinb. Review, Jan. 1837, p. 499.

[2] 'Essay on the External Corn Trade,' 1815, Part II, ch. ii: 'Is the general principle' of free trade 'liable to limitations in the case of a country more heavily taxed than other growing countries?' (To which Torrens answers: No), ch. iii. Should there be limitations where an artificial range of prices has been created by continued protection? (To which he answers: No, but the re-introduction of free trade should be gradual.) It was probably on such subjects as Tithes and Taxation that he differed most from Ricardo. On the whole, Torrens stands rigidly by Adam Smith as against his successors, especially Malthus. See Note to Letter XXIX.

[3] Malthus did not carry out his intention. Though there are occasional references in his later books to Torrens' 'Production of Wealth,' there seems to be nothing like a reply to the strictures in this 'Essay.'

and the friends of truth cannot fail to profit by the discussion. With regard to any remarks on my opinions, you must be governed by your own discretion. If those opinions are wrong, I should like to see them refuted, but, thinking as I do that they are in all essential points founded on correct principles, I ask for no mercy. I do not care how severely they are attacked; there is nothing you could say of them which would hurt me, if what you said did not express contempt, and that I know you do not feel for me. Act therefore towards me as if I were a perfect stranger, and notice me or not as you think best.

I cannot hesitate in agreeing with you that, if from a rise in the relative value of corn less is paid for fixed capital and wages, more of the produce must remain for the landlord and farmer together; this is indeed self-evident, but is really not the matter in dispute between us, and I cannot help thinking that you overlook some of the circumstances most important connected with the question. My opinion is that corn can only permanently rise in its exchangeable value when the real expenses [1] of its production increase. If 5000 quarters of gross produce cost 2500 quarters for the expenses of wages, etc., and 10,000 quarters cost double, or 5000 quarters, the exchangeable value of corn would be the same; but, if the 10,000 quarters cost 5500 quarters for the expenses of wages, etc., then the price would rise 10 p. c., because such would be the amount of the increased expenses. A rise of the price of corn and a fall in the corn price of labour is [*sic*] in my opinion incompatible, unless it be owing to something in the currency; and it is not necessary to enquire here what effects that would produce. Observe that I do not question that each individual labourer may receive a less corn price of labour, because I believe that would be the case, but I question whether the whole corn amount of wages, etc.,

[1] Here as elsewhere spelt in the old fashion 'expences.'

paid for the cultivation of the land can be diminished with an increase of the exchangeable value of corn. If no more labourers were employed and the price of corn rose, your proposition could not be disputed; but the cause of the rise of the price of corn is solely on account of the increased expense of production.

I have lost Lord Lauderdale's pamphlet [1], or rather it has been taken from my office. If I can get another, it sha[ll] accompany this. The improvement[s] in agriculture I believe have had more effect in kee[ping] down r[ents] than we have ever imagined. On my theory they fully account for rents being no higher; on yours they would tell the other way.

I meant to reproach you when I saw you [for [2]] speaking of Mr. Jacob's pamphlet with so much [praise [2]] as you did when Mr. Basevi [3] asked your opinion of it. I am glad you allow he is very deficient in scientific knowledge.

You will see by what I have said that a rise in the price of corn is always in my opinion accompanied by a less material surplus produce; but it may be of equal value as compared with other things. Of this produce the landlord gets so large a share that in spite of the rise of produce the situation of the farmer is constantly getting worse.

Yours very truly,
DAVID RICARDO.

XXVII.

My dear Sir,   London, 17 *March*, 1815.

If your statement [4] was correct, this extravagant consequence would follow from it: That in proportion as

---

[1] Probably one of the two he published on the Currency in 1812 and 1813 respectively.

[2] MS. hopelessly torn.

[3] The name appears as Baswi in Ricardo's letters to Say. Even in Ricardo's clear handwriting Basevi and Baswi would be hardly distinguishable.

[4] Probably the statement given at the beginning of next letter.

population increased and worse land was brought under
cultivation, the proportion of produce to the corn expenses of
procuring it would increase. If we now had twenty millions
of quarters with an expense of five millions of quarters, we
should when we expended ten millions of quarters obtain
more than forty [1], notwithstanding that in the latter period
many more than double the quantity of hands were employed in cultivation in consequence of the poorer quality
of the land. If this be true, the principle of population is
false, because the more you increase the people, the greater
surplus of abundance will appear. Your statement is however very ingenious, and carries a great deal of plausibility
with it; but I think you err in supposing it possible that
the proportion of the whole corn expenditure to the produce
obtained can fall, with an increase of the price of corn.
The two are incompatible ; either the whole corn expenses
of production will be increased or not. If they be, the price
of corn will rise ; but, if they be not, I can see no reason
for a rise in the price of corn. I admit that it is only the
last portion of capital employed on the land which will be
attended with an increased corn expense ; but, unless it
renders the whole produce together at an increased expense, the price of produce will not rise. Suppose the produce of the country ten millions of quarters with the price
at £4 per quarter, the number of labourers employed two-
and-a-half millions, each receiving two quarters of corn
annually as wages. Suppose too that the population increases and five millions of quarters more are required, but
that it cannot be obtained with less labour than that of two
millions of men. If we suppose the price to increase in proportion to the number of men employed, it will rise to £4 16s.,
because to raise ten millions of quarters an average of three

[1] This really happens in the cases made prominent by Mr. Carey, 'Social
Science,' I. iv (1858), where historical circumstances have made cultivation
begin with indifferent instead of fertile soils.

millions of men would be now required instead of two-and-a-half millions. Suppose now each man to consume one quarter annually for food and to exchange the remainder for other necessaries. Fourteen bushels will be sufficient wages for him[1]; the expenditure of corn for wages will then be for fifteen millions of produce 7.875.000, and for ten millions 5.250.000. Before, it was only five millions; consequently the proportion of surplus produce has diminished.

In making this calculation I have very much favoured your view of the question, because the price of corn would not, I think, rise in proportion to the greater number of men employed but to the greater amount of wages paid; it would not therefore rise to £4 16*s.*, but to £4 4*s.*, because as $5 : 5\frac{1}{4} :: £4 : £4$ 4*s.* But, if the price was only £4 4*s.*, more corn would be required by the labourer than fourteen bushels, that calculation being founded on a greater exchangeable value of corn. It appears too that your statement if true does not account for the less proportion of the population now emp[loyed upon] the land, because you always suppose more men to [be employed] but at less corn wages. It can never happen, I think, that profits can fall and encourage the cultivation of poor [land in] the manner assumed in my table without a rise in the price of corn. It is by the rise of the price of corn that all other profits are regulated to agricultural profits. If the price of corn remained low, money wages would not rise, and general profits could not fall. If it be true that capital has become more and more productive on the land, it can, I think, only be accounted for on the supposition that great improvements have taken place in agriculture, and that wages have been kept moderate by the improvements in those manufactures which supply the poor with the necessaries on which a part of their wages are expended.

What a dreadful change in our political horizon has

---

[1] Because the remaining six would purchase what eight purchased before.

occurred within a few days[1]! Will it be possible to remain at peace if Bonaparte establishes himself as sovereign of France? The prospect is very gloomy.

> . . . Ever yours,
> DAVID RICARDO.

XXVIII.

MY DEAR SIR,　　　　　　　　LONDON, 21 *March*, 1815.

On no subject that we have been lately discussing have we so materially differed as on the one now occupying our attention. Your position, if established, would, I think, overturn both your theory of rent and population, for I understand you to maintain that the higher the price of corn rises, in consequence of more men being employed on the poorer land, the greater will be, not only the surplus produce after paying the labourers, but the ratio of that surplus produce to the whole capital employed on the land. If this be true there is no check to the increase of population, and food can be increased in a ratio exceeding that at which mankind increase. Your statement requires that with every additional labourer not only an equal increase but a greater increase of surplus produce should be obtained. More labourers may then be employed without limit, and rent and profit together must not only increase, but increase in a geometrical progression. I am sure I am correct in thus stating your proposition, because if as you say the whole corn expense of production per quarter will be diminished with every rise of price, the surplus must increase in a geometrical ratio with the capital employed. If you meant only that the surplus produce would increase with every accumulation of capital on the land, though in a diminishing ratio to the capital employed on the land, that is not only advanced, but strenuously maintained as

---

[1] Napoleon landed near Frejus on 26th Feb., 1815.

the groundwork of my theory, and is the basis also on which my table is formed. You have misapprehended a passage in my last letter. I certainly never said, nor ever thought, that any good reason could be given for an increased number of men being required to produce precisely the same quantity of corn from precisely the same land. What I said was that, if at one period the number of labourers required to produce ten millions of quarters of corn was two-and-a-half millions of men, and at another, in consequence of increased demand, fifteen millions of quarters could not be produced with a portion of worse land at a less cost of labour than that of four-and-a-half millions, at this latter period a production of ten millions would require three millions of men, because fifteen is to four-and-a-half as ten to three, and if we supposed the price of corn under such circumstances to increase in the proportion of $2\frac{1}{2}$ to 3, a supposition much more favourable to your view of the question than we should be obliged to concede, yet that it would not support the conclusions to which you arrive, but, on the contrary, would prove my theory to be the correct one. If the calculation had been made, as you think would have been more correct, on an increase from ten millions to ten-and-a-half millions, the result would have been the same, but we should be puzzled with the decimals or fractions which must be employed on such a supposition. I agree with you 'that the natural price of corn depends entirely upon the price of the last addition, and it does not matter whether with regard to the old land a capital yields 50 per cent. rent and profit or 20 per cent. In either case the price of corn on such land has nothing to do with the cost of production.' I do not see how the admission of this fact can assist your argument, which relates only to the ratio of the surplus produce to the whole capital employed.

I cannot conceive by what argument you could shew

that it might be possible that the addition of another
labourer on the land would not pay his expenses, although
not more than a quarter of the population were employed upon the land. Allowing, as I most fully do, that
no pressure can destroy rents, yet as the last portions of
capital employed on the land pay no rent, it is to me
inconceivable that there would be no inducement to employ
more labourers whilst their average production should be
three times more food than they could themselves consume.
If the whole of this surplus, after maintaining in the most
frugal manner the owners of stock, were absorbed by the
landlords as rent, they would increase their revenue, and
employ more labourers on the land, if any among them
saved any part of his income and lent it at the common
rate of interest. I am sorry you do not come to town for
the next club.

Yours truly,

DAVID RICARDO.

XXIX.

My dear Sir,   London, *27th March*, 1815.

No particular event which I recollect ever occasioned so great a gloom as the late lamentable reverse.
At present we have the most dismal forebodings of war
and its consequences on our finances; the truth is our
courage is not screwed up to the proper pitch; like everything else, we shall be easy under our new situation in
another fortnight. I am glad, however, to turn my attention to other subjects.

I have observed in the bullion pamphlet[1] that many
who say they consider money only as a commodity, and
subject to the same laws of variation in value from demand and supply as other commodities, seldom proceed

---

[1] Or rather in the Appendix to it, p. 292 (McCulloch's ed.).

far in their reasoning about money without showing that they really consider money as something peculiar, varying from causes totally different from those which affect other commodities. Do you not fall into this error when you say, ' In the first place all depends upon the relation between corn and other commodities, and, as labour and corn enter into the prices of all commodities, the difference between corn and other commodities cannot possibly increase in any proportion to the increase in the money price of corn'? If money be a commodity does [*sic*] not corn and labour enter into its price or value? And, if they do, why should not money vary as compared with corn and labour by the same law as all other commodities do? As far as this question regards the importation of corn, you are much more interested than I am in maintaining the uniform value of commodities, because if the rise of the price of corn and labour will as you contend raise the price of our commodities, this is an additional reason why we should not impose restrictions on the importation of corn, as it will subject us to a decided disadvantage in our competition with foreigners for the sale of our commodities.

Not however to dwell on this very essential point, I agree with you that a rise in the price of corn occasions a different distribution of the produce from the old land. It does this by lowering profits. Instead of a manufacturer having it in his power to maintain a servant or mechanic who may contribute to his enjoyment, that power will be transferred to the landlord, and this will arise from the lower corn value of manufactured goods. Indeed I see no limit to the fall of the corn value of goods but the impossibility of manufacturing them with any the least return of profit, and this will not happen till the landlord has appropriated to himself in the form of rent nearly the whole surplus produce of the land. It appears to me that the progress of wealth, whilst it in-

creases accumulation, has a natural tendency to produce
this effect and is as certain as the principle of gravitation.

You have, I think, totally changed your proposition.
You before contended that, in consequence of increasing
wealth and the cultivation of poorer land, the whole *corn*
cost of production on the land would bear a *less* proportion
to the whole *corn* produce; but now you say that the
money cost of production on the land will bear a less
proportion to the *money* value of the whole produce. Between these propositions there is a very material difference,
as the latter might be true at the very time that the
former was false. To admit what you now contend for
would not affect my theory, as, though it would prove
that the landlord and tenant (together) got more money
revenue, or, if you will, a greater proportion of money
revenue as compared to the money capital employed, yet
the tenant might and I think would get a less proportion,
and therefore the rate of profits would fall. Such a state
of price [*sic*] is quite compatible with a greater proportion
of men, as compared with the produce obtained, being
employed on the land; but it is wholly irreconcileable
with the net corn produce bearing a larger proportion
to the gross corn produce, which was the principle before
contended for. I agree with you that the increased price
of corn in the order of things is rather a cause than a
consequence of a greater than the usual number of men
being employed to obtain the same quantity of produce
from new land, because profits from such an employment
of capital may be higher than other profits; but this difference of profit may be owing to a general fall in the
rate of profits on other concerns rather than to the actual
elevation of the profits on land; and I am of opinion that
a rise in the price of corn always lowers general profits
by increasing wages. I can in no way satisfy myself that
general profits can rise with a rising price of corn and

fall with falling prices, unless they are raised or lowered
by diminishing or increasing wages, and then they can be
but of short duration. In the ordinary course of things,
as a high price of corn attends a state of progression,
wages of labour will be really high, and profits cannot rise
because of wages being low.

I am decidedly of opinion that Torrens [1] has treated
you unjustly in his remarks in the preface of his book.
If I recollect, you acknowledged an alteration in your
opinion respecting the corn laws, since you wrote your
essay on population, in your 'Observations on the Corn
Laws.' I think too that you have always held the opinion
you now do that the difference between the value of gold
and paper was partly owing to the rise of the value of
gold. Is not his criticism very much strained as to the
use of the word depreciation? But, if he be right in all,
the instances are much too few to justify his severe
observation. At the Geological Club [2] his book was
spoken of the other day with great approbation. Mr.
Blake [3] and Mr. Greenough [4] think that he has exhausted
the subject, and that his arguments cannot be controverted.
I should think that he is very generally read. 'If I would
lay a tax on foreign corn,' you ask, 'on account of a tax
on our own, does not the same principle apply to the
indirect taxes that raise the price of labour?' I think
not, because a tax on corn will raise the price of corn
twice, once on account of the tax, and a second time on
account of the rise of wages; but, as this second rise is

[1] See the Note at the end of this letter.

[2] Ricardo was one of the original members of the Geological Society. See McCulloch's ed. of his Works, p. xvii.

[3] Blake, probably William Blake, author of 'Observations on the principles which regulate the course of Exchange and on the present depreciated state of the Currency,' 1810.

[4] Probably G. B. Greenough, F.R.S., F.S.L., and President of the Geological Society, who wrote on Geology, 1819.

common to all things in which labour enters, and will be corrected by a new value of money, it will not be of long duration. The indirect taxes which only raise the wages of labour produce, I think, the same effects as the second rise in the price of corn, of which I have just been speaking. Whenever a tax bore with unequal effect on the land, when it did not affect labour bestowed in other employments, a countervailing duty on importation should, I think, be also imposed. I fear I cannot be with you on Saturday. If you do not hear from me by Wednesday's post, conclude that I cannot leave home. . . .

Ever yours,

David Ricardo.

NOTE.—Robert Torrens, the soldier economist, began his literary career with 'The Economist Refuted' (1808), in answer to William Spence, who in 1807 tried to persuade his countrymen that Napoleon's blockade mattered little to them, Britain being 'independent of commerce.' In the winter of 1810-11, Torrens was Major Commandant of the Royal Marines, doing garrison duty on the island of Anholt in the Kattegat. The frost gave him time to re-read his Adam Smith and write his 'Essay on Money and Paper Currency' (publ. 1812). In his 'Essay on the External Corn Trade' (see above, page 65), Torrens characterizes the writings of Malthus as suggestive and candid and full of 'facts,' but ill-reasoned and inconsistent. Mr. Malthus, he says, scarcely ever embraced a principle which he did not subsequently abandon; his Essay on Population was a plagiarism from Wallace; and he refuted it himself by introducing the influence of Moral Restraint; in regard to Corn Bounties and in regard to the Currency, his later writings have contradicted his earlier. (Pref. pp. viii. to xii.) Torrens compared the Political Economy of Malthus with that of Ricardo, greatly to the advantage of the latter, in his 'Production of Wealth' (1821). See 'Malthus and his Work,' pp. 265-6. Compare also Note to Letter XLIV.

XXX.

MY DEAR SIR,   LONDON, 4 *April*, 1815.

You think that my theory of a diminishing rate of profit in consequence of being obliged to cultivate poorer lands is affected by my admission that there will be a greater quantity of surplus produce and a greater money value from the old land. This would be true if any part of either the additional quantity or additional value belonged to the owner of stock. You, however, expressly say that this additional value or quantity 'will remain to the farmer and landlord.['] Before my theory is affected it must be shown that the whole will not remain with the landlord, as, if the farmer gets no share of it, his rate of profits cannot be raised.

I agree with you that, when the exchangeable value of corn rises, 'the whole quantity of corn in the country will exchange for a greater number of coats than before, and consequently that there will be both the power and will to purchase, with the raw produce of the country, a greater quantity of manufactured and foreign commodities.' In a progressive country I can easily conceive this power and will to be doubled or trebled, as well as the commodities on which they are exercised; but this admission does not affect the question of profits. There may be a great demand for home and foreign commodities without their price being permanently raised, as no new difficulties may attend their production. When America becomes populous and wealthy in the same proportion as the most wealthy country of Europe, will not her corn exchange at a higher value both for money and commodities, although it will have much increased in quantity? Will not all foreign and home commodities in America be double or treble their present amount, yet will not the profits of stock be less there than they now are? On this question I could not have thought that the slightest doubt could exist; all theory, all experience is in favour of this opinion.

Whilst the labour of ten persons employed on land paying no rent can produce one hundred quarters of wheat, it appears to me possible and probable that one-third more labour might profitably be employed on that land, not indeed in producing only one hundred quarters of wheat, but an additional quantity more than the additional labourers would consume. Whilst the labour of ten men can produce one hundred quarters of wheat, it is difficult to suppose profits only ten per cent., and more difficult to conceive that many more men might not be profitably employed in increasing the produce off such land. In theory, land which yields no rent, according to your supposition, would have more and more capital profitably expended on it, whilst the additional quantity of produce obtained exceeded [the] quantity paid to the additional labourers. Capital [might] be so expended, whilst the profits of stock gave any return, not ten per cent. but one per cent. or a half per cent.

No doubt money varies more slowly than other commodities for the reason you mention; nevertheless its value, like every other foreign commodity, depends on the labour and expense of bringing it to market.

I expect some friends to dine with me on Saturday, and on Monday I am engaged out to dinner; yet, if the weather is tolerably fine, I will be with you by the time you leave chapel on Sunday, but I must get home next day. If this is not quite convenient, pray let me know.

Ever yours,

DAVID RICARDO.

XXXI.

MY DEAR SIR, LONDON, 17 *April,* 1815.

You, I think, agree with Mr. Torrens that a rise in
the price of corn will be followed by a rise in the price of
home commodities; but your theory requires that there
should be no rise in the price of those commodities on
which the wages of labour are expended, for, if they rose
.in the same proportion as corn, there could be no fall in
the corn wages of labour. Is it not, however, very impro-
bable that all manufactures should rise at home, and yet
that those on which [the wages of] labour are expended
should not rise? Is not the price of soap, candles, etc.,
though foreign commodities [1], necessarily affected by the
rise in the price of those home goods which are given in
exchange for them. Mr. Torrens' theory, however, on this
part of the subject appears to me defective, as I think that
the price of commodities will be very slightly affected
either by a rise or fall in the price of corn. If so, every
rise in the price of corn must affect profits on manufactures;
and it is impossible that agricultural profits can materially
deviate from them. I will, however, suppose that you and
Mr. Torrens are correct, and that commodities do rise in
price with every increased price of corn. The value of
fixed capital as well as of circulating capital employed on
the land will then rise also; and, although the money value
of the produce should be increased on the old land, it will
still bear the same proportion to the money value of the
capital employed; and, as this produce will be divided in
different proportions between the landlord and the farmer,
the rate of profits of the latter will fall. For the purpose
of examining the effects, let us suppose that all commodi-

[1] They were only foreign in the sense of being articles, not only manufactured in this country but also imported from abroad, e. g. soap (under
a heavy duty) from France, Italy, and Spain.

ties rise, with the rise of the price of corn, excepting those only on which the wages of labour are expended, and that in consequence the corn wages of labour fall. Suppose the price of corn £4, and that on the old land the labour of eight men was necessary to raise eighty quarters of corn, that no rent was paid, and that each labourer had eight quarters annually for his wages, of which one half was expended on commodities. The gain of the farmer, when the price was £4, would be £64 or sixteen quarters, and, besides his fixed capital, horses, seed, etc., he would require the value of sixty-four quarters, or £256, to pay the annual wages of his labourers; consequently his profits would be in the proportion of £25 to £100 of wages, for 256 : 64 : : 100 : 25. Now, suppose corn to rise to £4 10*s*., wages would vary only 10*s*. on four quarters, and consequently would rise to £34 annually per man, or £272 on the old land; but the eighty quarters of corn would sell for £360, leaving a produce of £88 to be divided between farmer and landlord; and 88 would be to 272 as 32 to 100.

But on the new land the labour of eight men and a half might be required to obtain eighty quarters or £360; the labour of eight-and-a-half men would cost, at £34 each, £289; consequently the profit would be £71, which is to the whole expense of £360 as £19.7 to £100.

£100 capital or expenses on the old land will yield £32
£100 capital or expenses on the new land „   „   £19.7
$$\overline{}$$
Rent   .   .   £[1]2.3.

It appears then that the profit on new land, which regulates the profit on all other land, would be 19.7 per cent. when the price of corn was £4 10*s*. It was 25 per cent. when the price was £4.

If indeed under the same circumstances we had supposed the price of corn to rise to £6, then profits would be increased, and would be much more than 25 per cent. ; but some adequate cause must be shown for [such] rise, and it cannot be arbitrarily assumed. Your theory supposes too what is impossible, that the demand for manufactures [could] increase in the same proportion as the demand for [corn] at the very time that more men are employed on the land to obtain a less proportion of produce. The whole appears to me a labyrinth of difficulties ; one is no sooner got over than another presents itself, and so on in endless succession. Let me entreat you to give my simple doctrine fair consideration, and you must allow that it accounts for all the phenomena in an easy natural manner.

I yesterday met Mr. Smyth [1], your friend, and Mr. Torrens at Mr. Phillips'. I passed a very pleasant day. Mr. Smyth was exceedingly agreeable. I like him very much. The corn question was occasionally introduced, and I had an opportunity of stating some of my objections to Mr. Torrens' theory. I have no reason to think that I convinced him. I defended the use of the word depreciation in the sense [in] which you had used it; and I believe I had every one with me. I fancy that his arguments in his book on currency are founded on the sense in which he uses the word. We spoke on the other points of difference between him and you. Mr. Smyth, Mr. Phillips, and Mr. Torrens have agreed to dine with me on Wednesday, which has induced me to write to you a day or two sooner than I otherwise should have done that I might express my wish that you would join us. If you will, we will dine as late as you please. There will be a bed at your service, and I need not say that you will add considerably to my pleasure.

Yours very truly,

DAVID RICARDO.

NOTE.—In many of his speeches, e. g. June 12, 1822, Ricardo

[1] Probably William Smyth, Professor of Modern History at Cambridge, friend of Mackintosh and Horner.

refers to the ambiguity of the word 'depreciation.' He himself always uses it to indicate that the currency had fallen below its own standard, as e. g. when coins are clipped. Others used it of a change in the *value* of the currency as purchasing a larger or a smaller quantity of goods. A currency might be depreciated in the first sense when it was actually, through counteracting causes, the opposite (or appreciated) in the second. Malthus, in Edinburgh Review, Feb. 1811, had used it in the first sense. (See pp. 341, 356, 365.) Torrens, in his 'Essay on Money,' 1812, had used it in the second. (See pp. 98, 99.) The word 'appreciation' occurs in Tooke's 'High and Low Prices' (1823), Part I. p. 76. Tooke himself distinguishes depreciation of the Currency (the first of the above senses) from depreciation of Money (the second of them) ; (l. c. p. 8.)

XXXII.

MY DEAR SIR,   LONDON, 21 *April*, 1815.

I was sorry you could not join our party on Wednesday. Mr. Smyth has left a pleasing impression on the minds of all those who met him, and I had every reason to confirm me in the favourable opinion which I had formed of him at our first meeting. Mr. Torrens is a very gentlemanly man. He had sent me his book on bullion before he came, and I fear that too much of the conversation was bestowed on the differences between his opinion and mine on the subject of paper currency and the exchanges. The latter he does not appear to me correctly to understand. I insisted on the consistency of your former and present opinions on the bullion question, and asked him from whence he had derived his knowledge of your views on that subject. He said that Dr. Crombie [1] and you had met pur-

---

[1] Dr. Alexander Crombie, schoolmaster, theologian, and economist, had published in the Pamphleteer, vol. x, in 1813, a 'Letter to David Ricardo, containing an analysis of his pamphlet on the Depreciation of Bank Notes.' About a year after the date of this letter he wrote ' Letters on the Agricultural Interest.' When Torrens did not get his inspiration from Adam Smith he seems to have got it from Dr. Crombie, for whom he had profound respect. See Torrens' Essay on Money and Paper Currency, 1812, and Essay on External Corn Trade (Preface), 1815.

posely to discuss the question, and from him he had understood that you ascribed the whole effects on the price of
bullion to the abundance of paper. He, as well as Monsieur
Say, finds it difficult to support his opinions and answer
objections in conversation—he says all such discussions
should be carried on in writing. . . .

On Saturday I shall meet you at the King of Clubs, to
which I am invited by Mr. Whishaw, and on Sunday I wish
you and Mrs. Malthus will oblige Mrs. Ricardo and me
with your company to dinner. If you can I will ask Mr.
Whishaw and Mr. Smyth to meet you. Perhaps too you
will breakfast with me on Saturday or Sunday morning.

It appears to me that my table is applicable to all cases
in which the relative price of corn rises from more labour
being required to produce it, and under no other circumstances can there be a rise, however great the demand may
be, unless commodities fall in value from less labour being
required for their production. It is not probable that the
relative price of corn will fall so low with an abundant
capital in the country as when capital was very limited,
but, if it could, the same effects on profits and on rent
would follow, as it would demonstrate that land only of the
best quality was in cultivation. You agree with me that
if a large tract of rich land were added to the Island it
would restore the state contemplated in my table. Though
we agree in the conclusion we differ materially in our
opinion of the means by which it would be brought about.
You think that ' before any fall of price had taken place
capital would be removing fast from the old land, *and from
manufactures*,'—I think that capital would go from the old
land to manufactures, because a given quantity of food only
being required, that quantity could be raised on the rich
land added to the Island with much less capital than was
employed on the old, and consequently all the surplus
would go to [manu]factures to procure other enjoyments for

the so[ciety[1]], and profits on the land would rise at the expense of the rent of the landlord, whilst the cheaper price of corn would raise the profits on all manufacturing capital. I confess it appears to me impossible that under the circumstances you have supposed the relative value of corn would fall, not from the facility of procuring it, but from a rise in the value of manufactures. You suppose that corn would remain at the same price whilst manufactures rose in price,—I on the contrary think that the price of manufactures would continue nearly stationary, whilst the price of corn would fall. Is not this the natural consequence of more capital being employed on manufactures and less on agriculture? Have you not too uniformly supported the opinion that a fall in the price of corn will occasion a fall in the price of commodities? If they act on each other as you think, but to which I do not agree, how can manufactures rise in price with a stationary price of corn? I should have thought that on your principles such an effect would be deemed impossible.

Ever truly yours,

DAVID RICARDO.

XXXIII.

(Addressed to Claverton House, near Bath.)

MY DEAR SIR,   UPPER BROOK STREET, *27th June*, 1815.

I have been for two or three days at Tunbridge Wells, and have been agreeably surprised to-day on my arrival in London, to hear of the great events which are taking place in France in consequence of the great victory obtained by the Duke of Wellington and his brave army over Bonaparte. With the deposition of Bonaparte I hope there may be no other obstacles to peace, and that we may at length be rewarded for the blood and treasure which we

---

[1] Hopelessly torn by the seal.

have expended with a long period of tranquil[l]ity, which I have no doubt will also prove a long period of prosperity. I think with Mr. Whitbread[1] that great credit is due to ministers for the energy which they have displayed in the prosecution of this contest. Having determined on war, their preparations have been on such a scale as to give from the commencement the best hopes of success, and we appear at last to have adopted the wise policy of making one grand effort in preference to a series of puny efforts, each just sufficient to keep the contest alive without making the least advance to its ultimate object.

The effect on the price of Omnium has been no more than what might have been expected. I am sorry that you have not profited by the rise. As for myself, I have all my stock, by which I mean I have all my money[,] invested in Stock ; and this is as great an advantage as ever I expect or wish to make by a rise. I have been a considerable gainer by the loan[2] ; in the first place by replacing the stock which I had sold before the contract with the minister [*sic*] at a much lower price, secondly by a moderate gain on such part of the loan as I ventured to take over and above my stock. This portion I sold at a premium of from 3 to 5 per cent., and I have every reason to be well contented. Perhaps no loan was ever more generally profitable to the Stock Exchange.

Now for a little of our old subject. It appears to me that there are two causes which may cause a rise of prices, one the depreciation of money, the other the difficulty of producing. The latter can in no case be advantageous to a society. It is always a sign of prosperity but never the cause of it. Depreciation of money may be beneficial, be-

---

[1] Probably they had had a private conversation on the subject. On the 28th June Whitbread made a lengthened speech in the House to this effect.

[2] A loan of 36,000,000 was contracted in 1815. See Gilbart's 'History and Principles of Banking' (2nd ed. 1835), p. 54.

cause it generally favours that class who are disposed to accumulate, but I should say that it augmented riches by diminishing happiness, that it was advantageous only by occasioning a great pressure on the labouring classes and on those who lived on fixed incomes. You and I concur in this opinion, for you say you are convinced that there are unobserved advantages attending the high price of corn and labour 'when not arising solely from difficulty of production,' [by] which I think you imply that no such advantages attend high prices if attended with difficulty of production.

This opinion is, however, a little at variance with that which you have long been supporting, for you have said that the high price of corn and labour in this country at this time was an advantage, although it is universally allowed that that high price is mainly owing to difficulty of production. The farmers and shopkeepers may suffer very general distress from a sudden and general fall of prices ; but I hold that this would be no criterion by which to judge of the general or permanent prosperity of a country.

The accounts in which I am at present engaged will I fear, keep me in London till the very latter end of July. I shall very much regret if you quit Bath without my seeing you. I quite depended on having a visit from you at Gatcomb this year, and I yet hope that it may be accomplished. I shall certainly leave London the very earliest day possible.

The price of labour in America appears to me enormously high as compared with the price of wheat; but we should not fail to remember how very low the exchangeable value of wheat is there, and how much of it must be given for the manufactured necessaries and comforts of life. . . .

Ever truly yours,

DAVID RICARDO.

XXXIV.

MY DEAR SIR,   GATCOMB PARK, 30 *July*, 1815.

I bore with great patience the fatigues of the last fortnight in London, in the hope that on my arrival at Gatcomb I should have the pleasure of your company for a few days previously to your return to London. It was a great disappointment to me to learn that you would be travelling to London the very day after I quitted it, and I see little prospect of having a visit from you here for some time to come, as your convenience or inclination will probably lead you to a different part of the country next year.

I most cordially join with you in the wish that the victory of the Duke of Wellington will be the means of giving Europe some permanent repose. There appears every probability that it will be attended with that happy effect, and I should hope that the late stormy times will afford instruction both to sovereigns and people, and will secure the world from the evils of anarchy as well as from those of tyranny and despotism.

David's ill health has induced us to take him from the Charterhouse. . . . . .

Mr. Clerk, a neighbour of mine here in Gloucestershire and who is brother to the East India Director of that name, has just sent his son George to the East India College, and knowing my intimacy with you has called upon me to request me to write to you on behalf of his son, that in case he may st[and] in need of any friendly advice or assistance you [would have] the goodness to give it to him. I hope [I] am not taking too great a liberty in asking you to comply with his father's wishes.

The immense concerns in business which I have lately had on my mind had nearly banished all consideration of subjects connected with political economy from it. Those concerns are now settled, but they have given me incessant

work in arranging and balancing my accounts ever since
I have been here. I recur now, however, with pleasure to
corn, labour, and bullion. A really high price of corn is
always an evil; in this opinion I think you would concur,
because it is always occasioned by difficulty of production.
I know of no other cause, and you allow difficulty of production not to be desirable in itself. In our own case the
high bullion price of corn is not wholly owing to the barrenness of the land to be taken into cultivation, but from whatever cause it has arisen it cannot, I think, have enabled us
to grant greater subsidies than we should otherwise have
done, for subsidies as well as all services performed for us
are paid for by the produce of the land and labour of
the people of England. It surely is a palpable contradiction to say that our power of commanding services is
increased, whilst our productions with which those services
are paid are diminished. The principle may be true when
confined to a few commodities of which we either have a
monop[o]ly or peculiar facilities in the production of them,
but as a general proposition it appears to me to be at
variance with the best established doctrines.

If a free trade in corn were allowed with America I should
not expect that the prices would differ more, here and there,
than the expenses and profits of sending it;—as it is I am
surprised the price should be so high. A high money price
of wages is I think quite natural.

Ever yours,

DAVID RICARDO.

XXXV.

MY DEAR SIR,   GATCOMB PARK, *10th Sept.*, 1815.

Nothing could be more unlucky than our missing
each other as we did this year. I should think there
would be no obstacle to our leaving town a little earlier

next year, when I hope we shall at length have the
pleasure of seeing Mrs. Malthus and you at Gatcomb.

It is the general remark in our part of the country
that a finer season was never remembered. The rain, of
which we have certainly had a deficiency, has generally
come at night, and the days which have followed have
been beautiful. The temptation to enjoy it has been so
great that I have been incessantly out with some one or
other of my friends who have been staying with me,
either riding or walking, which makes such inroads on
my time that I find I have much less leisure here for
reading and study than I have in London. Before I
came here I often saw Mr. Grenfell[1], who is very warm
on the subject of the Bank and the advantageous bargains
which it has always made with government, as well
for the management of the national debt, the composition
which it has hitherto paid for stamps, as for the compensa-
tion which government has received in the way of loan
for enormous average deposits left with the Bank. I am
quite of his opinion, and indeed I go much further; I
think the Bank an unnecessary establishment, getting rich
by those profits which fairly belong to the public. I
cannot help considering the issuing of paper money as a
privilege which belongs exclusively to the State; I regard
it as a sort of seignorage, and I am convinced, if the
principles of currency were rightly understood, that commissioners might be appointed, independent of all minis-
terial control, who should be the sole issuers of paper
money,—by which I think a profit of from two to three
millions might be secured to the public, at the same time
that we should be protected from the abuses of the country

---

[1] Pascoe Grenfell, member of the Bullion Committee, a strong supporter
of Wilberforce in the matter of Emancipation. His motions in Parliament
on the subject of the Bank of England are given in the appendix to Ricardo's
'Economical and Secure Currency' (Wks. p. 451), a pamphlet which by its
author's admission (p. 395) owes much to him.

banks, who are the cause of much mischief all over the kingdom. These commissioners should also have the management of the public debt, and should act as bankers to all the different public departments. They might invest the eleven millions which is the average of public deposits in Exchequer Bills, a part of which might be sold whenever occasion required. This of course (at least all of it) could not be effected till the expiration of the Bank Charter in 1833; but it is never too soon to give due consideration to important principles, which might be recognized, though not yet acted on. In looking over the papers which have from time to time been laid before Parliament, I think it might clearly be proved that the profits of the bank have been enormous. I should think they must have a hoard nearly equal to their capital. By their charter they are bound to make an annual division of their profits and to lay a statement of their accounts before the proprietors; but they appear to set all law at defiance. I always enjoy any attack upon the Bank, and [if I] had sufficient courage I would be a party to it.

Though I have been thinking on this subject lately, I am not less interested about our old subject, of the advantages or disadvantages of high prices for raw produce. If I agreed with Mr. Torrens that such high prices were accompanied with a rise in the prices of commodities, and, if I thought that such rise would not preclude the usual exchanges with foreign countries, I should of course agree with you that with such general high prices we should command a greater quantity of foreign commodities in exchange for a given quantity of ours; but I cannot admit in the first place that commodities would rise because corn rose[1]; and, secondly, if they did so rise there are but very few which we could sell in equal quantity at the advanced price to foreigners; and, if we sold less to them, we could buy less

---

[1] Cf. Ricardo's Pol. Econ. and Tax. ch. vi, Profits.

of them, and thus would our general commerce suffer. I
can see great advantages attending low general prices but
none in high prices. On this subject we are not likely to
agree. I hope you are diligently employed and that early
in the year we shall see something new from your pen.
I have some curiosity to see a pamphlet just advertised [1],
in the title page of which your name is mentioned.

Ever yours,
DAVID RICARDO.

. . . Have you seen Monsieur Say's [Catec]hisme d'Econo-
mic Politique? He has softened but not [expung]ed the
objectionable definitions.

NOTE.—Correspondence between Ricardo and J. B. Say is
given in the ' Œuvres Diverses' of the latter, published after his
death (Guillaumin, 1848), with notes by Ch. Comte, Daire, and
Horace Say. J. B. Say (born 1767) was the son of a Lyons merchant, of Huguenot origin. When a boy, he was sent with his brother
Horace to learn business in London, where he was struck, amongst
other things, by the fact that his Croydon landlord built up one of the
two windows of his lodgings to escape window tax. Having gained
familiarity with the English language and English ways he returned to France in 1789 and entered the employment of a Life
Insurance Company, the manager of which (Clavière) lent him a
copy of the ' Wealth of Nations,' not yet translated into French.
The reading of it made him an economist for life, as it did
for Ricardo ten years later. After serving in the revolutionary
army in 1792, he left commerce for journalism. His chief book,
Le Traité de l'Economie Politique, appeared in 1803. Too independent to please Napoleon, he was forced to quit his new pro-
fession for his old; and his commercial travelling landed him
eventually at Geneva, where he made the acquaintance of Necker,
Madame de Stael, and Benjamin Constant. He came back to
France (to Auchy, Pas de Calais) to spin cotton, retiring with a
moderate fortune in 1813. After the Peace he was sent by Government to report on the economical condition of England. He was

[1] Probably ' An Address to the Nation on the relative importance of Agriculture and Manufactures, with remarks on the doctrines of Mr. Malthus,'
1815.

cordially received by Ricardo, Bentham, and other economists; and on his return to Paris narrated with pride to his audiences at the Conservatoire des Arts et Metiers that the Glasgow professors had made him sit in the chair of Adam Smith. After an active life of teaching and writing, he died in Paris, 15th November, 1832.

Ricardo writes to him from Gatcomb Park on 18th Aug., 1815, thanking him for the copy of the (first edition of the) 'Catechisme de l'Economie Politique,' which he had just sent. Though complimenting him highly on the work, he thinks that Say has not, even yet, with sufficient clearness distinguished Value from Utility. No doubt to have value a commodity must be *useful*, but it is the *difficulty* of its production that is the sole measure of its value. 'The wealthiest man is he who has most values, and who is able, by giving them in exchange, to procure himself not the things which he himself and everybody else regard as the most desirable, and which can be had at a low price, but the things that are difficult to produce and consequently dear. A man is rich not by the moderation of his desires, but by the quantity of commodities that he possesses.' Say has also, in Ricardo's opinion, forgotten sometimes that the growth of the capital of a manufacturer cannot be safely estimated in money if we do not allow for the change in the value of money. Ricardo concludes : ' The pleasure which I take in reading and studying good works on political economy has not diminished since I saw you. I should devote all my time to the discussion of points which seem to me to need further elucidation, if I had any talent for composition. However, I have ventured to publish the pamphlet[1] which I sent you, and I should be glad to know your opinion on the doctrine which I maintain in it in relation to the rent of land and the rate of profits, in opposition to Mr. Malthus. I learn from Mr. Mill that several persons in this country do not understand me because I have not explained my views at sufficient length; and he is trying to induce me to undertake an explanation of them from the beginning and at greater length; but I fear that the undertaking is beyond my powers.' (Œuvres Diverses de Say, pp. 409–11. Ricardo wrote in English, but in this and the other cases the editors give only the French.)

Say's answer follows (pp. 411–13), 2nd Dec., 1815 : ' Nous nous occupons heureusement vous et moi de choses de tous les temps

---

[1] High Price of Corn, 1815.

plûtot que de celles du moment actuel, qui ne sont pas gaies, malgré les fêtes que l'on donne pour faire croire aux peuples qu'ils sont heureux.' Going to the subject of value, he says he did *not* say Utility was the measure of Value, but 'the value that men attach to a thing is the measure of the utility they find in it;' moreover he had not maintained the Stoical doctrine, 'the fewer wants, the greater wealth,' but had simply said that a man is the richer if all the things he wants (whatever they be) are cheap instead of dear, and would be richest of all if he had abundance of everything without any cost at all. He allows that Ricardo is right in regard to the growth of the manufacturer's capital, and promises to introduce the qualification suggested by Ricardo in his next edition. In the controversy between Malthus and Ricardo he finds it difficult to take a side, for he cannot for his part exclude from the question of profits 'the talent and industrial capacity of the man who brings out the resources of a land or a capital;' the profit inherent merely in land or in capital seems to him unimportant in comparison with the profit due to the source described. But he says he is too timid to insist on his opinion, and will wait for Ricardo's full explanations in the larger work. 'How I envy your lot, to study political economy in your beautiful retreat of Gatcomb Park! I shall never forget the too short moments I passed there, nor the charms of your conversation.'

XXXVI.

My dear Sir,

By facility of production I do not mean to consider the productiveness of the soil only, but the skill, machinery, and labour joined to the natural fertility of the earth. It does not therefore follow that because Otaheite[1] has an abundance of fertile land profits should be there at the highest rate, because the skill and the means of abridging labour may in Europe more than compensate this natural advantage of Otaheite. The question is this: If part of the skill and capital of England were employed in Otaheite to produce 100,000 quarters of corn, would not the persons

---

[1] Spelt throughout 'Othaeite.'

employing that capital obtain greater profits in Otaheite than they would if they employed the same capital for the same purpose here, and would not rent be lower there than here? You must at any rate allow that the quantity of corn produced with a given quantity of capital, supposing the same skill to be employed, must be greater there than here, or there is no meaning in fertility of soil. You must allow too that in proportion to the fertility of Otaheite and to its extent compared with the population will be the lowness of rent, notwithstanding its abundant rate of produce. I can easily *conceive* that, with the imperfect tillage the people of Otaheite now give their land, the population may be just sufficiently numerous to require that the whole of their lands should be in cultivation, and consequently that they should bear a rent; but let a hundred Europeans only join them with our improved machinery and perfectly skilled in husbandry, and the immediate consequence would be that three quarters of their lands would for a time become perfectly useless to them, as the quarter might produce them more food than all the inhabitants could possibly consume. Now I ask whether it be possible that three quarters of the land of a country can be suffered to pass from a state of tillage to a state of nature without occasioning a fall in rents? If land is less in demand, must not the rent of it fall? If you say no, there is no truth in the proposition that value depends upon the proportion between supply and demand. Now suppose England in the state in which I have been fancying Otaheite; and she is actually in that state, all or most of her land being in cultivation; and suppose further that there is another country totally unknown to us whose skill and machinery in husbandry as far surpasses ours as ours does that of the Otaheiteans. If a hundred of these persons were to come amongst us with their capital, skill, etc., would not the same consequences follow as I have just

stated? Now every improvement in machinery is precisely on a small scale what I have been here supposing on
a large scale; and I am quite astonished that you should
yet maintain that 'universally where land is limited in
quantity, the facility of production upon it will go mainly
to rent, and the soil of a country might be of such fertility
as to yield sixtyfold instead of eight or ten, and yet the
profits of stock be only six per cent. and the wages of
labour both nominally and really low.' Land, like everything else, rises or falls in proportion to the demand for
it; every improvement which shall enable you to raise the
same quantity of produce on a less quantity of land or,
which is the same thing, a larger quantity of produce on
the same quantity of land cannot increase the demand
for land and therefore cannot raise rents.

I do not clearly see the distinction which you think
important between productiveness of industry and productiveness of capital. Every machine which abridges
labour adds to the productiveness of industry, but it adds
also to the productiveness of capital. England with
machinery and with a given capital will obtain a greater
real net produce than Otaheite with the same capital
without machinery, whether it be in manufactures or in
the produce of the soil. It will do so because it employs
much fewer hands to obtain the same produce. Industry
is more productive; so is capital. It appears to me that
one is a necessary consequence of the other, and that the
opinion which I have advanced and which you are com-
bat[t]ing is that in the progress of society independently
of all improvements in skill and machinery the produce of
industry constantly diminishes as far as the land is concerned, and consequently capital becomes less productive.
That this diminution of produce is beneficial to all owners
of land, but that it is so at the expense of manufacturers,
amongst which [*sic*] I include farmers, first by rendering

the commodities which they manufacture of less exchangeable value than they before were for corn, and secondly by raising the cost of production by raising the price of labour.

I shall put this letter in the Post Office in London, where I am going to-morrow for a few days. I have been writing, in my unconnected and confused style, my opinions on the profits of the Bank and on the advantages of a paper and nothing but a paper currency. I am too little pleased with it to think of publishing. The whole is too little for a pamphlet. Mr. Grenfell is, I think, anxious that something should be said about the Bank before the meeting of Parliament, and I too wish some able hand would undertake it.

I am always glad to hear that you are preparing for the press; for, though I do not always agree in opinion with you, I am sure that your writings will contribute towards the progress of a science in which I take great interest. I should be more pleased that we did not so materially differ. If I am too theoretical (which I really believe is is the case), you I think are too practical. There are so many combinations and so many operating causes in Political Economy that there is great danger in appealing to experience in favour of a particular doctrine, unless we are sure that all the causes of variation are seen and their effects duly estimated. Mr. Whishaw and Mr. Warburton[1] have been at Mr. Smith's for some time. I have been absent from home unfortunately, and have seen but little of them. I yesterday dined with Mr. Whishaw; he talked of leaving Mr. Smith immediately. . . .

Yours,

7th Oct., 1815.   DAVID RICARDO.

[1] Probably Henry Warburton, mentioned e. g. in Personal Life of Geo. Grote, p. 75. In a MS. letter from Joseph Hume to Francis Place, 19th Oct., 1839 (in the Place Collection), he refers to Mr. Warburton as a friend of Place who had been too much neglected by the Whigs in office.

XXXVII.

[Not dated or headed, but fastened to preceding.]

MY DEAR SIR, [*Oct.* 1815?]

I have an account before me of the capital actually employed on a farm of 200 acres in Essex. It amounts to £3433 or about £17 per acre[1], of which not more than £1100 or £1200 is of that description which is not subject to the same variation of value as the produce of the land itself, for £2200 consists of the value of the seeds in the ground, the advances for labour, the horses and live stock, etc. etc. If then the money value of the produce from the land should fall *from facility of production* it must ever continue to bear a greater ratio to the whole money value of the capital employed on the land, for there will be a great increase of average produce per acre, whilst the fall in money value will be common to both capital and produce, and it cannot therefore be true that rent, profits, and wages can all *really* fall at the same time.

The effect of high or low wages on profits has always been distinctly recognized by me:—till the population increases to the proportion which the increased capital can employ, wages will rise, and may absorb a larger portion of the whole produce. But this effect will only take place with an increase of capital, and has nothing to do with new facilities of production. Wages do not depend upon the quantity of a commodity which a day's labour will produce, and I cannot help thinking you quite incorrect when you say that the natural consequence of the facility of production being so increased that a day's labour will produce 4 measures of corn, cloth and cotton instead of 2 measures, will be that 4 measures of corn, cloth and cotton will be worth only the price of a day's

---

[1] In Arthur Young's Farmer's Calendar, 1815, p. 501, £10 are said to be the average capital needed for stocking a farm in 1814, and £15 are counted high.

labour instead of 2. It appears to me that, if, instead of 4, 10 measures could be produced by a day's labour, no rise would take place in wages, no greater portion of corn, cloth or cotton would be given to the labourer, unless a portion of the increased produce were employed as capital, and then the rise in wages would be in proportion to the new demand for labour, and not at all in proportion to the increase in the quantity of commodities produced. This increase would be exclusively enjoyed by the owner of stock, and, if he consumed in his family the whole increased produce, without augmenting his capital, wages would remain stationary, and not be in any way affected by the increased facility of production.

I cannot agree with your proposition, namely, [']That the means of employing capital profitably can never co-exist with an abundant capital and produce and a stationary population, on account of the necessary effect of such a state of things in increasing the real price of labour,' because I consider the rise of wages as by no means a necessary effect of an abundant capital and produce, for it may be accompanied with new facilities in procuring corn, and then wages even if they should rise would not lessen profits, they will only keep them lower than they otherwise would be. In the case which we were considering the other night, if every lady made her own shoes, a part of the capital now employed in making shoes by the shoemakers would be otherwise employed. The same labour would be bestowed in the production of other objects desirable to these lady shoemakers, who would have both the power and the will to purchase them from the savings which would accrue to them by employing their labour productively. There is a great difference between [the] common effects of an accumulation of capital, and the employing the same capital more productively. The first is generally attended with a rise of wages and a fall of profits for a time at least,—but the second may exist for an indefinite length of time without producing any such effects. In the case of great improvements in machinery,—capital is liberated for other employments and at the same time the labour necessary for those employments is also liberated,—so that no demand for additional labour will take place unless the increased production in consequence of the improvement should lead to further accumulation of capital, and then the effect on wages is to be ascribed to the accumulation of capital and not to the better employment of the same capital. If the population were to be stopped whilst accumulation continued the effects which you enumerate would undoubtedly follow, but this would arise from the demand for labour not being adequately supplied,—it would be the effect of accumulation which would operate so powerfully that it would be but slightly checked by the facility of production, but it would not by any means be the consequence of such facility.

It is true that the rate of profits depends upon the scanty or abundant supply of capital compared with the means of employing it profitably,—and these means will as you say upon the common principles of supply and demand be increased either by a diminution of capital or by an extension of the market for it. Our inquiry is in fact what the causes are of an extension of the market, and I hold that the most powerful, and the only one which operates permanently, is a reduction in the relative value of food. You appear to me to concede a little respecting demand being regulated by the power of production,—but you are yet very far from yielding all that I demand. I hope we shall meet this month, but I cannot yet say whether I can leave London.

Yours very truly,

D. Ricardo.

XXXVIII.

MY DEAR SIR,   LONDON, 17 *Oct.*, 1815.

Mrs. Ricardo and I are sorry that Mrs. Malthus will be prevented from accompanying you when you pay us a visit at Gatcomb. We should have been very happy to have shown. her some of the beauties of our county. When you come, perhaps you will bring your gun with you. Though I am no sportsman myself, I will endeavour to procure you the best sport that my influence can command.

I am very much obliged to you for the attention which you have given to my MS.[1] I am fully aware of the deficiency in the style and arrangement; those are faults which I shall never conquer. I will however use my best endeavours to elevate it to the very low standard to which you compare it[2]. It would be unpardonable to write worse with more practice.

I expected that you would not quite agree with my plan of abolishing the metals from circulation; but the grounds on which you object to it may I think be answered, and then your objections would I hope be removed. You fear that without a metallic circulation we could not on an emergency supply a large sum of bullion for the exigencies of the State. The fact is however against you, for we have supplied large sums when the metals have been absolutely banished from circulation. This has been the case during the whole Peninsular War. If indeed on my system the Bank could keep a less quantity of bullion in

---

[1] Probably the 'Proposals for an Economical and Secure Currency, with observations on the profits of the Bank of England as they regard the public and the proprietors of Bank Stock.' See Works (McCulloch's ed.), pp. 391 sq. One 'proposal' was that the Bank should be obliged to deliver uncoined bullion, at the Mint price (instead of coined money) in exchange for its notes.

[2] Presumably Ricardo's first pamphlet, of 1810. Cf. Works (McCulloch's ed.) p. xxiii.

their coffers to answer the demands of the public, the objection would be well founded; but the only difference would be that in one case their hoards would consist wholly of coined gold and silver, and in the other they would consist of the uncoined metals; but, on both systems, if the Bank paid their notes on demand the currency must be equally reduced in quantity, if gold and silver should become more valuable. That argument then may be used against a currency convertible at all, into specie or bullion, but does not apply to one more than the other. I think with you that on the whole silver would be a better standard than gold, particularly if paper only were used. All objections against its greater bulk would be removed.

I find I did misapprehend your illustration respecting profits from Otaheite; but our difference is still very serious. I most distinctly allow that any causes which tend to make capital less in demand will lower profits; but I contend that there are no causes which will for any length of time make capital less in demand, however abundant it may become, but a comparatively high price of food and labour,—that profits do not *necessarily* fall with the increase of the quantity of capital, because the demand for capital is infinite and [is] governed by the same law as population itself. They are both checked by the rise in the price of food and the consequent increase in the value of labour. If there were no such rise, what could prevent population and capital from increasing without limit? I acknowledge the effects of the great principle of supply and demand in every instance; but in this it appears to me that the demand will enlarge at the same rate as the supply if there be no difficulty on the score of food and raw produce. Fertility is, as you justly observe, the essence of high rents; and low rents are the necessary result of barrenness, however scarce corn may be. I agree with you too that, in a country limited to 100,000 acres, all of the richest conceivable quantity, yet peopled and capital'd up to the utmost limits of its produce, the profits of stock and the wages of labour would both be very low, although the quantity of produce yielded by a given capital *including rent* might be 100 per cent.; but I ask, if by any miracle the produce of that land could at once be doubled, would rents then continue as high as before, or could they possibly rise? We are speaking of the immediate not the ultimate effects. The improvements in skill and machinery may in 1000 years go to the landlord, but for 900 they will remain with the tenant.

Yours very truly,

DAVID RICARDO.

I have been so busy and am yet so busy that I cannot return to Gatcomb till Friday.

XXXIX.

MY DEAR SIR,   LONDON, 17 *Oct.*, 1815.

My letter was sent to the post before I received yours of yesterday's date. The parcel you sent me has reached me safe. I am sorry you had so much trouble about it.

My views respecting the Bank are entirely prospective. The last return of bank notes in circulation was, I think, larger than any that preceded it. I have not the paper in London, but I think the circulation of bank notes then amounted (1815) to 28,000,000 or more [1].

It is dangerous to listen to reports respecting briskness or slackness of trade. It is I believe certain that the revenue has been uncommonly productive the last quarter, which is no indication of diminished trade. As you allow that the

---

[1] They amounted to 27,300,000 ('Econ. and Sec. Currency,' Wks., p. 450, but cf. p. 413).

loss of the sellers is the gain of the buyers, you appear to me to attribute effects much too great to the fall of raw produce which has lately taken place. It does not follow that, because prices are low, production will be discouraged. If money were to fall very much in value whilst a country was making great advances in prosperity, would not production be encouraged, notwithstanding a fall of prices ?

That profits may rise on the land, if population increases faster than capital, I am not disposed to deny; but this will be a partial rise of profits on a particular trade, for a limited time, and is very different from a general rise of profits on trade in general. This admission does not affect my principle.

Ever truly yours,

DAVID RICARDO. .

I ought to apologise for writing to you twice in one day.

XL.

MY DEAR SIR,   GATCOMB PARK, 24*th Dec.*, 1815.

I write to remind you that the time is come at which you once gave me hope almost to certainty that I should have the pleasure of seeing you here ; and even when I last saw you you promised, if you could make it convenient, to come and pass a part of your vacation with me. The weather is beautiful, and my desire to see you as ardent as ever. Come then and inhale the pure atmosphere of our hills, and be under no fear that your visit will retard any object to which your attention may now be devoted, for you shall be free to write, study, or read, as many hours in the day as you please, unmolested by any one's intrusion.

My lost MS.[1] is recovered. Mr. Mill recommends its

---

[1] Probably ' Econ. and Secure Currency.' See note to Letter XLII.

publication, but advises me to write an introduction, and to divide it into sections. I had almost resolved to throw it aside, but I have been again at work upon it, and, though I cannot put it in any shape to please me, it is I think rather better than when you saw it; and the probability at present is that I shall venture to publish it.

I attended the Bank Court the other day. I had no intention whatever of speaking; but some very bad reasoning on the other side and a total deviation from the question called me up, and I spoke for five or ten minutes with considerable inward agitation, but without committing any glaring blunder. My speaking is like my writing too much compressed. I am too apt to crowd a great deal of difficult matter into so short a space as to be incomprehensible to the generality of readers. The Chronicle, I see, has reported what he thought or heard I said, but he has imputed to me what I neither felt nor uttered. Allusions were made to the Bullion question, and it was said that it had been prophesied that, if the Bank directors were corrupt, they might with the power they had of issuing paper occasion the greatest public distress; no such distress, however, had been experienced. I observed in reply that the goodness of the system was not proved by the distress not having occurred,—that the speaker had been only paying a compliment to the integrity of the directors, in which no one in the court was more ready to join than myself,—but, if the directors had been corrupt, I still thought that they had been armed with the power of doing mischief. Though I was ready to declare my confidence in the integrity of the directors, there were many parts of their system of which I could not approve, etc. etc. This is very different from the report in the Chronicle; but I understand that the reporters were most carefully excluded from the court.

I hope the business at the college has been settled to your satisfaction, and that the result of the late unpleasant disturbance[1] will give you some security against its recurrence in future.

I conclude that you have quite finished writing the alterations and amendments which you projected for the new edition of your book[2]. When I last saw you I think you had made considerable progress, and therefore it is probable that you may be already in the press. What point will next engage your attention? For I hope, as M. Say says, that you will 'travaillez toujours' [*sic*] . . .

Ever yours,

DAVID RICARDO.

[Fragment. Within this year, or earlier. See Letter XI.]

[I began] by assuring you that I was not going to weary you with a repetition of my hundred times told tale, and I am ashamed to see that I have filled four sides with nothing else. There are some other points on which I shall make some remarks when I have the pleasure of seeing you. If you should come to town, will you do me the favour to call at the Stock Exchange, unless my house should not be much out of your way. I recommend your calling there because I am just about deserting Brook Street for some time. Mrs. Ricardo and all the family are going to Ramsgate to-morrow morning, and she will not consent to let me remain at home by myself, so that when I am in London I shall be chiefly with my brother at Bow; now and then I shall pass a night at home. My business is so uncertain that I cannot at all foresee what portion of the next two or three months I shall be able to spend at the sea side. It is probable that I shall be so much in town that I shall be found by you at the Stock Exchange. . . .

Yours most truly,

DAVID RICARDO.

[1] See Malthus and his Work, p. 422.

[2] ' Additions to the 4th and former editions of an Essay on the Principle of Population,' published in June 1817, both in the separate form and as part of the 5th edition of the Essay.

XLI.

MY DEAR SIR, GATCOMB PARK, 2 *Jan.*, 1816.

Your two letters have both reached me, and I am very sorry to find that I shall not have the pleasure of seeing you at Gatcomb this vacation. I left London, as you supposed, the day after the Bank Court. I should have considered it fortunate if whilst I was there I had met you. My house in Brook Street is not yet in a state to receive us ; nor will it be this season, unless we consent to go in it with the walls unpapered and unpainted, conditions to which we shall agree. It will bo we are told in a habitable state by the latter end of the month, at which time we shall probably quit Gatcomb.

As you have not given me the pleasure of your company here, and as I wish to speak to Murray concerning my book and to consult some Parliamentary papers which I have not got here, I intend taking a trip to town the beginning of next week. Do you think I shall havo any chance of meeting you there ? Remember that a letter will always find me at or follow me from the Stock Exchange[1].

It is exceedingly provoking that you should have been so much interrupted by college affairs as not to have made more progress with your new chapters. I shall regret your thinking it necessary to abridge or leave out anything which you may have to say connected with the subject, and particularly if you should so determine, because more time will otherwise bo required beforo you can publish. The question of bounties and restrictions is exceedingly important, and, unless you have already given your present opinions on that subject elsewhere, or mean to do so, it ought to form part of the present work[2]; and a little delay in tho publication is not very important.

---

[1] The Post Office London Directory of the time gives Ricardo's full City address as 4 Shorter's Court, Throgmorton Street.

[2] Tho advice was taken.

The edition which I have of your work is the first, and it is many years since I read it. When you wrote to me that you were looking over the chapters on the Agricultural and Manufacturing systems with a view to make some alterations in them, I looked into those chapters and saw a great deal in them which differed from the opinions I have formed on that part of the subject. At your house I observed that in a subsequent edition you had altered some of the passages to which I particularly objected, and in the chapters as you are now writing them it appeared to me that there was only a slight trace of the difference we have often discussed. The general impression which I retain of the book is excellent. The doctrines appeared so clear and so satisfactorily laid down that they excited an interest in me inferior only to that produced by Adam Smith's celebrated work[1]. I remember mentioning to you, and I believe you told me that you had altered it in the following editions, that I thought you argued in some places as if the poor rates had no effect in increasing the quantity of food to be distributed,—that I thought you were bound to admit that the poor laws would increase the demand and consequently the supply. This admission does not weaken the grand point to be proved.

As for the difference between us on Profits, of which you speak in your letter, you have not, I think, stated it correctly. You say that my opinion is 'that general profits never fall from a general fall of prices compared with labour, but from a general rise of labour compared with prices.' I will not acknowledge this to be my proposition. I think that corn and labour are the variable commodities, and that other things neither rise nor fall but from difficulty or facility of production or from some cause particularly affecting the value of money, and that no alteration

---

[1] Which gave him his first stimulus to economical study when he read it at Bath in 1799. See McCulloch's ed. of Wks., pp. xvii, xviii.

of price proceeding from these causes affect[s] general profits,—allowing always some effect for cheapness of the raw material. . . .

Yours very truly,

DAVID RICARDO.

XLII.

MY DEAR SIR,   LONDON, 10*th Jan.*, 1816.

I arrived in town yesterday and found your letter at the Stock Exchange. It is very uncertain whether I shall leave London to-morrow evening or Monday evening. I am desirous of getting home on many accounts, but I may not be able to accomplish the business for which I came so soon as I expected, and, if I do not get it done by to-morrow it will in all probability detain me till Monday. Thus then it is still uncertain whether we are to meet, and I do not exactly know how to make you acquainted with my movements. I will, however, let Mr. Murray know if I leave town to-morrow, and, if you are in the neighbourhood of Russell Square, by sending to No. 8, Montague Street (Mr. Basevi's), you will be sure to know. In the City, at the Stock Exchange, any of my brothers will inform you about me. If I should not be gone, will you do me the favour of dining with me on Friday at Mr. Basevi's? His dinner hour is six o'clock, and he begs me to say that he shall be much flattered by your favouring him with your company. I was in hopes of finding you in London and of having the benefit of your opinion of my book [1] in its present state, before I sent it to be printed. That advantage I must now forego, because I am desirous of getting it out before the meeting of Parliament, and have before experienced the inconvenience of too much hurry.

I cannot think it inconsistent to suppose that the money

---

[1] See note at end of this letter.

price of labour may rise when it is necessary to cultivate
poorer land, whilst the real price may at the same time fall.
Two opposite causes are influencing the price of labour, one
the enhanced price of some of the things on which wages
are expended, the other the fewer enjoyments which the
labourer will have the power to command. You think
these may balance each other, or rather that the latter
will prevail; I on the contrary think the former the most
powerful in its effects. I must write a book to convince you.

I am glad you are not going to cut your next edition
short.

Very truly yours,

DAVID RICARDO.

NOTE.—The MS. referred to in this letter was probably the
pamphlet on ‘Economical and Secure Currency,’ which internal
evidence would show to have been printed not earlier than Feb.,
1816. Ricardo, as appears from Letter XL, had already submitted the MS. to James Mill. In the fragment of a letter to Mill
(quoted in Bain’s ‘Life of Mill,’ p. 153, and dated Jan., 1816) he
writes : ‘Fill eight pages in the Appendix, will that be too much?’
Professor Bain thinks this must refer to the ‘Principles of Political
Economy and Taxation’ (1817). But that work has no Appendix;
and there seems no reason why it should not refer to the ‘Economical and Secure Currency’ (1816), which has one. The ‘Resolutions proposed concerning the Bank of England by Mr. Grenfell,’
and those proposed by Mr. Mellish, together, cover seven pages of
that Appendix in the original edition ; and Ricardo in the fragment quoted had probably been saying, that these Resolutions, if
he printed them, would fill nearly eight pages, etc.

XLIII.

MY DEAR SIR, LONDON, 7 *Feb.*, 1816.

I arrived in town yesterday, with the whole of my
numerous family. We are already as comfortably settled in
Brook Street as under all circumstances we can expect, and

I hasten to inform you that we have a bed ready for you, which I hope you will very soon occupy. I have forgotten on which Saturday in the month you meet at the King of Clubs, but conclude from your last meeting that it is the second. If so, you will probably be in town to-morrow or Friday, when I shall hope that you will lodge at our house and give us as much of your company as your numerous friends will allow you to do.

You have probably ere this seen my book [1]. I have been reading it in its present dress, and very much lament that I make no progress in the very difficult art of composition. I believe that ought to be my study before I intrude any more of my crude notions on the public.

It is said that the Bank have made some agreement with Government, but what it is is not exactly known. They talk of the Bank advancing to Government six millions at four per cent., besides continuing the loan of three millions without interest. We shall not, however, be long in suspense on this subject, as a general court of proprietors is to be held to-morrow, when the directors will make some communication to the proprietors to ask for their vote to sanction their agreement. They will ask for this without giving them any information either respecting their savings, their profits, or the amount of public deposits. Is not this a ridiculous piece of mockery, and an insult to our common sense ? I hope there may be a few independent proprietors present who may call for information, or who may at least demand a ballot, for which purpose nine only are necessary [2]. You would be surprised at the abjectness of the city men, and the great influence which the directors have in consequence of their power of discounting bills. I am persuaded many of the proprietors would vote very differently at a ballot, to what they would by a show of hands.

---

[1] 'Economical and Secure Currency.' See note to previous letter.

[2] Cf. ' Econ. and Secure Currency,' Wks., pp. 433, 434.

I have not thought much on our old subject; my difficulty is in so presenting it to the minds of others as to make them fall into the same chain of thinking as myself. If I could overcome the obstacles in the way of giving a clear insight into the original law of relative or exchangeable value, I should have gained half the battle. . . .

Very truly yours,
DAVID RICARDO.

XLIV.

[On the back of this are jotted figures and lists of books in Malthus' handwriting.]

MY DEAR SIR,   LONDON, *23rd Feb.,* 1816.

I beg to remind you that the first Saturday in the next month is to-morrow se'n-night, on which day or a few days before it, I hope to have the pleasure of seeing you in Brook Street. We have a bed always at your service, and I wish you would make the rule invariable to take up your lodging with us whenever you visit London.

I hope you have quite determined to extend your new edition to another volume, and that you are now making great progress in it. I wish much to see a regular and connected statement of your opinions on what I deem the most difficult and perhaps the most important topic of political economy, namely, the progress of a country in wealth, and the laws by which the increasing produce is distributed.

Have you seen Torrens' Letter to Lord Liverpool[1]? He appears to me to have adopted all my views respecting profits and rent; and, in some conversation which I had with him a few days ago, he unequivocally avowed that he was now of my opinion, that the price of labour, arising from a difficulty in procuring food, did not affect the prices

---

[1] Letter to the Earl of Liverpool on Agriculture, 1816.

of commodities. He confessed that his former view on that subject was erroneous. I should be glad to see all the arguments in favour of my view of the question clearly and ably stated. I should not wonder if Torrens undertook it.

The sale of my last pamphlet has far exceeded its merits. Murray is printing a second edition [1]. I had no idea that the subject was of much interest to the public, but it seems that they are curious about the amount of the Bank treasure. In the House of Commons the defence of the contracts with the Bank was very little satisfactory; they endeavoured to fix the attention of the House on what the public had got and saved by the operations of the Bank; they seemed to think that all the rest belonged of right to the Bank.

Will Ministers be able to carry the Income Tax [2]?

Very truly yours,
DAVID RICARDO.

NOTE.—Torrens came nearest to fulfilment of the above forecast in his 'Essay on the Production of Wealth' (1821), which was announced as 'a general treatise upon Political Economy, combining with the principles of Adam Smith so much of the more recent doctrines as may be conformable to truth and embodying the whole into one consentaneous system.' (Pref. p. v.) But he thinks out the subject vigorously for himself; and, though in all his later books he extols Ricardo above all his contemporaries, he finds frequent occasion to differ from him. Indeed he occasionally claims that Ricardo is the borrower, and he the lender. Ricardo, for example, is indebted to him (he says) for the doctrine that, when a nation has great advantage in one production but a much greater advantage in another, it will confine itself to producing the latter, and will even import the former (Ricardo, Works, pp. 76, 77; cf. Torrens, Preface to Essay on External Corn Trade, p. vii). Yet the doctrine has always passed as Ricardian *par*

---

[1] The edition reprinted in Wks., ed. McCulloch, pp. 391 seq.

[2] The question was whether the Income Tax, being a war tax, was to cease with the war. The Ministry were forced to yield.

excellence (see e. g. Cairnes, Leading Principles of Political Economy, Part III. ch. i. p. 371, and Logical Method, p. 81), and we should not guess, from Letter XLVII for example, that Ricardo was the convert. The Preface to the ' Production of Wealth' ends with the prediction that in twenty years' time there would be unanimity amongst Economists on all fundamental principles.

XLV.

MY DEAR SIR, LONDON, 5 *March*, 1816.

The public papers have ere this informed you of the result of yesterday's ballot at the India House ; Mr. Jackson's motion was lost by a majority of twenty-one or twenty-two. Mr. Jackson, in his reply, said everything of you that your most partial friends could wish ; and indeed the general tone of his speech, yesterday, was much more moderate than that by which he introduced his motion. Mr. Bosanquet's[1] comments on some passages in your pamphlet[2] lead me to think that he must have misunderstood you, as I conceive that it was not your intention by recommending the directors to appoint more young men than there were vacant writerships, that the unsuccessful candidates should be finally and irrecoverably dismissed from all chance of going out to India[3]. I imagine that it was your intention to let them be again competitors for one of the prizes of the following year, and therefore that the punishment of their neglect would rather be a delay in their appointment than an absolute dismission. Mr. Bosanquet appeared to me to argue on the latter supposition.

Mr. Elphinstone[4] spoke very kindly and very handsomely of the professors ; yet I thought that he was by far

---

[1] Not Chas. Bosanquet who wrote on the Bullion Report, but Jacob Bosanquet, a Director of the East India Company.

[2] Letter to Lord Grenville occasioned by his observations on E. India Co.'s education of Civil Servants, 1813.

[3] See Malthus and his Work, p. 424.

[4] Hon. Wm. F. Elphinstone, a Director of the East India Company.

I

the most formidable opponent of the College as at present constituted, and the one that I should have been least able to answer. His speech was short, but from the moderation of his language it produced, I think, a considerable effect, and gave great courage to Mr. Jackson's party. I hope this subject will not be again revived, or, rather, I hope that the proficiency of the young men, and the absence of all turbulence, will satisfy every one of the impolicy of interfering with the establishment.

I am sorry to be under the necessity of putting off my visit to you, but I shall not be able to be with you on Saturday[1]. . . . We are going . . into Gloucestershire, so that I must defer my visit to you to some more favourable opportunity. Perhaps you may be in London to the King of Clubs. If so, pray come to us. I wanted to show you my observations[2] on your pamphlets before they go to the printers. If I do not see you on Friday, I shall send them by the coach in a few days. As they are the last article in my very poor performance, the printer will probably not want them till my return[3]. When you have read them, pray send them with your observations to Brook Street by the coach. . . .

Very truly yours,

DAVID RICARDO.

XLVI.

MY DEAR SIR,   LONDON, *24th April*, 1816.

It is not too soon to remind you that Mrs. Ricardo and I expect to have the pleasure of Mrs. Malthus' and your company at our house on your visit to London in the next week. I hope it will be early in the week, and that

---

[1] Written without a capital, as the days of the week usually are in these letters.

[2] From the description which follows, this must be the last section ('Mr. Malthus's opinions on Rent') in 'Political Economy and Taxation,' 1817.

[3] From Letters LII, LIII, it is clear that the printer had to wait for the whole MS. much longer than was at first intended.

you will not be in so great a hurry to get home as you usually are. On the Monday, after your club meeting, I shall ask a few of your and my friends to meet you at dinner, and on Sunday or any other day perhaps Warburton and Mill will take a family meal with us. I have just received an invitation from Mr. Blake to dine with him on Friday the 3rd May, and I have taken upon myself to let you know from him that he hopes you will favour him with your company on that day. You will I trust be also agreeable to this arrangement.

I hope you have made better use of your time than I have done of mine, and that you are making rapid advances with the different works which you have in hand. I have done nothing since I saw you as I have been obliged to go very often into the city, and after leaving off for a day or two I have the greatest disinclination to commence work again. I may continue to amuse myself with my speculations, but I do not think I shall ever proceed further. Obstacles almost invincible oppose themselves to my progress, and I find the greatest difficulty to avoid confusion in the most simple of my statements.

Have you seen Torrens' letters to the Earl of Lauderdale in the 'Sun?' I think he has published five. They are chiefly on the subject of currency, and are ingenious, though I think they support some very incorrect doctrines. They are signed with his name.

Horner, I understand, will oppose the continuance of the restriction bill; he does not deny now the fall in the value of gold and silver since the termination of the war. There cannot be a better opportunity than the present for the Bank to recommence payments in specie. Silver is actually under the mint price. The change is surprising [and has been] brought about in a very unexpected [manner]. . .

Very truly yours,

DAVID RICARDO.

XLVII.

MY DEAR SIR,   LONDON, 28 *May*, 1816.

From what you said when you left London it is probable that you will not be at the Club on Saturday next. If your visit to town should be deferred till the following Tuesday we have a bed at your service—it is now occupied by Mr. and Mrs. Smith, our Gloucestershire friends. In case you should come sooner I hope you will be able to pass much of your time with us. Our breakfast hour is now at so reasonable a time that I hope you will take that meal with us the first morning you are in London, and then settle how often we shall see you at dinner.

I suppose you have been too busy in official occupations, since we last met, to have made much progress in the writings which you have in hand. I hope, however, that you will be prepared to give the public the result of your well considered opinions in due season. We have a right to look to you for the correction of some difficulties and contradictions with which Political Economy is encumbered [1].

Major Torrens tells me that he shall work hard for the next few months, so that we may expect a book on the same subject from him next year. He continues to hold some heretical opinions on money and exchange, notwithstanding Mr. Mill and I have exerted all our eloquence to bring him to the right faith. We, however, have succeeded in removing some of the obscurity which clouds his vision on the principles of exchange. He is, I think, quite a convert to *all* what you have called my peculiar opinions on profits, rent, etc. etc., so that I may fairly say that I hold no principles on Political Economy which have not the sanction either of your or his authority, which renders it much less

---

[1] This sentence is quoted by Empson, Edin. Review, Jan., 1837, p. 498.

important that I should persevere in the task which I commenced of giving my opinions to the public. Those principles will be much more ably supported either by you or by him than I could attempt to support them. My labours have wholly ceased for two months; whether in the quiet and calm of the country I shall again resume them is very doubtful. My vanity has not received sufficient stimulus to remove the temptation which is constantly offering itself to the indulgence of my idle habits.

The fine weather is come opportunely for your vacation. I suppose you will commence your travels without much delay. I hope we shall meet at Gatcomb before you return home.

Believe me,

Ever truly yours,

DAVID RICARDO.

XLVIII.

MY DEAR SIR, GATCOMB PARK, *9th Aug.,* 1816.

I am obliged to you for the interest you have taken about my boat. . . . I am glad that Mrs. Malthus and Miss Eckersall were pleased with their excursion to Easton Grey and Gatcomb. They and you would have better satisfied me that your visit was agreeable if you had not been in so great a hurry to put an end to it. Our friends at Easton Grey have been staying a few days with us, accompanied by Mr. Binda. We expected Mr. Warburton to join them here, but he wrote to delay his journey for a couple of days. . . . He appears pleased with the idea of his journey to Italy, though Mrs. Austin, who is returned, did not fail to represent in the strongest colours the disagreeables which she encountered. He I daresay is a very good traveller, and my daughter I have always thought the very worst I ever met with.

The Smiths leave Easton Grey on Monday for London. I suppose you have heard that they are going with Mr. Whishaw to the Netherlands and Holland. They will I am sure be very much delighted with their excursion. They always go a journey, as indeed I think they travel through life, with a disposition to be pleased. They view everything through a favourable medium, and are not eager to spy out the defects of every object they encounter.

I have no difficulty in agreeing with you 'that the rate of profits of stock depends mainly on the demand and supply of stock compared with the demand and supply of labour,' if by those words you mean the rise or fall of wages. That is my identical proposition. Now, if labour rises, no matter from what cause, profits will fall; but there are two causes which raise the wages of labour,—one the demand for labourers being great in proportion to the supply,—the other that the food and necessaries of the labourer are difficult of production or require a great deal of labour to produce them. The more I reflect on the subject the more I am convinced that the latter cause has an incessant operation. It is very seldom that the whole additional produce obtained with the same quantity of labour falls to the lot of the labourers who produce it; but, if it should, I should yet contend that the rate of profits would fall because the price of corn would fall with such an increased facility of production; capital would be withdrawn from the land, rents would fall, and profits rise. The causes you mention may operate in Poland and America; I have never denied it. The proportion between labour and capital will undoubtedly affect profits, because it will affect wages; but it is not the only element in the consideration of the subject of profits; there are other causes which also affect wages. Whether that demand can be general which increases price must, I apprehend, depend on whether the precious metals can be furnished as rapidly as other commodities. If the savings or acquisitions of labour are exchanged for all commodities in the same proportion, and the demand should increase in that proportion also, I can see no reason why any commodity should rise; but, if the demand for cloth or gold be either greater or less than the supply, they may rise or fall in their exchangeable value. That is to say, their market value might rise or fall; but their natural value would probably undergo little variation, and therefore after a time they would exchange at their usual rates. A new value thrown in the market always supposes a certain quantity of sales as well as purchases; if no part of that value consists of the precious metals, I do not see how all commodities could rise. I should expect some to rise and some to fall, but the general tendency would rather be to the latter.

Ever truly yours,

DAVID RICARDO.

. . . . .

XLIX.

MY DEAR SIR,   GATCOMB PARK, 5 *Oct.*, 1816.

Notwithstanding the bad weather I have not failed to enjoy myself, for I have been to Cheltenham, Malvern, and Worcester, and latterly to Bath. To be sure the continued rains make it less pleasant than it otherwise would be, but, as I am not at a loss for amusement within doors, I contrive to take my walks while it is fine, and return to my library with the recommencement of rain. . . . . .

I hope your additional volume will soon follow your new edition of the old work[1]. I shall be glad to see in a connected form your matured opinions on the progress of rent, profits, and wages, and in what manner they are affected

---

[1] Essay on Population.

by the increasing difficulty of procuring food, by the increase of capital, and the improvement of machinery. I fear we shall not agree on these subjects, and I should be very glad if we could fairly submit our different views to the public, that we might have some able heads engaged in considering it [*sic*][1]. Of this, however, I have little hope, for though I feel strongly the truth of my theory I cannot succeed in stating it clearly. I have been very much impeded by the question of price and value, my former ideas on those points not being correct. My present view may be equally faulty, for it leads to conclusions at variance with all my preconceived opinions. I shall continue to work, if only for my own satisfaction, till I have given my theory a consistent form.

You say that you think I have sometimes conceded that if population were miraculously stopped, while the most fertile land remained uncultivated, profits would fall upon the supposition of an increase of capital still going on. I concede it now. Profits I think depend on wages,—wages depend on demand and supply of labour, and on the cost of the necessaries on which wages are expended. These two causes may be operating on profits at the same time, either in the same, or in an opposite direction. In the case you put wages would have a tendency to keep stationary as far as the supply of food was concerned, but they would have a tendency to rise in consequence of the demand for labour increasing, whilst the supply continued the same. Under such circumstances profits would of course fall. You must, however, allow that this is an extraordinary case, and out of the common course of events, for the tendency of the population to increase is, in our state of society, more than equal to that of the capital to increase. I shall be in Lon-

---

[1] Part of this sentence is quoted by Empson in Edin. Review, Jan., 1837, p. 498.

don on Thursday or Friday next . . . . I should be glad if
some fortunate accident were to take you to town at the
same time. If so let me know where you are to be found ;
a line directed to the Stock Exchange will be certain to
find me. We shall not finally leave the country till January
or February. I wish you would come and see a little more
of Gatcomb during your Xmas vacation. . . .

Ever truly yours, .

DAVID RICARDO.

L.

MY DEAR SIR,   Bow, MIDDLESEX, 11 *Oct.*, 1816.

    I arrived in London this morning and found your
kind letter, which I ought to have answered immediately,
as you could not otherwise know whether I accepted your
kind invitation, before the time that you might expect me.
The truth is I forgot the day of the week, and was not
aware till I got home that we were so near Saturday. I
very much regret that I shall not be able to avail myself
of Mrs. Malthus' and your kindness, as I have engagements
here which will prevent me from leaving town till I return
to Gatcomb.

    You mistake me if you suppose me to say that under no
circumstances of facility of production profits could fall.
What I say is that profits will rise when wages fall, and,
as one of the main causes of the fall of wages is cheap food
and necessaries, it is *probable* that with facility of production, or cheap food and necessaries, profits would rise. At
the very time that the labour of a certain number of men
may produce on such land as pays no rent 1100 instead of
1000 quarters of corn, and when corn falls in consequence
from £5 to £4 10*s*. per quarter, the money as well as the
corn wages of labour *may* rise, for capital *may* have in-

creased at a very rapid rate, and labourers at a slow rate, in which case profits would fall and not rise. Under these very peculiar circumstances of higher money wages with a lower price of necessaries, the wages of labour would be in an unusual state, and would shortly revert to the old standard, when profits would feel the benefit. All I mean to contend for is that profits depend on wages, wages under common circumstances on the price of food and necessaries, and the price of food and necessaries on the fertility of the last cultivated land. In all cases it is perhaps true that rent will depend upon the demand compared with the supply of good land, and wages on the demand compared with the supply of labour, if it be allowed that the price of necessaries influence[s] the demand and supply of labour.

I do not quite understand the expression that profits depend on the demand compared with the supply of capital. What would you say of two countries in [which] there are precisely equal capitals, where wages [are] also equal, and where the population is precisely in the same number. Would the demand compared with the supply of capital be the same in both? If you say they would, I ask whether their rate of profits would be the same under any other supposition but that of their land being exactly of the same degree of fertility? To me it appears quite probable that the ordinary and usual rate of profits might in one be 20 and in the other only 15 per cent., or in any other proportions. . . .

Believe me,

Ever yours,

DAVID RICARDO.

LI.

MY DEAR SIR,

My stay in London will not be prolonged beyond Friday next. I hope it will be convenient to you to come up before. On Thursday I shall be disengaged and will meet you at any place in London that may best suit you, unless you will dine with me at my brother's at Bow. His house is small, and I fear he has not, now we are with him, a spare bed to offer, and you may not like to travel so far at night. If so, let us meet in the city and get our dinner there.

The money wages of labour are, I apprehend, generally regulated by facility of production. With an abundant production too I think that a less proportion of the whole will be given to the landlords, and more will remain for the other two classes, of capitalists and labourers; but of this increased quantity a greater proportion will be given to capitalists and a less proportion to labourers. Now, though what you call the real wages of labour[1] (but which I think a wrong term) will increase, the money wages will fall. But this will not be the case with profits ; what you would call real profits would increase, but so would also money profits. Under the circumstances then that I have supposed, the rate of profits would rise though money wages would fall. The difference between us is this. I say that with every facility or difficulty of production, of the quantity of necessaries, that is to be divided between profits and wages, different proportions will be given to each, and that money will accurately show those proportions. You appear to me

---

[1] See Malthus, Pol. Econ. (1820), p. 241 : ' The real wages of labour consist of their value, estimated in the necessaries, conveniences, and luxuries of life.' The 2nd ed. (1836) adds, ' which the money wages of the labourer enable him to purchase ' (p. 217). In ' Definitions' (1827) he says ' command ' instead of ' purchase,' (p. 239).

to think that profits do not depend on the division of the produce, and that money wages may as often rise with facility of production as fall.

You state the real question fairly; it is, ' What is the main cause which determines the rate of profits under all the varying degrees of productiveness ?' You do not appear to me [to] solve the question when you answer ' that it is the proportion which capital bears to labour.' In a rich country where profits are low, and where a great portion of produce is paid to the landlords for rent, the proportion of labour to capital will be the greatest, and yet according to your theory it should be the least. You will not, I think, deny that in a country where labour is high a manufacturer would employ more capital to produce the same commodities than what he would do in a country where wages were low, and there also would profits be low; that is to say, profits are high where capital bears a large proportion to labour, and low where labour bears a large proportion to capital.

I am writing amidst the noise of the Stock Exchange, and very much fear that I shall be more than usually incomprehensible.

Ever yours,
DAVID RICARDO.

LII.

My dear Sir,   GATCOMB PARK, *3rd Jan.*, 1817.

A long time has elapsed since I had the pleasure of seeing you, during which time I have often intended writing, as I did not hear from you; but my natural indolence prevailed, and I have procrastinated it till now. I had some faint hopes that you might be in the neighbouring county this vacation, in which case I should have hoped to prevail on you to pass a short time here; but I learnt from Mr. Binda, who is on a visit to Mr. Smith, that he had met with you at Holland House, and that it was not probable you would go far from home. I had previously enquired about you of our young neighbour George Clerk; he, however, could only tell me you were well; he knew nothing about your intended movements.

By an advertisement in the public papers I perceive that you have been occupied in writing about your College [1], which I regret, as I believe the task was not very agreeable to you, and as it may have prevented you from proceeding with other works in which I imagine you are more interested. I should be glad to hear that everything you think defective in the College was remedied, and that it was placed on such a footing as to require only the ordinary routine of your attention.

I have been occasionally employed, since we met, in putting my thoughts on paper, on the subjects which have often passed under our discussion. I have encountered the usual obstacles from difficulties of composition; but I have resolutely persevered till I have committed everything to paper that was floating in my mind. There are a few points on which there is a shadow of difference between my present and my past opinions; but they are not those on which we could not agree. I hope I shall succeed in putting my MS. in some tolerable order, as on that will depend whether I shall again appear before the public. What I have hitherto done is rather a statement of my own opinions than an attempt at the refutation of the opinions of others. Lately, however, I have been looking over Adam Smith, Say, and Buchanan, and where I have seen passages in their works contrary to the principles I hold to be correct I have noticed them, and shall perhaps make them the subject of some comment.

[1] 'Statements respecting the East India College,' etc., 1817.

I fear I shall not have the satisfaction of receiving your acquiescence to my doctrines, particularly as I have reverted to my former views respecting taxes on raw produce. Whatever may be correct on that subject, surely Adam Smith is wrong, as there are various passages in his book inconsistent with each other.

We shall, I hope, soon meet and renew our discussions on some of these difficult matters. I shall be in London on Friday next, and hope to see you in Brook Street as our inmate, as soon after that day as business or inclination may draw you to London.

I want to hear your opinion of the measures lately adopted for the relief of the poor[1]. I am not one of those who think that the raising of funds for the purpose of employing the poor is a very efficacious mode of relief, as it diverts those funds from other employments which would be equally if not more productive to the community. That part of the capital which employs the poor on the roads, for example, cannot fail to employ men somewhere, and I believe every interference is prejudicial. . . .

Believe me,

Ever yours,

DAVID RICARDO.

LIII.

UPPER BROOK STREET, LONDON, 24 *Jan.*, 1817.

MY DEAR SIR,

I have read your pamphlet[2] with great pleasure, and am very much satisfied with your arguments in favour of a college in preference to a school for the education of the young men destined to manage the complicated affairs

---

[1] See the long and interesting Report of Select Committee of House of Commons on the Poor Laws. Ann. Reg. 1817, Chron. pp. 263–302. Cf. Ann. Reg. 1816, Chron. pp. 151 and 345.

[2] 'Statements respecting the East India College,' 1817.

of our Indian Empire. The testimonies from India in favour of the young men sent from the College, as compared with those who went out to India before the establishment of the College make powerfully for you, and do not appear to have been answered by your opponents. I observe by the papers that the discussion on this subject will be renewed at the India House on the 6th February, at which time I conclude that you will be in London. If so, I hope you will make my house your headquarters. Mr. Murray promised to send copies of your book to the gentlemen you directed me to mention to him.

It appears to me that one great cause of our difference in opinion on the subjects which we have so often discussed is that you have always in your mind the immediate and temporary effects of particular changes, whereas I put these immediate and temporary effects quite aside, and fix my whole attention on the permanent state of things which will result from them. Perhaps you estimate these temporary effects too highly, whilst I am too much disposed to undervalue them. To manage the subject quite right, they should be carefully distinguished and mentioned, and the due effects ascribed to each.

I have been reading again your three last pamphlets on rent and corn, and cannot help thinking there is some ambiguity in the language. The word [*sic*], 'high price of raw produce,' is calculated to produce a different impression on your reader from what you mean. Your first and third causes of high price appear to me to be directly at variance with each other. The first is the fertility of land, the third the scarcity of fertile land. The second cause too, I think, never operates [1]. There is one passage in particular which expresses fully my opinions. I have not the book by me, and cannot refer you to the

---

[1] Rent, p. 8. The second is the fact that the necessaries of life create their own demand by leading to an increase of population.

page, but it begins, 'I have no hesitation in stating that independently of irregularities in the currency,' etc. It is in the essay on Rent [1].

Surely Buchanan is right and your comment [2] wrong; rent is not a creation but a transfer of wealth. It is the necessary consequence of rent being the effect and not the cause of high price [3].

Say and I would say that by turning revenue into capital we shall obtain both an increased supply and an increased demand ; but, if the same capital be so created, I do not approve of its present application, and taking it out of the hands of those who know best how to employ it, to encourage industry of a different kind and under the superintendence of those who know nothing of the wants and demands of mankind, and blindly produce cloth or stockings of which we have already too much, or improve roads which nobody wishes to travel. . .

Very truly yours,

DAVID RICARDO.

LIV.

MY DEAR SIR,

I am not in the least acquainted with the subject on which your papers [4] treat, but that is no reason why I should not mention what appears to me defective. In page 8 [5] you add $\frac{1}{8}$ to the births for probable omissions, and $\frac{1}{12}$ for deaths; but you do not tell your reader why these proportions are

---

[1] P. 40.   [2] Ibid., p. 15.

[3] The comments in this letter occur at greater length in the last chapter of Ricardo's 'Pol. Econ. and Tax.': 'Mr. Malthus's opinions on Rent' (1st ed., 1817), McC. ed., pp. 243 seq.

[4] 'Additions to the Fourth and Former Editions of an Essay on the Principle of Population,' etc., 1817.

[5] Should be p. 17.

taken rather than $\frac{1}{4}$ or $\frac{1}{3}$, nor can I discover on what grounds those numbers are chosen.

You sometimes take averages from the known facts of certain years; but your averages are formed on an arithmetical ratio while your application is to a geometrical series. I submit whether this is correct.

If, as you say in page 14[1], births are to burials as 47 to 30, and the mortality as 1 to 47, the addition to the population would be little more than $\frac{1}{82}$ instead of $\frac{1}{83}$, for out of every 1410 persons 30 would die and 47 would be born, and consequently there would be an increase of 17; but 1410 divided by 17 is 82·94, or 83 nearly; and therefore, if 1410 gives an increase of 17, 9,287,000 will give an increase of 111,970, or 1,119,700 in ten years, which will raise the population 9,287,000 + 1,119,700 = 10,406,700 instead of 10,483,000[2].

In page 16[3] the mortality is supposed to be as before, 1 in 47, and the births to the population as 1 to 29½, and the population to be 9,287,000. This latter sum divided by 29½ gives 314,813 the annual number of births, and divided by 47 gives 197,595 the annual number of deaths; deduct one from the other (197,595 from 314,813) gives 117,218 for the annual increase, which in ten years would be 1,172,180, which added to the former population of 9,287,000 gives 10,459,180 instead of 10,531,000.

I have marked in pages 35 and 36 some very trifling errors. These are all I can discover with the facts which are before me.

Ever truly yours,

DAVID RICARDO.

8 *Feb.*, 1817.

---

[1] P. 21.
[2] 10,488,000 is the figure given by Malthus, l. c. p. 18.
[3] Should be p. 21. Ricardo may have had a proof before him.

LV.

MY DEAR SIR,   LONDON, 21 *Feb.*, 1817.

I am very sorry that you were prevented from being in
London yesterday. I fully expected to see you, as I thought
the subject of debate at the India House was of too much
interest not to make you desirous of hearing it.

Mr. Grant[1] was, I assure you, a warm advocate in the
cause of the College. He spake admirably and with great
effect, improving in energy and eloquence as he proceeded.
He did justice to the various qualifications of the professors
for the responsible situations which they filled, and I believe
left nothing unsaid which might assist the cause which he
so ably defended. I thought him very severe on Randle
Jackson, who will find it difficult to answer some parts of
his speech. In the Times the report of what he said is very
correct, as far as it goes; but it is necessarily a very ab-
breviated statement. Mr. Kinnaird[2] began by speaking in
the most respectful manner of you, and indeed in terms of
great eulogy, but afterwards I think absurdly dwelt on
your being an interested party and an advocate for the
college, and imitated Mr. Jackson in his irony on those
whom he first declared were highly deserving of respect.
In what manner could we have any correct account of the
college and its concerns but from an interested party? Who
could speak of its management, attainments, and discipline,
but those who were acquainted with it ? He, however, gave
up the only strong grounds they had (if they had been true)
for inquiring into the affairs of the college, for he said that he
had no idea that there was more immorality and profligacy
in the East India College than in any other seminary;

---

[1] Charles Grant, M.P., later Lord Glenelg. He was a Director in the
preceding year (1816).
[2] Hon. Douglas J. W. Kinnaird.

neither did he say anything of a want of proficiency in the students; but his main argument was built on the general principle that a supply of intellectual attainments will as surely follow an effectual demand for it, as the supply of any material commodity will follow effectual demand.

Mr. Grant, I should mention, supported a directly contrary principle. Mr. Kinnaird dwelt very much on the compulsion under which parents were of sending their children to this particular institution. He seemed to me to adopt Mr. Mill's view of the subject, and his argument would have been quite as applicable to all colleges if parents were compelled to send their children to them. He passed over the compulsion under which parents were to send their children to college, who wished to bring them up to the church, etc. In a few minutes' conversation which I had with him after the debate I urged this objection, and he answered that they had a choice among a large number of colleges, whereas in your case they were confined to this one.

He finished by assuring me that my friend had a bad cause, that it could not be defended and must fall. Mr. Impey's speech was badly timed; he should not have immediately followed Mr. Grant, for he could not then say anything new, nor could he repeat anything that had been said half as well as Mr. Grant had said it before. The debate will be renewed on Tuesday. If you should come up, I shall expect you in Brook Street. If I do not see you, and you are disengaged on the Saturday evening following, I shall be glad to pass a day with you, commencing my visit at that time. . . .

Very truly yours,

DAVID RICARDO.

LVI.

MY DEAR SIR,   LONDON, *9th March*, 1817.

I leave London to-morrow morning very early for Gloucestershire, from whence I shall return some time before your next meeting at the King of Clubs, so that I hope you will do me the favour to come to Brook Street when you visit town on that occasion.

. . . This letter will accompany that part of my MS.[1] which refers to you. I hope I have not in any respect misapprehended you ; and, however we may differ in opinion on the subjects that we have so often discussed, I trust you will not think that I have exceeded the bounds of fair criticism in my remarks on the passages of your pamphlets which I have selected for animadversion. The printing goes on briskly. We have had a sheet a day since the commencement, and eleven sheets are now corrected. In their printed form they appear worse, in my eyes, than before ; and I need all the encouragement of my partial correctors[2] to keep alive a spark of hope respecting their reception. I wish it were fairly out of my hands ; and, that it may not be delayed, I have taken every precaution that it shall proceed uninterruptedly in my absence. As yet I have no misgivings about the doctrines themselves ; all my fears are for the language and arrangement, and above all that I may not have succeeded in clearly showing what the opinions are which I am desirous of submitting to fair investigation.

I hope that college affairs will no longer occupy an undue proportion of your attention, but that you will be able to give a finishing hand to the works which you are about to publish. Mrs. Marcet[3] will immediately publish a second

---

[1] Pol. Econ. and Tax. ch. xxxii.

[2] One of whom was probably James Mill. See 'Autobiography of John S. Mill,' p. 27.

[3] 'Conversations on Political Economy' (anon. 1816), in which the interlocutors are ' Mrs. B.' and 'Caroline.'

edition[1]. I have given her my opinion on some passages of her book, and have pointed out those which I know you would dispute with me. If she begins to listen to our controversy, the printing of her book will be long delayed; she had better avoid it, and keep her course on neutral ground. I believe we should sadly puzzle Miss Caroline, and I doubt whether Mrs. B. herself could clear up the difficulty.

From some conversation which I had yesterday morning with Mr. Murray, it appears that Torrens has been offering his book to him; but Murray is very lukewarm in the negotiation, and really very much underrates Torrens' talents. He thinks that the sale of Torrens' best work, that on corn[2], was very limited; he talked of it's not having exceeded 150 copies. Since writing the above I have seen Mr. Hume[3]; he tells me that he has heard that the directors are about to institute an inquiry into the state of the college themselves. . . .

Very truly yours,
DAVID RICARDO.

LVII.

MY DEAR SIR,   LONDON, 22 *March*, 1817.

I have been expecting you, both yesterday and to-day, and it is only after a most laborious calculation that I am led to suspect that the meeting of your Club is not till next Saturday. Next Friday then, or any earlier day, I hope we shall see you in Brook Street; and I am desired by Mrs. Ricardo to say that, if Mrs. Malthus will also favour us with her company, she will be very happy to see her. If you should come on or before Friday, the

---

[1] In original, 'addition.'   [2] On the External Corn Trade.

[3] Joseph Hume, M.P. for Melcombe Regis, and later for Montrose. He had much knowledge of India, and was at that time (vainly) endeavouring to get a seat on the Board of Directors.

printer will not before that day want that part of my MS.
which I sent to you; but, if he uses due diligence, he will
certainly be ready for it about that time. If you have any
remarks to make on it which will require much consideration on my part, be so good as to send it me before, for,
as the time approaches that I am to appear in print, I seem
to become more dissatisfied with my work, and less capable
to give any proposition contained in it a patient investigation.

It is now 5 o'clock; and, notwithstanding my doubts
have been gathering strength since the morning, I am but
just convinced, after tracing back with Mr. Hitchings the
day you were last here, that I shall not see you this day.

In great haste, yours very truly,

DAVID·RICARDO.

We returned from Gloucestershire on Tuesday last.

LVIII.

MY DEAR SIR,   LONDON, 26 *March*, 1817.

This morning I intended that my letter to you to-day
should inform you that I would have the pleasure of passing
next Saturday and Sunday with you at Haileybury; but a
circumstance has taken place which will make it necessary
for me to go to Bath on Friday next, from which place
I shall again return to London early in the next week. As
you say you will not be in town till after Easter, perhaps
it will be convenient to you to see me at Haileybury on
Saturday se'nnight. If so, I shall be with you on that day,
at your dinner hour; and, if I do not hear from you before,
I shall conclude that you have no engagement which will
render my visit inconvenient.

I mean this day to put the last of my papers in the
printer's hands, and hope he will be able to finish the
printing before my visit to you; but of this I have some

doubt, as he does not proceed regularly at the same even pace.

I agree with you that, after having so often heard your opinions, in contradiction to mine, it would not be of much use just now, when my book is actually in the press, to enter again on your reasons for differing with me. I did not send you the manuscripts with any such intention. I merely wished you to see that part which related to you before I published, that I might not inadvertently misrepresent your statement. I cannot have the least objection to insert the note you mention [1], although I cannot but regret that we should differ so much as to the just and fair import of the words *real price*. When you see my book altogether, you will not perhaps differ from me so much as you now think you do. You may, and I believe will, object to the correctness of many of my terms, as they will appear to you fanciful and not always properly applied; but, making allowance for such deviations, you will I am sure agree with much of the matter. On some points, indeed, there is no difference between us, and on others our chief disagreement would be in the mode of representing them. I have written this letter at intervals between other engagements, as I have been repeatedly interrupted. I now hear the postman's bell, and must hasten to conclude.

Very truly yours,

DAVID RICARDO.

LIX.

MY DEAR SIR,

I came up to London last night by the mail from Salisbury, and have just seen your letter. Mr. Whishaw

---

[1] I. e. the note which now appears Ric. Wks., p. 253, ('Upon showing this passage to Mr. Malthus at the time when these papers were going to the

told me when we last met that he was going to your house
on Saturday, and I feared that my projected visit might,
on account of numbers, be inconvenient to you. . . . You
have, however, suggested the getting me a bed out of your
house, with which I shall be well satisfied, let it be hard
or soft, narrow or roomy. . . . Pray make no ceremony
with me, and do not receive me if there be the least difficulty about the bed.

Yours very truly,

DAVID RICARDO.

LONDON, 3 *June*, 1817.

LX.

MY DEAR SIR,   LONDON, 25 *July*, 1817.

I am just returned from my six weeks' excursion
highly pleased with everything I have seen. I very much
regretted that you were not with me, as I am sure you
would have been gratified with the towns of Flanders and
the scenery of Namur, the Rhine and the castle of Heidel-
berg. I met Mr. Hamilton [1] at Luneville; he was going
through the country that I had just quitted, and I hope he
was as much pleased with it as I was. I fear that his
engagements at the college made him devote less time to it
than was required to enjoy all its beauties. We found
that we were obliged to hurry over it with more ex-
pedition than we wished. Mrs. Ricardo has been at
Gatcomb rather more than a week, and to-morrow I shall
quit town and join her there. Since Tuesday morning
when I left Paris I have been incessantly travelling in the
day and have not devoted many hours to sleep. I shall

press,' etc.). In that note Malthus is made to say he used the words real price
twice by mistake in Ricardo's sense, cost of production, instead of his own,
power of purchasing other commodities.

[1] Professor of Hindu literature and of the History of Asia, at Haileybury
College.

not be sorry to have a few days' rest. Your college was liberal to France, for I not only met Mr. Hamilton there but Mr. Le Bas[1] and the gentleman, whose name I forget, who teaches the French language at that institution[2].

I hope you have been enjoying your excursion and that you found less distress in Ireland than has been represented as existing there. The prospect of a good harvest is some consolation for the sufferings which the poor have been forced to endure; in every country of Europe they have endured much, and in every one they are anticipating a return of plenty.

M. Say was very much gratified with your present, and requested me to forward a letter and a small duodecimo volume which he has just published[3]. The letter I send you, but the book as well as his work on Political Economy, the 3rd edition of which he gave to me, has been detained at the Custom house at Dover, that they may have sufficient time to calculate the duty on them. As I did not wish to stay at Dover till the next day, I requested the master of the Inn to pay the duty and to forward them by Osman, who will be on his return from France in a few days. The book is an interesting little work in the manner of Rochefoucauld, and appears to me to be ably done. M. Say was very agreeable and friendly; he dined with me one day and I with him another. He is engaged in a commercial concern to which I believe he gives great attention.

I fear that it will be a long time before you and I meet, though I shall probably be in London once or twice in the next three months. I hope you will be disposed to bend your steps westerly in your winter vacation, and that you

---

[1] Professor of Mathematics.

[2] M. de Foligny, according to the E. India Register for this year, (1817).

[3] Probably the ‘ Petit Volume contenant quelques aperçus des Hommes et de la Société.’ See Œuvres Diverses, pp. 661 seq.

will not fail to pay us a visit at Gatcomb; but not such a
visit as the last,—I shall not be satisfied with a flying
excursion. Perhaps Mr. Whishaw will favour me with his
company at the same time; if so, with the assistance of my
friend Smith, we should, I hope, contrive to make the time
pass agreeably to both of you. Being very tired and very
sleepy I hasten to conclude.

Very truly yours,

DAVID RICARDO.

LXI.

MY DEAR SIR,   GATCOMB PARK, 4 *Sept.*, 1817.

I thank you very much for your kind letter of the
17th August. I am pleased to hear that your journey to
Ireland turned out so well. The account you give of the
improvements before the check which they received during
the last two years, as well as of the situation of the people,
agrees exactly with what I should expect to find. Hum-
bold[t] in his account of New Spain [1] points out the very
same evils as you do in Ireland, proceeding too from the
same cause. The land there yields a great abundance of
Bananas, Manioc, Potatoes, and Wheat, with very little
labour, and the people, having no taste for luxuries and
having abundance of food, have the privilege of being idle.
No other advantage would I think result from the dis-
posable labour being employed in manufactures than in
preventing its being turned to profligate and mischievous
pursuits, dangerous to the public peace. Happiness is the
object to be desired, and we cannot be quite sure that,
provided he is equally well fed, a man may not be happier
in the enjoyment of the luxury of idleness than in the

---

[1] See the passages quoted by Malthus, Pol. Econ. (1820), pp. 382 seq. Cf.
'Additions' to Essay, pp. 243 n., 235.

enjoyment of the luxuries of a neat cottage and good clothes. And after all we do not know if these would fall to his share. His labour might only increase the enjoyments of his employer.

Mr. Smith has heard from Mr. Whishaw; he was at Paris when he wrote, on the eve of recommencing his journey. I hope he may enjoy his tour. It is a pity that he is without an agreeable companion; he is of so sociable a disposition that he would have had pleasure in communicating his feelings and comparing them with those of another intelligent person. Mr. Smith has also heard from Mr. Warburton, who has set out on the very same tour that I have been taking, with the addition of Holland, through which country he means to pass. He has a very intelligent companion in Dr. Woolaston [1].

At the very moment that we were beginning to despair of the weather it has changed and is now beautiful. Our hopes will I trust not be disappointed, and we shall be enabled safely to house the abundant crops with which our lands in every country (*sic*) are loaded. I doubt whether we have, even during the late distresses, ceased to advance as a nation in wealth; but at present I think no one can doubt that we are again making forward strides in prosperity. A bad harvest does not perhaps very much check the progress of wealth; but it materially interferes with the general happiness.

You flatter me very much by your second perusal of my book; and I am happy to find that there are but a very few important points on which we materially differ. I certainly allow that my theory of value does not hold good in different countries when profits are different. If you look to page 156 and the following pages you will see my ideas on that subject [2].

---

[1] Probably Dr. W. H. Wollaston or Woolaston, F.R.S., the chemist.
[2] Pp. 81 seq. of McCulloch's edition of Works.

It is only yesterday that I received the book from Dover which M. Say entrusted me with for you; I send that and this letter together by Mrs. Ricardo, who is going to London for a few days; she has undertaken to send my parcel to the Hertford coach.

. . . If you go to Bath and do not come over to us I shall not know how to forgive you.

I have heard lately from Mill; he is still hard at work in correcting the press (*sic*) and finishing his book [1]. He tells me that Sir Samuel and Lady Romilly are expected at Ford Abbey. I fully expect that I shall see him here before he returns to London. I do not know when I shall be obliged to go to town, but whenever it may happen I will let you know, as I would not willingly forego any chance of meeting you. Mr. Smith's house is the centre of attraction for all his able London friends, and he is kind enough always to allow me to participate in the pleasure which their company affords him. We have already had Mr. Warburton and Mr. Belsham, and in a few days he expects to see Mr. Mallet. Mr. Smith continues to reign pre-eminent in the good-will of all his neighbours, and indeed I do not know any one who is entitled to dispute the palm with him. . . .

Ever yours truly,

David Ricardo.

This is a sad blundering letter, bad even from me, but you must excuse it, and will I am sure when I tell you that I am just recovering from the languor and weakness caused by the powerful medicines which I have been obliged to take . . . The night before last I was very ill; yesterday I was better, and to-day I have no complaint left but weakness.

---

[1] 'British India.'

LXII.

My dear Sir, Gatcomb Park, 10 *Oct.*, 1817.

I said I would write to you when I was going to London and therefore I now do it, but without much hope of seeing you there... It is not my intention, if I can get my business done, to stay in town beyond Tuesday morning, unless I had any chance of meeting you there, which would induce me to defer my return home one day longer. . . . Dr. Roget[1] has been on a visit for a few days at Mr. Smith's ; he stayed one evening with us at Gatcomb. We all very much admire his unassuming manners, and are well disposed to admit his claims on our esteem and affection. Sir Samuel Romilly and Lady Romilly have been on a visit at Mr. Phelps' a near neighbour of mine. They went from here to Bowood[2] and from thence they were going to Ford Abbey, Mr. Bentham's residence. I have since heard of their arrival there, and they are now probably returned to London.

. . . Our harvest in this part of the country is almost entirely got in. The crops are I believe generally good, and we are very grateful for the fortunate change in the weather which enabled us to reap and house them in a state of perfection. We shall now, I hope, for some years sail before the wind. You and I have always agreed in our opinions of the power and wealth of the country ; we were not in a state of despair at the discouraging circumstances with which we were lately surrounded. We looked forward to the revival which has taken place. . .

Ever truly yours,
David Ricardo.

If you should write me a line, it will reach me sooner by being directed to the Stock Exchange.

[1] The physician who, along with Dr. Marcet, attended Sir Sam. Romilly on the day before his death (Nov. 1818).

[2] Lord Lansdowne's house in Wiltshire.

LXIII.

My dear Sir,   Gatcomb Park, 21 *Oct.*, 1817.

I hope we shall be more fortunate in meeting, when I again visit London.

You think that the low price of labour which has lately prevailed contradicts my theory of profits depending on wages, because the rate of interest is at the same time very low. If interest and profits invariably moved in the same degree and in the same direction, my theory might be plausibly opposed; but I consider this as by no means the case. Although interest is undoubtedly ultimately regulated by profits, rising when they are high and falling when they are low, yet there are considerable intervals during which a low rate of interest is compatible with a high rate of profit; and this generally occurs when capital is moving from the employments of war to those of peace. If goods do not vary in price and the cost of manufacturing them falls, it is self-evident that profits must rise; and, if goods do fall in price generally, then it is not the value of goods or of labour which falls, but the value of the medium in which they are paid which rises, and then my theory does not require any rise of profits; they may even fall.

You ask me if I can show you the fallacy of the following statement: 'Capital is wholly employed in the purchase of materials and machinery and the maintenance of labour. If, from any cause whatever, materials, machinery and the maintenance of the labourer and his wages fall considerably in money value, is it *possible* that the same amount of monied capital can be employed in the country?' I answer that it is *possible* but by no means probable. Suppose the mines were to produce a diminished quantity of the precious metals, at the same time that materials and machinery were greatly increased in quantity, might not the increased aggregate quantity of materials and machinery be of a greater money value than before, although each particular portion should be at a less? Might we not by importation appropriate to ourselves a larger proportion of the mass of money distributed amongst all the countries of the world? I cannot doubt the *possibility* of the case.

In your argument about the stimulus of increased value and the effects of demand and supply on future wealth, you do not really differ from my views on this subject so much as you suppose, for I make profits and wealth to depend on the real cheapness of labour, and so do you, for you say that the evils of a dearth will often be more than counteracted as regards wealth, by the great stimulus which it may give to industry. I say the same, for I contend that the evils of a dearth fall exclusively on the labouring classes, that they perform frequently more labour not only without receiving the same allowance of food and necessaries, but often without receiving the same value for wages or the same recompense in money, whilst everything is dearer. When this happens, profits, which always depend on the value of labour, must necessarily rise.

I thought I had written to you about the additional matter in your excellent work [1], although I had not given it all the examination I intended. I read it as I was travelling and noticed the pages wherever I saw the shadow of a difference between us, that I might look at the passages again when I got home and give them my best consideration* [2]. On my passing through London when I returned from France, I looked for your book, as I expected you had sent me a copy, which I think you

---

[1] Essay on Pop., 4th ed. See above, p. 128.
[2] See next page.

kindly told me you would do; but Mrs. Ricardo had
jumbled that and many other books in a wardrobe, and
it could not be got at till I went to town. I have it now
here and have been reading all the new matter again, and
am surprised at the little that I can discover, with the
utmost ingenuity, to differ from.

* [*Foot-note, eventually ousting the text.*] In every part you
are exceedingly clear, and time only is wanted to carry
conviction to every mind. The chief difference between us
is whether food or population precedes. I could almost agree
with the statement of the question in p. 47 of third vol.,
which I think is in strict conformity with Sir J. Steuart's
opinion. In speaking of the fall of wages you only once
mention *corn* wages, but must always mean corn wages
and not money wages. In the note to p. 438 of the third vol.
you agree to my doctrine, but I think in pp. 446, 456
and 457 you forget the admission you had before made,
497 [*sic*]. You agree with Smith that the monopoly of
the Colony trade raises profits. 502 is in my opinion
wrong and inconsistent with 438. I differ a little from
your views in 506. You do not always appear to me to
admit that the tendency of the Poor Laws is to increase
the quantity of food to be divided, but assume in some
places that the same quantity is to be divided among a
larger number. I can neither agree with Adam Smith nor
with you in 326, 328: a maximum tends to discourage
future production; an undue increase of wages, or poor
laws, tend to promote it. 360, a fall in the price of commodities and a rise in the value of money are spoken of
as the same thing. 361, a diminution of production is
another way of expressing an abatement of demand. 371,
a combination among the workmen would increase the
amount of money to be divided amongst the labouring class.
These you will observe are slight objections, and I make
them that I may preserve my consistency. They would

not be understood by the mass of readers, but to you who are acquainted with my *peculiar* views, if you please, they need no explanation. . . .

Ever yours,

DAVID RICARDO.

LXIV.

MY DEAR SIR,   GATCOMB PARK, 16 *Dec.*, 1817.

I believe I am within the time stated in your letter for your visit to Surr[e]y, and consequently that this will reach you there. I am sorry that you were not sufficiently loyal to give her majesty some mark of your attention at Bath[1], during your present vacation, as in that case I might have hoped to have seen you here. As it is we may probably be in London nearly at the same time. We have not yet absolutely fixed on the day for our journey, but it will not be deferred beyond the middle of next month. I hope I may see you before your return home.

I am glad to find that we may soon expect another volume[2] from your pen, although, if you attack me, I am prepared for nine tenths of our readers deciding in favour of your view of the question. I want an able pen on my side to put my opinions in a clear light, and to divest them of that appearance of paradox which they now wear. I wish I could assist you to a good title but no one is more able to give a work the best air and arrangement than yourself. Have you seen the Review of M. Say and myself in the British? In some of the remarks you would I believe agree; yet it is some consolation to me that, after designating every part of my performance absurd and nonsensical, they attack you on the subject of Rent, and say that both you and I have endeavoured to make the

---

[1] Queen Sophia went there with Princess Elizabeth at the end of November. (Ann. Register, 1817, Chron., p. 123.)

[2] Probably the 'Political Economy,' 1820.

nature of rent, which was before so clear, obscure. Rent is nothing more than the hire paid for land. I feel delighted that they have given me so desirable a companion. In the Scotsman, a Scotch newspaper, I have been ably defended—the writer[1] has evidently understood what I meant to say, which the reviewer has not done.

I have been reading Mill's book[2] for this last week, and have got through about half of the first volume. I am not qualified to give an opinion of its merits, but I am very much pleased with it. It is very interesting, and is, I think, calculated to excite a great deal of attention, for it not only descants on the religion, manners, laws, arts, and literature, of the Hindus, but compares them with the religion, manners, etc. of other nations which the world has generally considered as much inferior to the Hindus ; and, if these in the Hindus are to be deemed marks of a high state of civilization, Africa, Mexico, Peru, Persia, and China, might also lay claim to the same character. He also gives his own sentiments as to what constitutes good laws, a good religion, a high state of civilization, and shews at what a very low degree Hindostan deserves to be estimated for these acquirements[3]. The Political Economy is, I think, excellent, and the part that I have read may be considered as the author's view of the progress of the human mind. I hope it will bring him fame and reputation,—his perseverance as well as his other qualities well deserve it. . . .

Like the Patriarchs of old I am surrounded by all my descendants, sons, daughters and grandchildren—they have assembled from all quarters to visit us, and if I were not afraid that they would soon become too numerous for the limits of our house I should insist on its being an annual custom.

You have probably seen in the papers that I am gazetted

---

[1] J. R. McCulloch, in all probability.   [2] 'British India.'

[3] Mill's estimate, however, has seldom been accepted by later authorities.

as one of the three from whom the choice of Sheriff is to
be made, and as Col. Berkeley, the first named, will in all
probability be excused on account of his intended application to the House of Lords for the Peerage which must
otherwise be given to his brother, who is nearly of age,
I shall no doubt be selected. This honour I could well
have dispensed with. . . .

Ever yours,

DAVID RICARDO.

NOTE.—In Say's ' Œuvres Diverses' (vol. i. p. 413) is printed
a letter of Ricardo to Say, dated from Gatcomb, 18th Dec. 1817.
He says amongst other things: ' Since your visit to England, I
have been by degrees retiring from business ; and, as our debt is
enormous and the price of stock very high, I have from time to
time withdrawn my capital, and have laid out much of it in land.
. . . My life is made up of successes and cares; hence I am
providing for the future as much as I can, that I may get rid of
anxiety altogether. Our friend Mill is about to publish his book
on India, on which he has been at work for several years. With
powers like his, nothing can fail to become interesting and instructive under his pen; and I am convinced that this book will
exceed the expectations of his closest friends. It is in type; and
he has kindly given me an early copy. I have read more than
half of the first volume, and I hope it will produce on competent
judges the same impression that it has made on me. What he
says on the government, laws, religion, and manners of the country
is of great weight; and the comparison he draws between the
former condition of Hindostan and its present condition seems to
me to decide the question of the high state of civilization attributed
to the former. . . . Your *Traité d'Economie Politique* increases in
reputation among us, in proportion as it becomes better known.
Extracts from it (and from my own book) have recently appeared
in the British Review, and its merit has been recognised. I have
not fared so well; the reviewer has found in my book ample
material for criticisms, and hardly a single passage worthy of
praise.'

LXV.

MY DEAR SIR,   LONDON, 30th Jan., 1818[1].

During your visit in London next week I hope you will stay with us in Brook Street, and I am commissioned by Mrs. Ricardo to add her solicitations to mine to induce Mrs. Malthus to accompany you.

Lord King[2], Mr. Whishaw and you have done me a great deal of honour in making my work[3] the subject of your discussions, but I confess it fills me with astonishment to find that you think, and from what you say they appear to agree with you, that the measure of value is not what I have represented it to be ; but that *natural price*, as well as *market price*, is determined by the demand and supply,—the only difference being that the former is governed by the average and permanent demand and supply, the latter by the accidental and temporary. In saying this do you mean to deny that facility of production will lower natural price, and difficulty of production raise it ? Will not these effects be produced after a very short interval, although the absolute demand and supply, or the proportion of one to the other, should remain permanently the same ? At any rate then demand and supply are not the sole regulators of price. I should be glad to understand what Lord King and you mean by supply and demand. However abundant the demand it can never permanently raise the price of a commodity above the expense of its production, including in that expense the profits of the producers. It seems natural therefore to seek for the cause of the variation of permanent price in the expenses of production.

---

[1] Written by oversight 1817. The postmark and all the internal evidence show that 1818 must be the year.

[2] Less famous perhaps by his numerous writings and speeches on the currency than by his Letter to his leaseholders in the spring of 1811, calling on them to pay their rents in gold or else in such an amount in notes as would cover the depreciation since the date of their leases. The text of the letter is given by Cobbett, Paper against Gold, letter xxv.

[3] 'Political Economy and Taxation.'

Diminish these and the commodity must finally fall, increase them and it must as certainly rise. What has this
to do with demand? I may be so foolishly partial to my
own doctrine that I may be blind to its absurdity. I
know the strong disposition of every man to deceive himself in his eagerness to prove a favourite theory, yet I
cannot help viewing this question as a truth which admits
of demonstration and I am full of wonder that it should
admit of a doubt. If indeed this fundamental doctrine of
mine were proved false I admit that my whole theory falls
with it, but I should not on that account be satisfied with
the measure of value which you would substitute in its place.

I am sorry that you have determined not to publish this
spring.

I have not seen Torrens, and do not know what his in-
tentions are respecting the work which he promised to
give to the public.

Sir James Mackintosh is indeed a great acquisition in
more respects than one to your College[1]. It must be
particularly agre[e]able to you.

I thank you for your congratulations on the hono[u]r
[which] has been conferred on me by the appointment [to]
the office of Sheriff[2], an honour which I could well have
dispensed with. Under all circumstances I think it best
not to offer an objection to it.

I wish you were of our party to-day. Mr. Whishaw,
Mr. Smyth, Mr. Mallet, Mr. Sharp and Mr. Warburton dine
with me.

I am glad that you have heard Mill's book[3] favourably
spoken of. I hope it may be as well thought of by others
as it is by me.

Very truly yours,

DAVID RICARDO.

[1] Mackintosh entered on his duties as Professor of Law there 1818.
[2] 1818. See Ann. Register, 1818, Chron., p. 207.
[3] British India, publ. 1818.

LXVI.

My dear Sir, London, 25 *May,* 1818.

I have again to regret that I shall not have you as an inmate of my house on your next visit to London. . . . I hope, however, that you will be our daily visitors, or as often as engagements will permit. I trust that those on our part will be exhausted before you come, for at no period have I led so dissipated a life as during this season. The King of Clubs will meet on the 6th. Let me know whether Mrs. Malthus and you will favour us with your company on the 8th, as we should be glad to ask a few friends to meet you on that day.

The general opinion here is that Parliament will be dissolved immediately after the prorogation [1], but as the election in that case will interfere with the Circuit I cannot believe that ministers will choose so inconvenient a time.

To-morrow evening there is to be a long debate in the House of Lords on the Bank Restriction Bill [2], on which occasion Lord Grenville means to speak. Lord King mentioned to me his idea of proposing that the Bank should be forbid making any dividend on their stock while the price of gold was above the mint price. I have no doubt that practically such a measure would operate a reduction of the currency and its rise to par; but, if the bank directors were obstinate, it might be attended with the most serious consequences to widows, orphans, and others, who might depend on the bank dividends only for their support.

My walks with Mill continue almost daily. I hope you will sometimes honour us with your company when in

---

[1] It was dissolved on 10th June.

[2] The Bill for renewing Restriction for another year had passed the Commons, and was to be moved by Lord Liverpool on 26th May, 1818. Lord Grenville spoke against it at great length.

London. We could make a very tolerable reformer of you
in six walks, if your prejudices be not too strongly fixed.
Indeed I should expect to find that our differences were
not very great, as, if you are favourable to reform at all,
and that I believe you are, we should agree on all the important principles. Sir James Mackintosh has been reading
Bentham, and was just beginning to give me his opinion of
the book [1] when we were interrupted. I hope I shall find
another opportunity of hearing his sentiments, which I am
very eager to do. In a conversation which I yesterday
had with Sharp he told me what he conceived Sir James'
sentiments on reform to be [2]. If he is correct, I do not
think that Sir James and I should be so much opposed to
each other as he now thinks. . .

Very truly yours,

DAVID RICARDO.

LXVII.

[Addressed to Albury, Guildford.]

MY DEAR SIR,   LONDON, 24*th June*, 1818.

Your letter arrived here whilst I was in Gloucestershire. I came to town last night, having on Monday pre-
sided at the County meeting, and made a return of our two
members.

I thank you for your inquiries after the infant [3] that you
left so ill. . . It died . . . on the day you left London.
Dr. Holland was surprised at the rapidity with which the
disease advanced. . . .

l believe it is now finally settled that I am not to be in
Parliament, and truly glad I am that the question is at any

---

[1] ' Plan of Parliamentary Reform in the Form of a Catechism, with reasons
for each article. With an Introduction, showing the necessity of Radical and
the inadequacy of Moderate Reform ' (1817).

[2] A glimpse of his mental history is given in the remarkable letter to
Sharp, written from Bombay, on 9th Dec. 1804. He had even then outlived
his reaction against the ideas of the French Revolution. See Life, vol. i.
128-136.   [3] A grandchild.

rate settled, for the certainty of a seat could hardly compensate me for the disagreeables attending the negociation for it. Mr. Clutterbuck's [1] answer announced to me that the seat he had in view for me was disposed of; and thus end my dreams of ambition.

Having once consented to yield to the opinion of my friends, I let no opportunity slip of getting into the Honourable House; but I am fully persuaded that, if I consult my own happiness only, I shall do wisely in stopping where I am. It is easier to animadvert on the actions of others than to act with wisdom ourselves; and I strongly fear that I want both the judgment and discretion which are requisite to make a tolerable senator. I am surprised at the kindness and consideration with which my friends now treat me, and it would be a great want of prudence to afford them more easy means of sifting my claims.

I am equally pleased with you that Sir Samuel Romilly's election is going on so well in Westminster, and more pleased than you will be at Sir Francis Burdett's recent success on the poll [2]. Sir Francis is, I think, a consistent man. I believe Bentham's book has satisfied him that there would be no danger in universal suffrage; but his main object, I am sure, is to get a real representative government; and he would think that object might be [secur]ed by stopping very far short of universal suffrage. [With] such opinions it is a mere question of prin[ciple] [3] (as to the obtaining of his object) whether he shall ask for the more or the less extended suffrage. I agree with you that it would be more prudent to ask for the less, and I agree also with you in thinking that with our present experience we should not venture on universal suffrage if it

---

[1] Ricardo's son-in-law. See above, p. 41. Ricardo eventually sat for Portarlington in Queen's County.

[2] The poll was open for fifteen days, and on Saturday, July 4th, the result was declared : Romilly (Whig) 5339, Burdett (Whig) 5238, Maxwell (Tory) 4808, Orator Hunt 84.   [3] We should expect 'detail.'

could be had. I am glad, however, to find that you think the election in Westminster will afford us a fair sample of the sense of the nation.

I will take care that all demands against you shall be faithfully discharged.

I have not left myself room to enter at any length into the question of the comparative advantage of employing capital in agriculture or on manufactures[1]. If by wealth you mean as I do all those things which are desirable to man, wealth I think would be most effectually increased by allowing corn to be grown or imported as best suits those concerned in the trade. You say that in the one case the corn obtained would only be sufficient to support the workmen employed *and pay fully the profits of stock;* and in the other case it would pay in addition the increased amount of rent, and support an additional population proportioned to it. Now, *if the profits of stock to be paid fully* in one case would be much greater both in value as defined by you, and in value as defined by me, than in the other, it is evident that the difference might not only equal the additional amount of rent but exceed it. I contend that the profits of stock would be higher than this whole amount if we consented to import corn, and therefore, although I will admit that in the case supposed our wealth has increased by the increase of rent from 1790 to 1818, yet I would contend that, if the trade had been free, and corn had been imported in preference to growing it, under the new and improved circumstances of agriculture, our wealth would have increased in a still greater ratio than it now has done. . . .

Truly yours,
DAVID RICARDO.

---

[1] He had added (and then cancelled): ' but it appears to me that our difference is occasioned by what I think the improper sense in which you use the word Wealth.'

NOTE.—In the new Parliament of 1818 Portarlington was represented, as in the last Parliament, by Richard Sharp, who seems to
have retired in the course of six or seven months, for we find
Ricardo's name in a division list as early as March 2, 1819.
(Hansard, *sub dato*, p. 846.)   It was a pocket borough, and there
is nothing to show that Ricardo ever visited his constituents ; but
this did not prevent him from strongly denouncing the system of
election.   The biographer of J. B. Say asserts (apparently on pure
conjecture) that Ricardo had bought an estate at Portarlington,
and with it the seat in Parliament as one of its appurtenances
(Say, Œuvres Diverses, p. 406) : ' Possesseur de vastes domaines,
il s'en trouvait qui, par un abus déploré par lui-même, lui donnaient
entrée au parlement.'   In his Biography of James Mill, p. 172,
Professor Bain speaks as if Ricardo had entered Parliament at the
General Election in 1818.

LXVIII.[1]

[On outside of letter with the frank MINCHING HAMPTON (*sic*), *Aug.* 20, 1818.]

MY DEAR SIR,

I am very much obliged to you for the kind manner
in which you express yourself respecting the praise that
has been so lavishly bestowed on me by the reviewer of
my book, in the Edinburgh Review[2].   Immediately on
reading it, I guessed that the writer of the article was Mr.
M'Culloch[3], for from the publication of my book he appears sincerely to have embraced the views which I wished
to impress on all my readers.   I cannot but feel highly
gratified at his praise, which I should not have been in
anything like an equal degree if it had come from Mr. Mill,
because, though I should not have doubted his sincerity, I
should have imputed much to his friendship and good

---

[1] Franked by H. J. Shepherd (M.P. for Shaftesbury, Dorsetshire).

[2] June, 1818. ' Mr. Ricardo,' says the reviewer, ' has done more for the
improvement [of Political Economy] than any other writer with perhaps the
single exception of Dr. Smith ' (p. 60).   He follows up this laudation with a
full analysis of the doctrines of the book (' Political Economy and Taxation '),
finding nothing with which he disagrees.

[3] Here, as frequently elsewhere, written M'Cullock.

opinion. The praise indeed is far beyond my merits, and would perhaps have really told more if the writer had mixed with it an objection here and there.

I do not remember what the question was which I answered consistently with my general principles in my last letter, and not having your letter here I cannot refer to it. I admit that by improvements in agriculture an enormous quantity of wealth may be created, and that in the natural progress of society much of that wealth may ultimately go to landlords in the shape of rent, but that does not alter the fact of rent being always a transfer, and never a creation of wealth—for before it is paid to the landlords as rent it must have constituted the profits of stock, and a portion is made over to the landlord only because lands of a poorer quality are taken into cultivation. . . .

. . . You must have found your excursion to the Isle of Wight very pleasant. . . .

You will have seen by the newspapers that I have been through all the parade and expense, which my office of sheriff imposes on me, when the judges attend the Assizes, without any advantage. The judge came into the town after midnight, by which his commission became void, and, after sending to London, Jury, Witnesses, Counsel, and Sheriff were all dismissed to their respective homes. It is expected that we shall have a new commission in two or three weeks. . . .

I am sorry that you have not made any great progress in the work that you are about. After the reflection you have given to the subject I am not surprised that my reviewer has not shaken your confidence in your opinions. It would have been little flattering to me if he had, for I have had many opportunities, and have taken a great deal of pains to bring you round to my way of thinking without success. Why should he be so fortunate on the first trial ? The truth I begin to suspect is that we do not differ so much as we have hitherto thought. I differed very little from the opinions expressed in that part of your MS. which you read to me, but I wish to h[ave an] opportunity of judging of your system as a whole, and therefore shall be glad when it comes forth in its printed form.

I am glad to hear that Sir J. Mackintosh and Mr. Whishaw are well, pray remember me kindly to them. If either, or both of them, should go to Bowood [1] this season, I shall take it very kind of them if they will come for a few days to me. The Marquis of Lansdown has promised me a visit, and it would be particularly agreeable if they would all come at the same time. Should Mr. Whishaw be as near to me as Bowood he is already under an engagement to come. I met the Marquis and Marchioness of Lansdown at Gloucester; they entered the town on their way home from a tour, just as I was about leaving it; and owing to the breaking up of the courts were detained some time for want of horses. I suppose that you will be confined at Hertford till the Xmas vacation. I very much wish that Mrs. Malthus and you would pass a part of that vacation with us. . . Mr. Mill arrived here yesterday evening to pay me his long promised visit. He brings me no news, excepting that he dined at Mr. Bentham's with Mr. Brougham, Mr. Rush [2] the American Ambassador, and Sir Samuel Romilly. The old gentleman is becoming gay. A party of four must to him be a formidably large one [3]. . . .

Ever truly yours,

D. RICARDO.

[1] The estate of Lord Lansdowne, about three miles from Chippenham, Wilts. As Lord Henry Petty, this statesman had been Chancellor of the Exchequer in the short-lived government of 'All the Talents' in 1806. He held office in Grey's Reform Ministry 1831. He joined with Malthus and others in founding the Statistical Society 1834. He outlived his most famous contemporaries, and died in 1863 in his 83rd year.

[2] Famous by association with the Oregon dispute. He recorded his impressions of England in a book called ' Narrative of a Residence at the Court of London from 1817 to 1825,' (publ. 1833), and ' Memoranda of a Residence at the Court of London, comprising Incidents Official and Personal, from 1819 to 1825,' (touching on Oregon and other questions) (1845).

[3] Bentham was then over 70.

NOTE.—Between this letter and the next come probably the two quoted by McCulloch (Ricardo, Works, p. xxvi), to whom (if not to Mill) they were no doubt addressed: 7th April, 1819, ' You will have seen that I have taken my seat in the House of Commons. I fear that I shall be of little use there. I have twice attempted to speak; but I proceeded in the most embarrassed manner; and I have no hope of conquering the alarm with which I am assailed the moment I hear the sound of my own voice.' 22nd June, 1819, ' I thank you for your endeavours to inspire me with confidence on the occasion of my addressing the House. Their indulgent reception of me has, in some degree, made the task of speaking more easy to me; but there are yet so many formidable obstacles to my success, and some, I fear, of a nature nearly insurmountable, that I apprehend it will be wisdom and sound discretion in me to content myself with giving silent votes.' Happily he did not keep this resolution. It was at this time that George Grote was introduced to Ricardo, breakfasting with him at Brook Street (March 23 and 28, 1819), and walking with him and Mill in St. James's Park and Kensington Gardens afterwards. Grote used to submit his papers to Ricardo's judgment, and vied with Mill in admiration of him (Personal Life of George Grote, p. 36). A letter from Ricardo to Grote, dated March 1823, is given in Grote's Life (p. 42); Ricardo thanks Grote for having expressed approbation of his political conduct. One of Ricardo's last public appearances, outside Parliament, was at a Reform dinner, where he proposed the chief resolution of the evening in a speech which Grote helped him to prepare (Bain's Life of J. Mill, p. 208).

LXIX [1].

MY DEAR MALTHUS, GATCOMB PARK, 21 *Sept.*, 1819.

I must not longer delay answering your kind letter. I have had you often in my mind, and was on the point of writing to you a short time ago, when I received a letter from Mill enclosing one from Mr. Napier, the editor or manager of the Encyclopedia Britannica, requesting him to apply to me to write an article on the Sinking Fund [2] for his publication. The task appeared too formidable to me to think of undertaking; and I immediately wrote to

---

[1] Franked by himself.   [2] See Note 1 at end of this letter.

Mill to that effect; but that only brought me another letter from him which hardly left me a choice, and at last I have consented to try what I can do, but with no hope of succeeding. I am very hard at work, because I wish to give Mr. Napier[1] the opportunity of applying to some other person, without delaying his publication, as soon as I have convinced Mill and him that I am not sufficiently conversant with matters of this kind. This business has lately engrossed all my time, and will probably continue to do so for at least a week to come.

So you moved from Henley to Maidenhead! You were determined not to lose sight of the Thames. I shall expect to see your name entered as a candidate for the annual wherry.

I am glad that you are proceeding merrily with your work. I now have hopes it will be finished. You have been very indolent, and are not half so industrious nor so anxious as I am when I have anything on hand.

I have not been able to give a proper degree of attention to the subject of your letter. The supposition you make of half an ounce of silver being picked up on the sea shore by a day's labour is, you will confess, an extravagant one. Under such circumstances silver could not, as you say, rise or fall, neither could labour, but corn could or rather might. Profits I think would still depend on the proportions of produce allotted to the capitalist and the labourer. The whole produce would be less, which would cause its price to rise, but of the quantity produced the labourer would get a larger proportion than before. This larger proportion would nevertheless be a less quantity than before, and would be of the same money value. In the case you suppose the rise of money wages does not appear to be neces-

---

[1] See Macvey Napier's Correspondence (Macmillan, 1879), p. 23, where Jas. Mill (writing on 10th Sept. 1819), says of Ricardo to Napier, 'it is unaffected diffidence that is the cause of his unwillingness, for he is as modest as he is able.' Cf. also Bain's Life of Jas. Mill, p. 187.

sary in the progress of cultivation to its extreme limits ; but the reason is that you have excluded the use of capital entirely in the production of your medium of value. You know I agree with you that money is a more variable commodity than is generally imagined, and therefore I think that many of the variations in the price of commodities may be fairly attributed to an alteration in the value of money. It is difficult to conceive that in a great and civilized country any commodity of importance could be produced with equal advantage without the employment of capital. By what you tell me in your letter[1] you have respected my authority much too highly, and I do not consent that you should attribute to that respect the little activity you have displayed in getting your work finished. I wish that Mrs. Malthus and you would come to us here at Christmas. I shall then be quite in the humo[u]r to discuss all the difficult questions on which we appear to differ. My family is now in a settled state, and I think I can promise you more comfortable entertainment than I have yet been able to give you here. You must no longer plume yourself on being the principal object of Cobbett's[2] abuse. I have come in for my share of it, and just in the way that I anticipated. Even when he agrees with you he can find shades of difference which calls [*sic*] forth his virulence.

I had the pleasure of passing a few days lately in Mr. Whishaw's company at Mr. Smith's at Easton Grey. He was in very good spirits and very agreeable. We had some political discussion, particularly on Reform, and he was more liberal in his concessions than I have usually found him. I had Miss Hobhouse heartily on my side ; and Mrs. Chandler, an enthusiast for the Whigs, declared that mine were the true Whig principles. Mr. Belsham

[1] Probably, that deference for Ricardo's authority was delaying his new book on 'Political Economy.'   [2] See note 2 at end of this letter.

was of the party, but he did not take a decided part. Mr.
Macdonnel, who came with Mr. Whishaw was, I thought,
all but an ally. Are you not weary? . .

Believe me, Ever yours truly,

DAVID RICARDO.

NOTE 1.—The Sinking Fund was a frequent topic of Ricardo's
speeches in the House of Commons. It was a delusion to the
people, who fancied it was paying off their National Debt, and a
snare to the Government, who were constantly tempted to divert
it from its proper purpose. So he declared in his first session
(e. g. May 13, June 9, and June 18, 1819), and so he persisted, in
his last. The following apologue on the subject from his speech
of 28th Feb. 1823, is in the manner of Cobden, and shows
how economists will rather read a difficult truth 'writ small'
than 'writ large:'—'I have (he says) an income of £1000
a year, and I find it necessary to borrow £10,000, for which
I agree to give up to my creditor £500 per annum. My steward
says to me: "If you will live on £400 a year and give up another
£100 out of your income of £500, that will enable you in a certain
number of years to get completely rid of your debt." I listen to
this good advice, live on £400 a year, and give up annually £600
to my steward in order to pay my creditor. The first year my
steward pays the creditor £100; then the debt would be £9,900,
and therefore the income [or interest] due to the creditor would be
only £495. But I continue to pay to my steward £600 per annum;
and in the next year the steward pays over £105, and so from
year to year the debt is diminished, £600 being still received by
the steward. At the end of a certain number of years the result
is this—that out of a yearly reserve of £600, half the debt is paid
off; only £250 is due to the creditor, and £350 remains in the
hands of the steward, his master continuing to live on £400 per
annum. At this period some object occurring to the steward
which he thinks might be of benefit to me or to himself, he
borrows £7000, and devotes the whole £350 in his hands to pay
the interest on that sum. What then becomes of my sinking
fund? Originally I was in debt only £10,000; now I find myself
indebted altogether £12,000; so that instead of possessing a sinking fund, as I had hoped, I am positively so much more in debt.'
Ricardo's moral was that we should honestly give up pretending

to have a sinking fund. One of his own friends remarking that this was to believe, with the French lady, that the best way to overcome temptation was to yield to it, Ricardo retorts (speech of 6th March, 1823): 'If I knew I was going to be robbed of my purse, I should spend its contents myself first.'

NOTE 2.—It is worth while to quote some parts of the passages of Cobbett, to which this letter refers. They were too violent to be taken seriously. If Dr. Johnson really loved a good hater, he lost much enjoyment by ending his days before Cobbett wrote. In the letter which appears in the Political Register for 4th Sept. 1819, Cobbett delivers himself as follows: 'I see that they [the borough-mongers] have adopted a scheme of one Ricardo (I wonder what countryman he is), who is I believe a converted Jew. At any rate he has been a 'Change Alley-man for the last fifteen or twenty years. If the Old Lord Chatham were now alive, he would speak with respect of the muckworm, as he called the 'Change Alley people. Faith, they are now become- *everything*. Baring assists at the Congress of Sovereigns, and Ricardo regulates things at home. The muckworm is no longer a creeping thing; it rears its head aloft, and makes the haughty borough-lords sneak about in holes and corners.' ... He goes on to say that the doctrines preached in the 'Courier' and elsewhere about the inutility of ready money and the convenience of paper show that cash payments are not really thought practicable by these people. 'This Ricardo says that the country is happy in the discovery of a paper money, that it is an improvement in political science. Now if this were true it would be better to have a paper money in *all* countries. And what standard of *value* would there then be? It is manifest that there could be none, and that commerce could not be carried on. Besides, what would be the peril in case of war?' Even as it is, the French expect us to be in their power in a very few years from this very cause, &c. In another letter to Hunt in the following number of the Register he goes on (p. 112): 'I wonder that Ricardo, hot from the 'Change, who talks of the *lower orders* in such goodly terms, and was shocked at the idea of their increasing, ... had not thought of the fine and copious *drain* that is continually going on from England to America. This was a little thing of sunshine amidst the gloom.' There are other references to Ricardo in the Register not much more complimentary.

Ricardo and Malthus, however, wear their rue with a difference. Cobbett reaches his spring-tide level of vituperation in the letter written from Long Island on 6th Feb., and printed in the Political Register for May 8, 1819 (vol. 34, no. 33): 'To Parson Malthus, on the Rights of the Poor and on the cruelty recommended by him to be exercised towards the Poor.'

'Parson, I have during my life detested many men, but never any one so much as you. Your book . . . could have sprung from no mind not capable of dictating acts of greater cruelty than any recorded in the history of the massacre of St. Bartholomew. Priests have in all ages been remarkable for cool and deliberate and unrelenting cruelty; but it seems to have been reserved for the Church of England to produce one who has a just claim to the atrocious preeminence. No assemblage of words can give an appropriate designation of you; and therefore, as being the single word which best suits the character of such a man, I call you Parson, which amongst other meanings includes that of Borough-monger Tool' (pp. 1019, 1020). He goes on to say he has drawn up a list of 743 obnoxious parsons, who have dared to exclude his Register and 'Paper against Gold' from their parish reading-rooms. 'I must hate these execrable Parsons; but the whole mass put together is not to me an object of such perfect execration as you, a man (if we give you the name) not to be expostulated with but to be punished' (1021).

The best commentary on this scurrility may be found in a speech of Ricardo himself (July 1, 1823, on the 'Petition of Christian Ministers for free discussion'), where he says that ribald language should always be allowed full publicity, for it 'offends the common-sense of mankind' and can hope to make no serious converts.

LXX.

My dear Malthus,   Gatcomb Park, 9 *Nov.*, 1819.

. . . . I shall go to London alone, on the 22nd, and of course I shall continue there until Parliament adjourns for the holidays :—perhaps you may have occasion to visit town during that time, if so, I shall have a bed at your service, and such fare as can be furnished by my factotum in Brook Street.

I am glad that Mr. Whishaw has expressed satisfaction with his very short visit here. I was very much pleased with his company—no one could be more agreeable, nor more disposed to be satisfied with everything about him. We had many conversations on the subject of Parliamentary Reform, and I was glad to find that our sentiments accorded much more than I had previously imagined. I should be quite contented with such a reform as Mr. Whishaw was willing to grant us. I am certainly not more inclined than I was before to Radicalism[1], after witnessing the proceedings of Hunt, Watson, and Co., if by Radicalism is meant Universal Suffrage. I fear, however, that I should not think the moderate reform, which you are willing to accede to, a sufficient security for good government. Your scheme of reform, if I recollect right, is as much too moderate as the universal suffrage plan is too violent: something between these would give me satisfaction. Do you think that any great number of the people can really be deluded with the idea that any change in the representation would completely relieve them from their distresses? There may be a few wicked persons who would be glad of a revolution, with no other view but to appropriate to themselves the property of others, but this object must be confined to a very limited number, and I cannot think so meanly of the understandings of those who are well disposed, as to suppose that they sincerely believe a reform in Parliament would give them work, or relieve the country from the payment of the load of taxes with which we are now burthened; neither do I observe in the speeches which are addressed to the mob any such extravagant ex-

[1] 'The principal domestic events of the year [1819] are intimately connected with the movements of a set of men who have received the name of Radical Reformers,' Annual Register, 1819, Hist. p. 103.

pectations held out to them. If there were I am sure they know better than to believe the speakers who make such delusive promises. I expect that we shall have a very stormy session of Parliament.

With respect to my calculations, I have only this to say in defence of them, that I never brought them forward for any practical use, but merely to elucidate a principle. It is no answer to my theory to say that ' it is scarcely possible that all my calculations should not be necessarily and fundamentally erroneous,' for that I do not deny; but still it is true that the proportion of produce in agriculture or manufactures, retained by the capitalist who sets the labourers to work, will depend on the quantity of labour necessary to provide for the maintenance and support of the labourers.

You ask me 'whether, when land is thrown out of cultivation from the importation of foreign corn, I consider the new rate of profits as determined by the state of the land, or the stationary prices of manufactured and mercantile products compared with the fall of wages.' You have correctly anticipated my answer. ' Capital will,' I think, ' be withdrawn from the land till the last capital yields the profit obtained (by the fall of wages) in manufactures, on the supposition of the price of such manufactures remaining stationary.[']

I am glad to hear that your book will be so soon in the press, but I regret that the most important part of the conclusions from the principles which you endeavour to elucidate, will not be included in it, I mean taxation. In a letter which I have lately received from Turner [1], he is full of regret that the important subject of taxation receives so little attention from Political Economists ;—at this time he thinks it peculiarly important, and I cannot but agree with him. As soon as you have launched your present work, I

[1] Name not clear in MS.

hope you will immediately prepare to give us your thoughts on a subject in which [we] are all practically interested.

I have received a letter also very lately from M'Culloch, he has been writing an article on Exchanges for the Ency. Brit., which is very well done, I think; although I cannot agree with one or two of his definitions.

I finished in my hasty way the article I had undertaken to do on the Sinking Fund, and then became so disgusted with it, that I was glad to get rid of it. I have given so many injunctions not to regard my supposed feelings in deciding whether it shall or shall not be published, that I much doubt whether it will ever see the light. . . . .

Ever yours,

D. RICARDO.

NOTE.—The gap between the above letter (of 9th Nov. 1819) and the following (of 4th May, 1820) may be filled up by a letter of Ricardo to J. B. Say, dated from London, 11th January, 1820 (Œuvres Diverses, p. 414). After thanking him for a present (which appears from Say's reply to have been a French translation of his 'Pol. Econ. and Taxation') and a letter, he goes on to say: ' I remember hearing you tell me when I saw you in Paris that in each successive edition of our respective works our opinions would approximate to each other more and more, and I am convinced that the truth of the remark will be demonstrated.' Our differences (he goes on) are becoming rather verbal than substantial. Your chapter on Value has in my opinion gained considerably. You misrepresent me, however, on that subject when you say I consider the *value* of labour to determine the value of commodities ; I hold, on the contrary, that it is not the value, but ' the *comparative quantity of labour* necessary to production which regulates the relative value of the commodities produced.' Also in regard to Rent, Profits, and Taxation, you do not observe that my reasoning proceeds on the assumption that there is in every country ' a land which yields no rent, *or* there is a capital employed on the land with a view to profit merely, and paying no rent for it.' [See ' Pol. Ec. and Tax.' (McC.'s ed.), ch. xii. p. 107.] The latter you pass over without answer. I forward you the 2nd edition of my book, which 'has nothing new in it, as I have not had the courage to recast it.' He concludes by saying: 'Political Economy is gaining ground. Sounder principles are now brought forward. Your treatise is rightly in the first rank of authorities. The debates in parliament last session were satisfactory to the friends of the science. The true principles of currency are at last recognised. I think that on that point we shall not again go astray. Jeremy Bentham and Mill are well; I saw them a short time ago.'

Say answers (2nd March, 1820) that their controversy would certainly end in agreement, if it were not cut short by death, as a recent fit of apoplexy had made him think probable. He then briefly defends himself against Ricardo's criticisms. How can you (he says) determine the quantity and quality of the labour except by the price paid to obtain it? As to the two parts of your proposition on Rent, I see no reason for disagreeing with the second when I differ from the first, and I think (with you) that taxation in the second case will be shifted to the consumers.

LXXI[1].

MY DEAR MALTHUS,   LONDON, 4 *May*, 1820.

. . . I have read your book[2] with great attention. I need not say that there are many parts of it in which I quite agree with you. I am particularly pleased with your observations on the state of the poor; it cannot be too often stated to them that the most effectual remedy for the inadequacy of their wages is in their own hands. I wish you could succeed in ridding us of all the obstacles to the better system, which might be established.

After the frequent debates between us you will not be surprised at my saying that I am not convinced by your arguments on those subjects on which we have long differed. Our differences may in some respects, I think, be

[1] Franked by himself.

[2] ' Principles of Political Economy considered with a view to their practical application ' (Murray), 1820.

ascribed to your considering my book as more practical than I intended it to be. My object was to elucidate principles, and to do this I imagined strong cases that I might show the operation of those principles[1]. I never thought, for example, that practically any improvements took place on the land which would at once double its produce; but, to show what the effect of improvements would be, undisturbed by any other operating cause, I supposed an improvement to that extent to be adopted; and I think I have reasoned correctly from such premises. I am sure I do not undervalue the importance of improvements in agriculture to landlords, though it is possible that I may not have stated it so strongly as I ought to have done. You appear to me to overvalue them; the landlords would get no more rent while the same capital was employed as before on the land, and no new land was taken into cultivation; but, as with a lower price of corn new land could be cultivated and additional capital employed on the old land, the advantage to landlords would be manifest. Because the landlord's corn rent would increase without these conditions, you appear to think he would be benefited; but his additional quantity of corn would exchange for no more money nor for any additional quantity of other goods. If labour were cheaper, he would be benefited in as far as he would save on the employment of his gardeners and perhaps some other menial servants, but this advantage would be common to all who had the same money revenue, from whatever source it might be derived. The compliment you pay me in one of your notes[2] is most flattering. I am pleased at knowing that you entertain a favourable opinion of me; but I fear that the world will

---

[1] The three foregoing sentences are quoted by Empson, Edin. Review, Jan. 1837, p. 478, though the letter is wrongly dated.

[2] Probably the note on p. 485: 'Mr. Ricardo deserves the thanks of the country' for having suggested to it a comparatively easy means of returning to Cash Payments.

think, as I think, that your kind partiality has blinded you in this instance.

I differ as much as I ever have done with you in your chapter on the effects of the accumulation of capital[1]. Till a country has arrived to [*sic*] the end of its resources from the diminished powers of the land to afford a further increase, [I hold] it to be impossible that there should [be at the] same time a redundancy of capital and of [commodities (?)]. [I] agree that profits may be for a time very l[ow] because capital is abundant compared with [labour][2], they cannot both, I think, be abundant at one [and the same time].

Admitting that you are correct on this [point, I doubt] whether the inference you draw is the correct one, and it [does not seem to me] wise to encourage unproductive consumption. If individuals would not do their duty in this respect, government might be justified in raising taxes for the mere purpose of expenditure.

McCulloch[3] has a short review of your book in the last Scotsman; it is chiefly on the subject of value; he differs from you but does so with the greatest civility and good humour. Torrens has an interest in (I believe he is editor of) the Traveller[4], and as his arguments are on my side, I of course think his criticism just. . .

> Believe me, ever truly yours,
> DAVID RICARDO.

---

[1] Ch. vii. sect. iii. pp. 351 seq.

[2] Several words wanting. Page much torn. But cf. Letter LXXIII, p. 173.

[3] Hitherto 'McCullock.' Ricardo at last falls into the Scotch way of spelling.

[4] 'An important Liberal organ,' of which in 1822 the editor was Walter Coulson a friend of Jas. Mill. (See Bain's Life of the latter, p. 183.) In 1811 the editor was Mr. Quin, and its views were at least not liberal enough for Cobbett. See Paper against Gold, p. 310.

LXXII [1].

MY DEAR MALTHUS, GATCOMB PARK, *Sept.* 4, 1820.

I was very desirous of hearing from you, and was on the point of telling you so when your letter reached me from Brighton. Mr. Hump[hre]y Austin, a neighbour of mine, told me he saw you at Paris and I had heard of your safe arrival in England. I am quite pleased to hear that your journey has been agreeable to you; it could not fail to be so when it gave you the opportunity of seeing and conversing with the principal literary men of France and of hearing their opinions on the present state of that important country. I hope in that quarter there will be no interruption of the present order of things for some time to come; but, if they do make a movement, I trust it will be for the purpose of securing more effectually the liberty of the people by perfecting as far as human means can perfect the representative system. There is nothing on which the happiness of the great body of the people so much depends. I did not expect that I had so many readers in France as the number of copies of the French translation which you tell me have been sold would seem to imply. I am not surprised that you found few who understood my theory correctly and still fewer who were disposed to agree with me. I have not yet succeeded in making many converts in my own country; but I do not despair of seeing the number increase; the few I have are of the proper description, and do not want zeal for the propagation of the true faith.

I have seen Say's letters to you [2]; it appears to me that

---

[1] Franked by himself.

[2] Lettres à M. Malthus sur différents sujets d'économie politique, notamment sur les causes de la stagnation générale du commerce (Paris, 1820). In addition to these 5 open letters, a letter of Say to Malthus (Feb. 1827) together with the reply of Malthus is given in Œuvres Diverses de J. B. Say, pp. 502-515.

he has said a great deal for the right cause but not all that could be said. In one point I think he falls into the same error as Torrens in his article in the Edinburgh Review[1]. They both appear to think that stagnation in commerce arises from a counter set of commodities not being produced without which the commodities on sale are to be purchased, and they seem to infer that the evil will not be removed till such other commodities are in the market. But surely the true remedy is in regulating future production; if there is a glut of one commodity, produce less of that and more of another, but do not let the glut continue till the purchaser chooses[2] to produce the commodity which is more wanted. I am not convinced by anything Say says of me; he does not understand me and is frequently at variance with himself, when value is the subject he treats of. In his 4th edition[3], vol. ii, page 36, he says everything falls in value, as the quantity is increased, by the facility of production. Now suppose that you have to pay for what he calls 'services productifs' in these commodities which have so fallen in value, will you give the same value if you give for them the same quantity of commodities as before? Certainly not, according to his own admission; and yet he maintains, page 33, that productive services have not varied if they receive the same quantity of a commodity, notwithstanding the cost of production of that commodity may have fallen from 40 to 30 francs per ell. He has two opposite notions about value, and I am sure to be wrong if I differ with either of them[4].

I am sorry that the government of France is prejudiced

---

[1] Perhaps Oct. 1819 (see e.g. p. 471), 'on Mr. Owen's Plans for relieving the National Distress.'

[2] Spelt here, as elsewhere, 'chuses.'

[3] Of the 'Traité d'Économie Politique' (1819). See Œuvres Diverses, p. xiii. Say had made considerable alterations.

[4] See Ricardo, Pol. Econ. and Tax., ch. xx. 'Value and Riches,' Wks. pp. 165 seq., 3rd ed.

against Political Economy. Whatever differences of opinion may exist amongst writers on that science, they are nevertheless agreed upon many important principles, which are proved to demonstration. By an adherence to these, governments cannot fail to promote the welfare of the people who are submitted to their sway. What more clear than the advantages which follow from freedom of trade, or than the evils resulting from holding out any peculiar encouragement to population?

I have been reading your book a second time with great attention, but my difference with you remains as firmly rooted as ever. Some of the objections you make to me are merely verbal; no principle is involved in them; the great and leading point in which I think you fundamentally wrong is that which Say has attacked in his letters. On this I feel no sort of doubt. With respect to the word value, you have defined it one way, I another. We do not appear to mean the same thing, and we should first agree what a standard ought to be and then examine which approaches nearest to an invariable standard, the one you propose, or that which I propose.

I have not heard of anything further having been written against you either by McCulloch or Torrens, nor do I know that they have anything in contemplation. McCulloch has written me two letters since I saw you last; he does not say anything about value, and it will probably be a year or two before he can publish anything on that subject in the Supplement to the Encyclopedia. In the next Review there will be an article of his on Tithes, which I have seen; his principles are right, but I do not like his remedy for the existing evil [1].

Mill has been with me here for a fortnight and will stay

---

[1] Edin. Review, Aug. 1820. McCulloch proposed to make the tithes a poundage on Rents, varying therefore with the net income and not with the gross produce.

some time longer. He has it in contemplation to write a popular work on Political Economy[1], in which he will explain the principles which he thinks correct in the most familiar way for the use of learners. It is not his intention to notice any person's opinions or to enter into a controversy on the disputed points.

I have been looking over my first chapter with a view to make a few alterations in it before the work goes to another edition. I find my task very difficult, but I hope I shall make my opinions more clear and intelligible. I did intend to defend myself against some of your attacks, but on reflection I think that, to do myself justice, I must say so much that I should very inconveniently enlarge the size of my book, besides which I should be constantly drawing my readers' attention from the [proper?] subject. If I defend myself at all, I must do it in [a] separate publication[2].

Respecting the trial of the Queen I am more than ever convinced of the impolicy and inexpediency of the proceedings which have led to it, and am quite sure that the plea set up that it is a State question is a false one: it is entered into merely to ·gratify the resentment and hostility of one individual who has himself behaved so ill that whatever he may have to complain of he so fully merits that no one is bound to enter into his quarrels or wish for punishment to follow offences to which his own conduct has been so instrumental. . . . Gatcomb is very delightful. I wish you and Mrs. Malthus could give us your company here before we go to London. Mr. Mill desires to be kindly remembered.

Ever yours,
DAVID RICARDO.

---

[1] Elements of Political Economy, 1821. See J. S. Mill, Autobiography, pp. 27, 28, for whose use (in the first place) it was prepared. For clear logical precision it stands alone among economical text-books.

[2] See Wks. (ed. McCull.), Preface, p. xxxi.

LXXIII[1].

My dear Malthus, GATCOMB PARK, 10 *Oct.*, 1820.

The Queen's defence appears to be going on well; a few more such evidence [*sic*] as Sir Wm. Gell and I think the Lords cannot pass the bill; in that case I shall not be called to town, and if you are in this part of the world at Christmas perhaps we shall see you at Gatcomb.

Warburton is staying at Easton Grey and has paid us a visit of two or three days with the Smiths; he was very agreeable. He does not speak quite positively, but I think he is one of my disciples and agrees with me on some of those points which you most strongly dispute.

I quite agree with you in thinking that M. Say's letters to you are not very well done. He does not even defend his own doctrine with peculiar ability, and on some other of the intricate questions, on which he touches, he appears to me to be very unsatisfactory. He certainly has not a correct notion of what is meant by value when he contends that a commodity is valuable in proportion to its utility. This would be true if buyers only regulated the value of commodities; then indeed we might expect that all men would be willing to give a price for things in proportion to the estimation in which they held them; but the fact appears to me to be that the buyers have the least in the world to do in regulating price; it is all done by the competition of the sellers, and, however the buyers might be really willing to give more for iron than for gold, they could not, because the supply would be regulated by the cost of production, and therefore gold would inevitably be in the proportion which it now is to iron, although it

---

[1] Franked by himself 9th Oct., which is therefore the real date of the letter.

probably is by all mankind considered as the less useful metal.

I think more may be said in defence of his doctrine of services; they are, I think, the regulators of value, .and, if he would give up rent, he and I should not differ very materially on that subject. In what he says of services he is quite inconsistent with his other doctrine about utility. He appears to me to talk very ignorantly of the taxation of England. In the note, page 101, he concedes too much. The difficulty of finding employment for capital in the countries you mention proceeds from the prejudices and obstinacy with which men persevere in their old employments; they expect daily a change for the better, and therefore continue to produce commodities for which there is no adequate demand. With abundance of capital and a low price of labour there cannot fail to be some employments which would yield good profits; and, if a superior genius had the arrangement of the capital of the country under his control [1], he might, in a very little time, make trade as active as ever. Men err in their production; there is no deficiency of demand. If I wanted cloth and you cotton goods, it would be great folly in us both, with a view to an exchange between us, for one of us to produce velvets and the other wine; we are guilty of some such folly now, and I can scarcely account for the length of time that this delusion continues. After all, the mischief may not be so great as it appears. You have fairly represented the point at issue between us;—I cannot conceive it possible, without the grossest miscalculation, that there should be a redundancy of capital and of labour at the same time.

When I say mine is the true faith, I mean to express only my strong conviction that I am right; I hope you do not attach anything like arrogance to the expression.

[1] Written 'controul.'

I am in the habit of asserting my opinion strongly to you, and I am sure you would not wish me to do otherwise. I am satisfied that you should do the same by yours, and I dare say you will agree with me that you are not more inclined to yield to mere authority without being convinced than I am[1]. I affirm with you that 'if the farmer has no adequate market for his produce, he will soon cease to distribute more necessaries to his labourers,' with a view to the production of more necessaries; but will he therefore leave that part of his capital inactive, will not he or somebody else employ it in producing something which will meet an adequate market? You speak of the relative *utility* of our two definitions of value. I confess that your definition[2] does not convey to my mind anything approximating to the idea I have ever formed of value. To say that real value as applied to wages implies the quantity of necessaries given to the labourer, at the same time that you agree that those necessaries are as variable as anything else, appears to me a contradiction. Political Economy you think is an enquiry into the nature and causes of wealth; I think it should rather be called an enquiry into the laws which determine the division of the produce of industry amongst the classes who concur in its formation. No law can be laid down respecting quantity, but a tolerably correct one can be laid down respecting proportions. Every day I am more satisfied that the former enquiry is vain and delusive, and the latter only the true object of the science. You say that my proposition, 'that with few exceptions the quantity of

---

[1] The foregoing three sentences are quoted by Empson, Edin. Review, Jan. 1837, p. 499.

[2] 'Real value in exchange may be defined to be the power of an object to command in exchange the necessaries and conveniences of life, including labour,' Malthus, Pol. Econ. (1820), p. 62. 'Wages are to be estimated by their real value, namely, by the quantity of labour and capital employed in producing them,' Ricardo, Pol. Ec. 2nd ed. 1819, p. 44, Wks., p. 32.

labour employed on commodities determines the rate at which they will exchange for each other, is not well founded.' I acknowledge that it is not rigidly true, but I say that it is the nearest approximation to truth, as a rule for measuring relative value, of any I have ever heard. You say demand and supply regulates value [*sic*]; this I think is saying nothing, and for the reason I have given in the beginning of this letter: it is supply which regulates value [1], and supply is itself controlled by comparative cost of production. Cost of production, in money, means the value of labour as well as profits. Now, if my commodity be of equal value with yours, its cost of production must be the same. But cost of production is, with some deviations, in proportion to labour employed. My commodity and your commodity are both worth £1000; they will therefore probably have the same quantity of labour realized in each. But the doctrine is less liable to objections when employed not to measure the whole absolute value of the commodities compared, but the variations which from time to time take place in relative value. To what causes, I mean permanent causes, can these variations be attributed? To two and to two only, one insignificant in its effects, a rise or fall of wages, or what I think the same thing a fall or rise of profits, the other of immense importance, the greater or less quantity of labour that may be required to produce the commodities. From the first cause no great effects may follow because profits themselves constitute but a small portion of price, and no great addition or deduction can be made on their account. To the other cause no very confined limit can be assigned, for the quantity of labour required to produce commodities may vary to double or treble.

The subject is difficult, and I am but a poor master of

[1] See Pol. Econ. and Tax. ch. xxi. 'Effects of Accumulation on Profits and Interest.'

language, and therefore I shall fail to express what I mean. My first chapter[1] will not be materially altered; in principle I think it will not be altered at all. . . .

Ever truly yours,

DAVID RICARDO.

LXXIV [2].

MY DEAR MALTHUS, GATCOMB PARK, 24 *Nov.*, 1820.

I have been living in a state of great uncertainty whether I should be obliged to go to London or not. It seems to be settled that Parliament will be prorogued, and therefore I do not think it necessary to take a journey to town for the sole purpose of hearing the usher of the black rods give his three taps at the door of the House of Commons with his rod of office, and which [*sic*] we are assured by Hobhouse would be laid about his back, if he presumed so to disturb a reformed House of Commons. The political horizon does not appear to be clearing up. It is always unwise for a Government to set itself against the declared opinion of a very large class of the people, and it is more particularly so when the point in dispute is one trifling in itself, and of no real importance to the state. Should the public be kept in this agitated state on a question whether the Queen should be allowed a palace, or whether her name should be inserted in the Liturgy? Nothing can be more unjustifiable than to risk the public safety on such questions as these, for after raising the discussion there is no safety either in yielding or resisting.

You say in your last letter 'that you are fortified with

---

[1] The arrangement is altered, and we have such significant changes as ' almost exclusively' instead of ' solely.'

[2] Franked by himself.

N

new arguments to prove demonstratively that a neat
revenue is absolutely impossible under the determination
to employ the whole produce in the production of necessaries, and consequently that if there is not an adequate
taste for luxuries and conveniences or unproductive labour,
there must necessarily be a general glut.' I shall not
trouble you to bring forward these arguments, for with a
very slight alteration I should entirely concur in your
proposition. If I recollect right, it is the very exception
which I made[1] and which you mention in your book.
You must collect your stock of arguments to defend more
difficult points than this.

I am quite sure that you are the last man who would
misstate an adversary, knowingly, yet I find in your book
some allusions to opinions which you represent as mine
and which I do not really hold. In one or two cases you,
I think, furnish the proof that you have misapprehended
me, for you represent my doctrines one way in one place,
and another way in another. After all the difference between us does not depend on these points; they are very
secondary considerations.

I have made notes on every passage in your book which
I dispute, and have supposed myself about publishing a
new edition of your work, and at liberty to mark the passage with a reference to a note at the bottom of the page.
I have in fact quoted three or four words of a sentence,
noting the page, and then added my comment. The part
of your book to which I most object is the last. I can see
no soundness in the reasons you give for the usefulness of
demand on the part of unproductive consumers. How
their consuming, without reproducing, can be beneficial to
a country, in any possible state of it, I confess I cannot
discover. I have also written some notes on M. Say's
letters to you, with which I am by no means pleased. He

---

[1] See Wks. p. 176. 'Malthus and his Work,' p. 294.

is very unjust to me, and evidently does not understand my doctrine; and for the opinions which we hold in common he ˙does not give such satisfactory reasons as might, I think, be advanced. In fact he yields points to you, which may almost be considered as giving up the question, and affording you a triumph. In Say's works generally, there is a great mixture of profound thinking, and of egregious blundering. What can induce him to persevere in representing utility and value as the same thing? Can he really believe that our taxation operates as he describes [1], and can he think that we should be relieved, in the way he represents, by the payment of our national debt [2]?

I shall not dispute another proposition in your letter. 'No wealth,' you say, 'can exist unless the demand or the estimation in which the commodity is held exceeds the cost of production.' I have never disputed this. I do not dispute either the influence of demand on the price of corn or on the price of all other things; but supply follows close at its heels and soon takes the power of regulating price in his [*sic*] own hands, and in regulating it he is determined by cost of production. I acknowledge the intervals on which you so exclusively dwell, but still they are only intervals. 'Fifty oak trees valued at £20 each do not contain as much labour as a stone wall in Gloucestershire which costs £1000['] [3]. I have answered your question; let me ask you one. Did you ever believe that I thought fifty oak trees would cost as much labour as the stone wall? I really do not want such propositions to be granted in order to support my system. . . .

I am, Ever truly yours,

DAVID RICARDO.

---

[1] See Ricardo, Wks. pp. 110 ·112.   [2] A Sinking Fund.
[3] This simile is used by Malthus in Quart. Rev. Jan. 1824, with ' old wine ' in place of ' oak trees.'

LXXV[1].

MY DEAR MALTHUS,   [MINCHINHAMPTON, 29 *Nov.*, 1820.]

. . . I am very glad to hear of your intention of
paying me a visit here. I hope it will be for a longer time
than you mention. I am desired by Mrs. Ricardo to say
that it would give her great pleasure to see Mrs. Malthus
and your three children. . . There is a coach which leaves
London three times a week at five o'clock in the evening,
on Monday, Wednesday, and Friday. This coach goes to
Minchinhampton, one mile from our house ; it carries four
inside, travels at a very good pace, and sets off from the
Angel Inn, St. Martin's-le-Grand. There is also a morning
coach which goes from Gerard's Hall, Basing Lane, Cheap-
side, three times a week in the morning at a quarter before
six. I believe this coach goes on Tuesday, Thursday, and
Saturday; it is a Stroud coach and does not come nearer
to our house than within four miles on the Cirencester
Road. If you prefer this coach, we will send for you to
the place where the roads diverge. This is of course in
case Mrs. Malthus does not accompany you. . . .

It is true the case[2] in my book is stated to be temporary, and in my opinion it can only be temporary
because it cannot exist when the population has increased
with the demand for people. When we meet we must
agree upon the meaning to be attached to ' a neat surplus
from the land '; it may mean the whole material produce
after deducting from it what is absolutely necessary to

---

[1] Franked by himself. Date only on cover.

[2] Perhaps the passage beginning at foot of p. 41 of Wks. and pp. 65-6
of 2nd ed. of Pol. Ec. and Tax. (where he is describing the effect of agricultural
improvements), ' With the same population and no more, there can be no
demand for any additional quantity of corn,' etc. etc., as far as the sentence,
' A considerable period would have elapsed attended with a positive diminution
of rent.'

feed the men who obtained it, or it may mean the value of the produce which falls to the share of the capitalist, or to the share of the capitalist and landlord together. If the first be neat surplus it is equally so whether given to labourers, capitalists, or landlords. If the second it may fall short of giving as great a value to the capitalist as he expended in obtaining it, and therefore for him there would be no neat produce. This term neat produce is used ambiguously in your book, and is made the ground of an observation on something [which I s]aid about neat and gross produce. The observation is [just] or not just, according to the meaning attached to the term neat produce; but more of this when we meet.

Knowing as I do how much we are influenced by taking a particular view of a subject, and how difficult it is to destroy a train of ideas which have long followed each other in the mind, I will not say I am right about the effects of unproductive demand, and therefore it is possible that five years hence I may think as you do on the subject, but at present I do not see the least probability of such a change, for every renewed consideration of the question confirms me in the opinion which I have long held.

Ever truly yours,

DAVID RICARDO.

NOTE.—On the 8th May, 1821, Ricardo writes to J. B. Say from London (Say, Œuvres Diverses, p. 416), acknowledging receipt of Say's 'Letters to Malthus,' and sending him an early copy of the 3rd edition of his 'Pol. Econ. and Tax.' He finds fault again with Say's use of the word Value. He adopts Say's doctrine of 'productive services'; but 'rent being the effect and not the cause of the rise of prices, I submit afresh to you the question whether it is not well to leave rent out of account when we are estimating the comparative value of the productions of the soil. Suppose that I have before me two loaves, the one from the best land in the country, a land yielding

three or four pounds sterling per acre, the other from a land rented
at about three or four shillings. The two are precisely of the same
quality and the same price. You would say that the price of the
one is largely a payment for the service of the soil, while it gives
little profit for the capital and the labour that have made that
land produce. This is incontestable; but what consequence can
you draw from it for our practical guidance? What we want
to know is the general law which regulates the value of bread
relatively to the value of all other things; and I believe that we
shall find that one of those loaves, the one that comes from the
land that pays little or no rent, determines the value of the whole
of the bread; consequently its value, compared with that of all other
things, depends on the quantity of labour employed in its production, comparatively with the quantity of labour employed in every
other production. Your book (the Traité) would have gained much
if you had considered the laws of rent and profits more deeply: 'Adam
Smith was certainly wrong in supposing that the rate of profits depends on the amount of accumulated capitals without regard to the
population, and the means of providing for it.' In other points
I agree with your book and with the greater part of your 'Letters
to Malthus.' 'Mr. Malthus and I see each other frequently, without
convincing one another. I am glad to be able to inform you that
economical science is more and more studied by the youth of this
country. We have recently formed a club of political economists,
in which we are proud to include Messrs. Torrens, Malthus, and
Mill. Many others besides are actively maintaining the principles
of free trade, though their names are not so well known to the
public.'

In his reply (Paris, 19th July, 1821) Say points out that Ricardo
neglects the distinction between 'natural wealth' and 'social
wealth,' or he would agree more than he does with Say in his
view of value. 'Value in use,' if it means anything, means
utility pure and simple, and we may leave out the 'value.'
But utility may be gratuitously presented to us by nature, or
added by our labour and outlay. We measure the new utility
thus added, not as you say by the *quantity of labour* it costs us,
but by the different *quantities of another product* which are given
for it (for the new utility not for the nature-given utility) by others.
For instance, a pound of iron is perhaps 2000 times less valuable
than a pound of gold, though the utility of the iron may be equal,

if not superior, to that of the gold; and the reason is that nearly all the utility of the iron is a gratuitous gift of nature to us. I neglect, therefore, the distinction of value in use and value in exchange deliberately, for I think Political Economy has to do only with the latter. As to the two loaves, the phenomenon you speak of is due, first, to the appropriation of land, apart from which such produce of the soil as was got without labour would cost nothing to anybody,—second, taking things as they are, to the fact that progress in production essentially consists in the substitution of nature's gratuitous services for our own costly ones—our ideal being the complete displacement of the latter by the former, which would make us all ' richer than David Ricardo.' Again, I consider that the determining causes of value include the causes that influence demand as well as supply, the cost to the demander of the productive services he offers in exchange, and not only the cost in labour of the article supplied. I am glad to hear of your Club. ' What I desire above all is that such economical principles as are not abstract, but are only the frank exposition of facts and their consequences, should be diffused among all classes of citizens. We have need not of controversialists expert in syllogistic weapons, but of practical economists; and all that is wanted, for that, is notions accessible to plain common sense, which I fear we repel by our too abstract reasonings.' If you admit strangers, I should be glad to be a member. He adds in a postscript that his eulogies (in the letters to Malthus) of the Essay on Population have been taken by some English writers as ironical; and he would like Ricardo to tell Malthus this is not so; he considers the position of the Essay impregnable, and has a genuine esteem for the author (Œuvres Diverses, pp. 418–22). Say was of opinion that the time had not yet come for setting up a dogmatic orthodoxy in economical doctrines; and he begins the above letter by saying to Ricardo:—' I see in your book a new proof that the subjects of political economy are prodigiously complicated, for, though you and I are both seeking the truth in good faith, yet after devoting whole years to sounding the depths of its fundamental questions we find several points on which we do not agree. It is well we are agreed on the essential point, the possibility of the progress of man in wealth and happiness, as well as on the means needful to that end. We reach the same conclusions, though sometimes in different ways' (p. 418).

LXXVI [1].

[Addressed to St. Catherine's, Bath.]

GATCOMB PARK, MINCHINHAMPTON, 9 *July*, 1821.

MY DEAR SIR,

I am sorry that you will not spare me a few days before you return to London. Pray reconsider your determination, and, if you can alter it, do. On Saturday I expect Mr. Tooke ; it is a long time since he fixed on that day to come to me, and I am sure the pleasure of his visit will be much increased, both to him and to me, if you also formed one of our party.

McCulloch has specifically and strongly objected to my chapter on Machinery [2]; he thinks I have ruined my book by admitting it, and have done a serious injury to the science, both by the opinions which I avow, and by the manner I have avowed them [3]. Two or three letters have passed between us on this subject; in his last, he appears to me to acknowledge that the effect of the use of machinery may be to diminish the annual quantity and value of gross produce. In yielding this, he gives up the question, for it is impossible to contend that with a diminished quantity of gross produce there would be the same means of employing labour. The truth of my propositions on this subject appear to me absolutely demonstrable. McCulloch is lamenting over the departure from my plan of currency, and means to make it the subject of an article in the Edinburgh Review, as he has already done in the Scotsman. I very much regret that in the great change we have made

---

[1] Franked by himself.

[2] Ch. xxxi, in which he explains his change of mind with great frankness. Cf. Author's Advertisement to 3rd ed. of Pol. Econ. and Tax., Wks. p. 3. McCulloch's views were too early stereotyped. For his character and habits generally, see Bain, Life of Jas. Mill, p. 183, etc.

[3] It is due to McCulloch to say that in his published notices of Ricardo he conceals his consternation.

from an unregulated currency to one regulated by a fixed standard we had not more able men to manage it than the present Bank directors. If their object had been to make the revulsion as oppressive as possible, they could not have pursued measures more calculated to make it so than those which they have actually pursued. Almost the whole of the pressure has arisen from the increased value which their operations have given to the standard itself. They are indeed a very ignorant set.

You are right in supposing that I have understood you in your book not to profess to enquire into the motives for producing, but into the effects which would result from abundant production. You say in your letter—'We see in almost every part of the world vast powers of production which are not put into action, and I explain this phenomenon by saying that from the want of the proper distribution of the actual produce adequate motives are not furnished to continued production.' If this had been what I conceived you to have said, I should not have a word to say against you; but I have rather understood you to say that vast powers of production are put into action and the result is unfavourable to the interests of mankind; and you have suggested as a remedy either that less should be produced or more should be unproductively consumed. If you had said 'After arriving at a certain limit, there will in the actual circumstances be no use to try to produce more; the end cannot be accomplished, and, if it could, instead of more, less would belong to the class which provided the capital,' I should have agreed with you; yet. in that case I should say the real cause of this faulty distribution would be to be found in the inadequate quantity of labour in the market, and would be effectually cured by an additional supply of it. But I say with you there could be no adequate motive to push production to this length, and therefore it would never go so far. I do not know whether I am correct in my observation that 'I say so with you,' for you often appear to me to contend not only that production can go on so far without an adequate motive, but that it actually has done so lately, and that we are now suffering the consequences of it in stagnation of trade, in a want of employment for our labourers, etc., etc.; and the remedy you propose is an increase of consumption. It is against this latter doctrine that I protest, and give my decided opposition. I acknowledge there may not be adequate motives for production, and therefore things will not be produced; but I cannot allow first that with these inadequate motives commodities will be produced, and secondly that, if their production is attended with loss to the producer, it is for any other reason than because too great a proportion is given to the labourers employed. Increase their number and the evil is remedied. Let the employer consume more himself and there will be no diminution of demand for labour; but the pay of the labourer, which was before extravagantly high, will be reduced. You say in your letter, 'If an increased power of production be not accompanied by an increase of unproductive expenditure, it will inevitably lower profits and throw labourers out of employment.' In this proposition I do not wholly agree. First I say it must be accompanied with an increase either of productive or of unproductive expenditure. If the labourer receives a large proportion of the produce as wages, all that he receives more than is sufficient to prompt him to the necessary exertions of his powers, is as much unproductive consumption as if it were consumed by his master, or by the State; there is no difference whatever. A master manufacturer might be so extravagant in his expenditure, or might pay so much in taxes, that his capital might be deteriorated for many years together; his situation would be the same if, from his own will or from the inadequacy of the population, he paid so much to his labourers as to leave himself without adequate profits or without any profits whatever. From taxation he might not be able to escape, but from this last most unnecessary *unproductive* expenditure he could and would escape, for he could have the same quantity of labour with less pay, if he only saved less; his saving would be without an end, and would therefore be absurd. You perceive then I fully admit more than you ask for; I say that, under these circumstances, without an increase of unproductive expenditure on the part of the masters profits will fall; but I say this further that even with an increased unproductive consumption and expenditure by the labouring classes profits will fall. Diminish this latter unproductive expenditure and profits will again rise; this may be done two ways, either by an increase of hands which will lower wages, and therefore the unproductive expenditure of the labouring class, or by an increase of the unproductive expenditure of the employing class, which will also lower wages by reducing the demand for labour.

I fear I have been guilty of needless repetition, but I have really a great wish to show you what the points are on which our difference really exists. I am glad to hear that you are in a pleasant country. . .

Ever yours,
DAVID RICARDO.

LXXVII [1].

[To St. Catherine's, Bath.]

MY DEAR MALTHUS,   GATCOMB PARK, 21 *July*, 1821.

I think that the concession which I have made will not bear the construction you have put upon it. 'An increased power of production must be accompanied with an increase

---

[1] Franked by himself.

of productive or unproductive expenditure.' This is the sentence on which you have remarked, and you say could not be true if the gross produce were diminished. Certainly not, but I have never said that with an increased power of production the gross produce would be diminished; I have never said that machinery enables you to get a greater quantity of gross produce ; my sole complaint against it is that it sometimes actually diminishes the gross produce.

With respect to the particular subject of discussion between us, you seem to be surprised that I should understand you to say in your book ' that vast powers of production are put into action, and the result is unfavourable to the interests of mankind.' Have you not said so? Is it not your objection to machinery that it often produces a quantity of commodities for which there is no demand, and that it is the glut which is the consequence of quantity which is unfavourable to the interests of mankind ? Even as you state your proposition in your present letter, I have a right to conclude that you see great evils in great powers of production from the quantity of commodities which will be the result, and the low price to which they will fall. Saving, you would say, would first lead to great production, then to low prices, which would necessarily be followed by low profits. With very low profits the motives for saving would cease, and therefore the motives for increased production would also cease. Do you not then say that increased production is often attended with evil consequences to mankind because it destroys the motives to industry, and to the keeping up of the increased production ? Now in much of this I cannot agree with you. I indeed allow that the case is possible, to conceive of saving being so universal that no profit will arise from the employment of capital; but then I contend that the specific reason is because all that fund, which should, and in ordinary cases does, constitute profit, goes to wages and immoderately swells that fund which is

destined to the support of labour. The labourers are immoderately paid for their labour, and they necessarily become the unproductive consumers of the country. I agree
too that the capitalists being in such a case without a sufficient motive for saving from revenue to add to capital, will
cease doing so, will, if you please, even expend a part of
their capital; but I ask what evil will result from this?
None to the capitalist, you will allow, for his enjoyments
and his profits will be thereby increased, or he would continue to save; none to the labourers, for which we should
repine, because their situation was so exceedingly favourable that they could bear a deduction from their wages and
yet be in a most prosperous condition. Here it is where
we most differ. You think that the capitalist could not
cease saving on account of the lowness of his profits, without a cessation in some degree of employment to the people.
I, on the contrary, think that with all the abatements from
the fund destined to the payment of labour, which I acknowledge would be the consequence of the new course of
the capitalists, enough would remain to employ all the
labour that could be obtained and to pay it liberally, so
that in fact there would be little diminution in the quantity of commodities produced; the distribution only would
be different; more would go to the capitalists and less to
the labourers.

I do not think that stagnation is a proper term to apply
to a state of things, in which for a time there is no motive
to a further increase of production. When in the course of
things profits shall be so low from a great accumulation of
capital and a want of means of providing food for an increasing population, all motive for further savings will
cease; but there will be no stagnation; all that is produced will be at its fair relative price, and will be freely
exchanged. Surely the word stagnation is improperly applied to such a state of things, for there will not be a

general glut, nor will any particular commodity be necessarily produced in greater abundance than the demand shall
warrant.

You say, 'We know from repeated experience that the
money price of labour never falls till many workmen have
been for some time out of work.' I know no such thing;
and, if wages were previously high, I can see no reason
whatever why they should not fall before many labourers
are thrown out of work. All general reasoning, I apprehend, is in favour of my view of this question, for why
should some agree to go without any wages while others
were most liberally rewarded? Once more I must say that
a sudden and diminished demand for labour in this case
must mean a diminished reward to the labourer, and not a
diminished employment of him; he will work at least as
much as before, but will have a less proportion of the produce of his work, and this will be so in order that his
employer may have an adequate motive for employing him
at all, which he certainly would not have if his share of the
produce were reduced so low as to make increased production an evil rather than a benefit to him. 'It is' (never)
'said that an increase of unproductive consumption among
landlords and capitalists may not sometimes be the proper
remedy for a state of things in which the motives for production fail.' I know of no one who has recommended
a perseverance in parsimony even after the profits of
capital have vanished. I have never done so, and I should
be amongst the first to reprobate the folly of the capitalist
in not indulging himself in unproductive consumption.
I have indeed said that nothing can be produced for which
there will not be a demand, unless from miscalculation,
while the employment of stock affords even moderate
profits; but I have not said that production may not in
theory be pushed so far as to destroy the motive on the
part of the capitalist to continue producing to the same

extent. I believe it might possibly be pushed so far, but we have never witnessed it in our days, and I feel quite confident that, however injurious such a state of things may be to the capitalist, it is so only because it is attended with disproportionate and unusual benefits to the labourers. The remedy, therefore, and the sole remedy, is a more just distribution of the produce; and this can be brought about only, as I said in my last letter, by an increase of workmen or by a more liberal unproductive expenditure on the part of the capitalists. I should not make a protest against an increase of consumption as a remedy to the stagnation of trade, if I thought as you do, that we were now suffering from too great savings; as I have already said, I do not see how stagnation of trade can arise from such a cause.

We appear then not to differ *very* widely in our general principles, but more so respecting the applications of them. Such and such evils may exist; but the question is do they exist now? I think not; none of the symptoms indicate that they do, and in my opinion increased savings would alleviate rather than aggravate the sufferings of which we have lately had to complain. Stagnation is a derangement of the system, and not too much general production, arising from too great an accumulation of capital.

Mr. Tooke has been here since Saturday last. I am going with him to-morrow to Bromesberrow[1], from whence he will go to Ross and down the Wye to Chepstow. We have had plenty of talk on subjects of political economy, and have found out points on which there is partial difference of opinion between us. He brought with him two pamphlets, in which you are often mentioned as well as myself; perhaps you have seen them: their titles are An Inquiry into those principles advocated by Mr. Malthus relative to the Nature of Demand and the necessity of

---

[1] Or Bromeberrow, one of Ricardo's estates, afterwards left to his son Osman.

Consumption [1], the other Observations on certain Verbal Disputes in political economy [2]. Mrs. Ricardo unites with me in kind regards to Mrs. Malthus and yourself. Mr. Tooke also desires to be kindly remembered.

Ever truly yours,

DAVID RICARDO.

LXXVIII [3].

MY DEAR MALTHUS,   GATCOMB PARK, 18 *Sept.*, 1821.

Without imputing the least blame to you, I fear that I do not quite understand your 'knotty point.' You appear to me to compare things together, which cannot, under any supposable circumstances, be made the subject of comparison. You compare a commodity, in the production of which the advances in labour remain the same while the profits of stock diminish, to another commodity 'obtained by a given quantity of labour, a given quantity of capital, and a given rate of profits.' Is not this supposing two rates of profit at the same time? Perhaps this was not meant, and your question was asked on the supposition of profits varying equally in all trades. If so, I have no hesitation in answering that, if, from an increased quantity of labour on the land, corn should appear to have doubled in money price, and not from any increased facility in the production of money, we ought to say, as we always do say, that corn had risen a hundred per cent., and not that money had fallen fifty. In differing on this point we in reality come to our old dispute, whether the quantity of labour in a commodity should be the regulator of its value, or whether the value of all things should, under

---

[1] Anon. London, 1821. The writer criticises Malthus closely though in a friendly spirit. He is less polite to Say.

[2] Also anonymous.   [3] Franked by himself.

all circumstances, be estimated by the quantity of corn for which they would exchange. You say ' we cannot surely assume that the cost of producing the necessaries of the labourer is low absolutely when the land is productive, if what is gained by the small quantity of labour employed is counterbalanced by the very high rate of profits.' I, of course, should say the cost of these necessaries was low if they were produced with little labour, but would not you, who adopt another measure and *sometimes* think value is to be estimated by the quantity of things generally which the commodity could command, would you not say, that the cost of these necessaries was small in value, agreeing, as you would, that they would not command an abundance of other things ? I do not know what you mean by the low cost of necessaries being counterbalanced by the very high rate of profits. If a hundred quarters of corn be to be divided between my labourers and me, its cost being made up of wages and profits, its cost will be the same, whether profits be high or low, and this division will in no degree affect the price of the corn; but, if at a subsequent time eighty quarters only can be obtained with the same labour and capital, and in consequence a greater proportion of the eighty be given to the labourers than was before given of the hundred, corn will rise absolutely both in my measure and in yours. It is I who am willing to take some one or more of the external commodities[1] in the production of which, while the advances in labour increase in money value, the profits of stock diminish, as a steady measure, but which you so often reject, and insist that, whether the produce of a given quantity of labour be a hundred or eighty quarters, in either case, corn has remained a steady measure of value. In the case you have supposed, you say that the commodity, in which the same advances for labour were made, while profits diminished, 'would not only fall

[1] Imported foreign goods. See below.

one half relatively to corn, but it would appear to do so estimated in any common external commodity which had all along been produced by the same quantity of labour, *and at the same rate of profits.*' I wish you had named this commodity. In the first place I deny that it would be produced at the same rate of profits, for there cannot be two rates of profit at the same time in the same country, and secondly I contend that this commodity would also fall to one half relatively to corn, and therefore would appear invariable when compared with the other commodities.

Perhaps by external commodity, you mean a foreign commodity to be imported from abroad. If so, why should not that commodity vary in reference to corn in the same degree as any home made commodity? If a hogshead of claret were worth a certain quantity of cloth, of hats, of hardware, etc., etc., would its relative value to these things alter because it was more difficult to raise corn in England, and its price rose because we refused to import it from other countries? To me it appears most clear that claret would not vary as compared with the things which I before enumerated, and that it would vary as compared with corn. Pray think of this and tell me whether I am not right. In the postscript to your letter you ask ' In the two extreme cases of the highest profits, and the lowest profits on the land, may not corn and labour remain of the same value estimated in some external commodity, although in the interval considerable variations may have taken place from supply and demand?' I answer, no, it could not remain of the same value estimated in home commodities, and as it is by means of these home commodities that we should purchase the external commodities, I cannot see the slightest reason for supposing that these commodities so exchanged could alter in relative value. I hope I have made myself understood. I am glad you approach a little towards my views, I wish you had told me to what extent.

Torrens told me he should send me his book [1]; he has not
done so, and I have not seen it.

Ever yours,

DAVID RICARDO.

LXXIX [2].

MY DEAR MALTHUS,   [28 *Sept.,* 1821.]

The case you put to me appears to me to be an impossible one. How can all countries produce their commodities with the same quantity of labour, all, except one,
produce their *corn* with the same quantity of labour also,
and yet all, the one not excepted, have their profits on
capital at the same rate? The one which you suppose to
raise its corn with only half the quantity of labour required
in the others would in all probability obtain its labour at
a much cheaper price, and consequently profits would be
higher in that country. If indeed a free trade should be
established between all these countries, then their profits
might be all nearly at the same rate, because the price of
corn and necessaries estimated in quantity of labour would
be nearly the same in all. In carrying on this supposed
case we must be informed whether the country in which
corn is obtained with comparatively little labour can continue to obtain it on the same terms, after she is called upon
to supply the markets of other countries; if she can, then
the comparative prices of corn and commodities will be
altered in all countries; in the country producing the cheap
corn, money will be rather at a higher level than before, and
therefore corn rather dearer; but commodities generally
will be at no higher price;—they will be indeed rather
cheaper, because they will be imported from abroad and

---

[1] 'An Essay on the Production of Wealth, with an Appendix, in which the
principles of Political Economy are applied to the actual circumstances of this
country,' London, 1821. The Preface is dated June 30, 1821.

[2] Franked by himself. Date only on cover.

O 2

from countries where the level of currency will be somewhat reduced ; and therefore the cost price of commodities
in those countries will be lower, and consequently they can
be sold cheaper to the country importing them. Bulky
commodities and the price of labour will only be raised in
this particular country, because the level of currency will
be somewhat raised; labour will in the real measure of
value be rather lowered, that is to say, the portion of
produce paid to the labourer, manufactured and raw produce, together, will probably be rather increased, but in
consequence of free trade and a better distribution of
capital, the proportion of the whole produce of a given
capital which the labourer will receive, will be diminished; his proportion will really be obtained with less
labour.

The benefit to other countries cannot be doubted; corn
and labour will fall very greatly in those countries, and
consequently profits will rise, and, as part of their exports
in return for corn must in the first instance be money, the
general level of currency will be reduced and commodities
generally will fall, not because they can be produced
cheaper but because they are measured by a more valuable
money. This is on the supposition that corn can continue
to be produced with little labour in the excepted country ;
but suppose the increased demand for corn should oblige
this country to cultivate poorer land, then the price of corn
would rise from another cause besides the higher level of
currency ; and, if this difficulty should be nearly as great
as in other countries, corn would be nearly as high ; but,
while it could afford on any terms to export corn for
commodities, there would be previously to the importation
of commodities an influx of the precious metals and a
higher level of currency. Without such higher level of
currency commodities could never be imported from
countries where they were before at the same price, and

where they required the same quantity of labour to produce them. Your case is an impossible one, first because you suppose the profits in two countries to be the same although the cost of producing necessaries in one of them be only one half of what it is in the other, secondly you assume as a matter of course that with a free trade the price of corn in the exporting country would rise to the price of corn in the importing country whereas it would fall in the importing country to the price in the exporting country if its cost of production was not increased in that country, and if it rose it would rise only in proportion to the increased cost of production. When there is a free trade between countries it is impossible that profits can differ very much, the only cause of difference in such case will be the different modes of living of the labourers; in one country they may be contented with potatoes and a mud hovel; in another they may require a decent house and wheaten bread. You say: 'Proceeding from this point it is obvious that in the course of a hundred years (if accumulation were supposed) labour and corn might continue at nearly the same price, while domestic commodities from the fall of profits to the level of other countries would fall to half their price estimated in the money of the commercial world.' Domestic commodities are to fall, because profits fall. If profits fall, *I* do not see why domestic commodities should fall; but why should profits fall if corn and labour continued at nearly the same price? I know of no cause of the fall of profits but the fall [1] of labour. You say: 'A striking approximation to this case actually exists in America.' 'The only difference,' you continue, 'is that circumstances in America have made labour high'; but this is the only important feature in the case. I am however decidedly of opinion that, if in America labour was very low and profits consequently

---

[1] *Sic,* a slip of the pen for 'rise.'

much higher than they are, there would be very little fall in the domestic commodities of America.

I agree indeed with you that in the progress of the cultivation of America her corn must rise with the increased difficulty of producing it; this circumstance must have a tendency to reduce the relative quantity, or rather lower the level of American currency, which will not fail by increasing the value of money to lower, the value of those commodities in America which are too bulky to be exported[1]. The commodities which America exports will not be similarly affected. Nothing is to me so little important as the fall and rise of commodities in money; the great enquiries on which to fix our attention are the rise or fall of corn, labour, and commodities, in real value, that is to say the increase or diminution of the quantity of labour necessary to raise corn and to manufacture commodities. It may be curious to develop the effect of an alteration of real value on money price; but mankind are only really interested in making labour productive, in the enjoyment of abundance, and in a good distribution of the produce obtained by capital and industry. I cannot help thinking that in your speculations you suppose these much too closely connected with money price.

I have read a very good critique on Godwin in the Edinburgh Review[2]; and I am quite sure that I know the writer. It is very well done and most satisfactorily exposes Godwin's ignorance as well as his disingenuousness.

Ever yours,

DAVID RICARDO.

[Postscript.] I cannot agree with you that in the progress of the cultivation of America a mean between her corn and

---

[1] [Note by Ricardo.] On reading over my letter I am doubtful whether this opinion respecting exportable commodities is correct.

[2] July 1821, no. LXX. See Malthus and his Work, p. 368. Ricardo evidently suspected Malthus to be the author. See conclusion of next letter.

labour will remain nearly at the same price as it now is, estimated in money or in hogsheads of claret; it will in my opinion rise. Let me take your own supposition. A country produces her corn with half the labour of another country; consequently she employs only half the capital in producing a given quantity[1]. In this country corn will be at only half the price at which it is in another; 100 quarters will sell for £200, while in another it sells for £400. Suppose profits in both countries to be 20 per cent.; in one a capital of £166 will be employed in the raising of 100 quarters of corn, in the other £333 will be so employed, and 20 per cent. on each of these capitals will be on one £33, and on the other £66. To get £33 the one must have 16½ quarters for his share of the 100 quarters, the other must have precisely the same quantity, and consequently 83½ quarters are paid in both cases for wages and other charges. But the farmer in the fertile country employs only half the labour that the other employs, and consequently with the same money wages each labourer will have the command of double the quantity of corn, he will have what you call double real wages.

Now suppose that in the progress of the fertile country it [will] at last arrive at the state in which it is necessary to [emplo]y £333 instead of £166 to raise 100 quarters of corn; it is indeed possible, under the extravagant supposition with which we have commenced, that labour might continue at the same money price; but it is quite impossible that corn should not be doubled in money price, for twice the quantity of labourers at these uniform money wages would be required to produce it. If corn doubles in price and wages remain stationary, the mean between the two must necessarily rise, and consequently, estimated in claret or in money, a mean between her corn and labour

---

[1] The writer added but struck out: 'and wages must be necessarily high, in which case she may employ nearly the same amount of capital.'

cannot as you say remain nearly the same. If (as I had a right to suppose) labour in such a country was at a low money price, when corn could be produced with so much facility, the conclusion, when corn rose, would be much more in my favour.

I cannot allow that hats would fall in a progressive country because of a fall of profits. How can it be said that the cost of producing hats is reduced by a fall of profits, if a fall of profits must be accompanied by a rise of wages? Show me that a fall of profits may take place without a rise of wages in any fixed measure of value, and then I will yield this point. But *you* have no right to talk of a fall of profits; your case is that of a progressive country with low profits and enormous wages. If of every 100 quarters of corn, where it can be produced with little labour, eighty-three be given to the labourers, while no more is given in countries where double the quantity of labourers are employed to produce 100 quarters of corn, *you* are bound to say that wages are enormously high. In my measure of value they would not be enormously high : but the commodity on which wages were expended would be extravagantly low; at any rate we should both agree that profits in such a state of things would be very moderate.

It is hardly fair to tax you with so long a letter and so soon too!

LXXX [1].

MY DEAR MALTHUS,   GATCOMB PARK, 11 *Oct.*, 1821.

It is certainly probable that the fault is with me in not understanding the proposition you submit to me ; and it may arise as you say from my being too much pre-possessed in favour of my own views; but I do not plead guilty to the charge of not giving the requisite degree of

---

[1] Franked by himself.

attention to the propositions themselves. You now say
' where have I made the supposition you impute to me?
Surely not in my last letter. My first supposition was
that profits would be 100 per cent. in the country where
corn was obtained with double the facility, while it was
10 per cent. in all others.' If you had done so, then indeed
I should be justly chargeable with inattention; but these
were your words in the letter which I was answering, ' I
will try an illustration. Suppose that corn, money and
commodities were obtained in the great mass of nations,
connected with each other by commerce, at a rate of 10
per cent., but that in one country half the quantity of
labour only was necessary to produce corn, while other
commodities were produced with as much labour as in the
rest of the world;' not one word is said of profits being
at a different rate in this country; and, as you had said
that in the great mass of nations profits were at 10 per
cent., I concluded that in this country also profits were supposed to be at 10 per cent. In this instance then you must
acknowledge the fault was yours and not mine. You do indeed afterwards suppose that this single country exports
its corn and obtains the high price of other countries for it,
and by such means raises its profits to 100 per cent.; but
this evidently would depend on the fact whether she would
get the price of other countries or whether domestic competition would lower the price of corn, in the countries to
which it was exported, to the growing price of the exporting country. This I now understand to be your case. If
the country which raised its corn, with such great facility,
were completely insulated from all other countries, you
would probably allow that corn, in that country, would be
cheap in proportion to the facility of producing it. You
would allow this also if all other countries were determined
to protect their own agriculture and absolutely refused to
import foreign corn. But in the case of a free trade, then

you think the price would rise in the exporting country to the level of the price of other countries, and consequently profits would be enormously high. If I could admit the fact of a high price, which I cannot do, I should adopt your conclusion. I should say that general profits would be higher than they had been before the rise in the price of corn. Rents would undoubtedly be higher, for the land-lord would have at least the same portion of corn as before, and that portion would be greatly enhanced in value. Labour would be higher, because the labourer would require higher money wages when corn was doubled in price. And profits would be higher because the capitalist would have more corn than before at the same time that it bore a higher price. All these classes would be benefited by the high relative value of corn to manufactured commodities, and the capitalist more particularly so, because amongst those manufactured commodities are to be found some of the necessaries of the labourer, and therefore by the payment of a less portion of corn to the labourer he would still have the command of a increased quantity of food and necessaries for himself and his family. The question then between us is—would the price of corn rise permanently or would it not, in the country which continued to possess the great facility of producing it?

There is only one case in which I think such a rise possible, and that is on the supposition that the whole capital of the country was employed in producing corn, and yet could not produce it in sufficient quantity to satisfy the demand of other countries. In that case corn would be at a monopoly price, in the same manner as those rare wines which can only be produced in particular districts are at a monopoly price, because competition could not have its full effect. In the article of corn it would be limited by the scarcity of capital, which gave to the growers of corn large profits, in the same way as the East India Company or any

other Company might make large profits. In the article
of wine the price would be augmented by the scarcity of
the land on which the grapes were grown, and would chiefly
go to the landlord in [the] form of rent. But, supposing no
monopoly, supposing capital to be so abundant that all the
corn demanded could be supplied, then I hold it to be demonstrable that the price would sink to the growing price
of it in the exporting country.

There is however another point on which we differ; you
say a striking approximation to this actually exists in the
case of America; the only difference is that the demand
for labour has awarded a larger quantity of corn to the
labourer, the effect of which has been to keep the rate of
profit comparatively low. But you surely do not mean
that the exchangeable value of the commodities exported
by America are (*sic*) in the least degree affected by the
quantity of corn awarded to the labourer. I do not think
you are justified in your expectation that in consequence
of the accumulation of capital in America any commodity
should fall there until it ceased to possess the character of
a monopolized commodity. Corn and the bulky commodities of America (which latter are always regulated by the
price of corn) could not fall until corn was sold at a price
depending on the quantity of labour actually expended on
its production, and not on the demand of our countries.
When that time came, it would cease to be a monopolized
commodity, and would fall as well as profits to the fair
competition rates. I deny that America comes at all within
your supposed case; and the proof is that, if you were to
isolate America from all other countries, you would not
lower her rate of profits, otherwise than by preventing her
from receiving a supply of labour from other countries;
but do the same thing to a country circumstanced as you
have supposed, and profits would immediately fall from
100 to perhaps 20 per cent. Your case in fact is that of a

country possessed of a particular commodity in very general
demand, and on which competition operates most feebly.
We have often discussed this peculiar case, and have
always agreed in our opinions on it. I confess, however,
I am astonished to hear you say that this is the case of
America; you might with as much reason contend that it
was also the case of Russia, of Poland, of the Cape of Good
Hope, of Botany Bay. If indeed America could send her
produce from the interior to Europe without expense, and
if the ports of all countries were open freely to receive the
corn with which America could, under the circumstances I
have supposed, supply [them], then I should say the cases
were similar; but, with the enormous expenses of sending
corn from the interior of the country, America can really
produce a very inconsiderable supply to Europe at an expense much less than Europe can grow it. You ask what
can entitle me to suppose that corn will be at half the price
in America that it is in other countries, and then argue
on that supposition so contrary to the fact. I answer I
did not apply my argument to America but to your case,
which supposed a country to produce corn with half the
labour which was required to produce it in other countries.
If America can do this, then I apply it to America. You
complain that I do not reason fairly with you, that my
theory requires labour to be low in America; but you dispute my theory and refer to the actual state of things in
America, where labour is high, and yet I contend that I
have a right to suppose labour low. I was dealing with
your case and not with America. With respect to America
I am not in possession of the facts of her case, and I cannot
admit that my theory requires the price of labour to be low
in that country. It requires rent to be low, for without
that there cannot be a great surplus produce to divide between the two other classes, after satisfying the landlord.
You will always make me say that profits depend on the

low price of corn. I never do say so ; I contend that they depend on wages, and, although in my opinion wages will be mainly regulated by the facility of obtaining necessaries, they do not entirely depend on such facility. You wish to confine me to that theory, but I reject it ; it is none of mine, and I have often told you so. I think I *do* show that your fact does not invalidate my theory, which you say I am bound to do, and I do not assume a different fact than the one you refer to in order to refute you. Surely it is fair to say 'for such and such reasons your conclusion is not correct, but my argument would have been still stronger against you, if, as I have a right to suppose, labour in such a country were cheap, because the necessaries of the labourer are there obtained with facility.' In a country situated as you suppose America to be I do not see what is to make her corn rise ; it is already according to your arguments at a monopoly price and cannot rise above that price unless there should be a greater demand and a higher price in Europe, which you say regulates the price in America, or unless America should become so populous that the price of her corn should be regulated by the expense of growing it, as in other countries, and that expense should exceed the present expense in Europe. If your theory be correct, this may not happen in 150 years, notwithstanding the greatest accumulation of capital ; but will not labour fall during all that time? If it does fall, then the mean between corn and labour will fall. But suppose the other case. Suppose the *cost* price of corn in America should rise above the present cost price in Europe ; is it conceivable that labour should fall under such circumstances? To me it appears impossible unless we suppose money to alter in value. In this case then also the mean between corn and labour would vary in value. If hats were produced under the same circumstances as money they would not fall in price in consequence of a fall of profits. If hats were pro-

duced by the employment of capital, and money were produced, as you suppose, without any capital, then I allow and
have said so in my book[1], hats would fall in price with a
fall of profits. But I say again that too much importance
is attached to money; facility of production is the great
and interesting point. How does that operate on the interests of mankind? You ask what is to become of the
money before produced in a country which should grow its
own corn with 10 per cent. profit, if it had its facility of
producing corn doubled, and profit, were to rise to 100 per
cent.; you ask further whether she would not continue to
produce money as well as other commodities as the profits
of producing it would be also 100 per cent. If the facility
of producing corn were doubled, a great deal of labour
would be employed on other things, and therefore the corn
and commodities of the country would altogether be of
as great a money value as before, and would require the
same quantity of money to circulate them. With respect
to the production of more money that would depend on the
demand for it and the prices of other things. I think the
production of money would continue as before, but it is
quite possible that there might be less encouragement to
produce money than other things, and therefore capital
might afford 100 per cent. profit in all employments except
that one. I wonder you should refuse to assent to this obvious conclusion. You say it is your opinion that, if labour
were to fall in consequence of improvements in agriculture
before an increase of population had taken place, it could
only be from glut and want of demand. Is this opinion
consistent with another, which I think you hold, and in
which I agree, that one of the regulators of the price of
labour is the price of the necessaries of the labourer?

I have mentioned my suspicions respecting the writer of
the article on population in the *Edinburgh Review* to several

[1] See 'Political Economy and Taxation,' chapter on Value.

persons. I will not utter them from this time. I hear
nothing about Murray and Place. I hope your visit at
Holland House was an agreeable one. Mrs. Ricardo unites
with me in kind regards to Mrs. Malthus; we are all well
and are leading gay lives, one week at Worcester Music
meeting and Bromesberrow, another at Bath, etc.

Ever truly yours,

DAVID RICARDO.

NOTE.—Francis Place, the radical tailor, is well known to every
reader of Prof. Bain's Life of Mill (see e. g. p. 77). His book
on Population, perhaps the best of the long series that followed
the ' Essay' of Malthus, was published by Longman early in 1822.
He differed from Malthus mainly on the nature of the preventive
checks. The collection of Scrap Books known by his name in the
British Museum library contains the following autograph letter of
Malthus (whom he seems to have first known through Ricardo):—
' Mr. Malthus sends to Mr. Place, at the request of Mr. Ricardo,
the edition of the Essay on Population which was first published
in reply to the speculations of Mr. Godwin and other writers.
The copy sent is the only one which Mr. Malthus has left. He
will be much obliged to Mr. Place, therefore, as soon as he has
done with it, to send it to Mr. Ricardo's house in Upper Brook
St., to be kept till Mr. M. is in town, which will be in a fortnight.
Mr. Godwin, in his last work, has proceeded to the discussion of
the principles of population with a degree of ignorance of his
subject which is really quite inconceivable.' E. I. Coll. Feb. 19,
1821.

LXXXI[1].

GATCOMB PARK, 27 *Nov.*, 1821.

MY DEAR MALTHUS,

Your excuse for not going on with the discussion
which you commenced is ingenious, and I ought to be
satisfied with it, as it is accompanied with a pretty compliment to me—indeed as pretty an one as could well be
paid to a person who is so uniformly your adversary.

---

[1] Franked by himself.

I however agree with you;—we know each other's sentiments so well that we are not likely to do each other much good by private discussion. If I could manage my pen as well as you do yours, I think we might do some good to the public by a public discussion.

I am sorry that I shall be obliged to miss two of the Political Economy meetings[1], as I shall not be in London till towards the latter end of the month of January.

On the 7th of December I am to dine at Hereford, by invitation, with Hume, at a public dinner, which is to be given to him for the purpose of presenting him a silver tankard and a hogshead of cider, in token of the respect and gratitude of the inhabitants of Hereford for his public services. Hume comes from town on the occasion, and is to be met at Ross at 11 o'clock in the forenoon, and escorted with due honour into Hereford. I hope everything will be conducted in an orderly and peaceable manner. I have a great aversion to a row.

I have not yet seen Torrens' book[2], nor shall I see it in all probability till I get to London. Torrens has some concern in the Champion, in which there is a paper weekly on Political Economy[3]. I think these essays are well done, but you probably would not agree with me in that opinion.

Ever yours,

D. RICARDO.

---

[1] The Political Economy Club was founded by Tooke in 1821, though there had been informal meetings of the members for some time before in Ricardo's house. See Bain's Life of Jas. Mill, p. 198, where the programme of the club is given. It included discussion and propaganda, replies to unsound newspapers, and the circulation of sound literature.

[2] 'Essay on the Production of Wealth,' 1821. See above, p. 195.

[3] This had been its feature for some time. 'There is a canting Scotchman in London who publishes a paper called the "Champion," who is everlastingly harping upon the virtues of the "fireside," and who inculcates the duty of quiet submission.' Cobbett, Pol. Reg., Nov. 2, 1816, p. 460. Cobbett, like many others, took the received Political Economy for a doctrine of political quietism.

NOTE.—This wide gap of more than a year between the eighty-first and the eighty-second letter of this collection may be filled up by a letter to Say (Œuvres Diverses, p. 423), dated from London, 5th March, 1822, and being a somewhat tardy answer to Say's letter of July, 1821, quoted above, p. 182. He says in effect: We are nearer agreement than I thought, and your distinction of natural and costly utility illustrated by the iron and the gold is objectionable only in point of expression. But it follows that commodities have a value equal to the quantity of labour spent on them, and that therefore if a pound of gold for example could be produced with less labour it would fall in value. You for your part therefore are bound to maintain it would be a less portion of our [social] wealth. Whereas for my part I do not estimate wealth by value, but by utility from whatever source derived. Your ' Catéchisme ' (of which Francis Place has just given me the 2nd edition) says that a man's wealth is in proportion to the value and not to the quantity of the things he possesses, but, as you add that that same value is estimated by the quantity of other things these same things will buy, wealth turns out to be in proportion to quantity of goods after all. If wealth is value, then to lessen all costs, so as to produce all things with less labour, would be to make the wealth of the world no greater. After some remarks on the ' two loaves,' he concludes by saying that the Political Economy Club had made Say an honorary member. ' We hope in time to raise ourselves from a Club to the dignity of an Academy, and become a learned body with ever-increasing numbers.'

Say replies (1st May, 1822) that he gratefully accepts the honorary membership. As to the points discussed, some of their differences are merely verbal. His most important contention is that in production we exchange productive services for products, and the more products we obtain for them the more *value* they have, and the richer we are. ' Moreover, I do not think that we should aim at giving abstract definitions especially of wealth, —definitions, that is to say, in which we should abstract from the possessor and the thing possessed. This was the method of medieval disputants, and this was the very reason they could never come to an understanding. Too general a definition, which enters into none of the peculiarities of each several object, teaches us nothing.'

He concludes his letter by lamenting that his countrymen paid
so little attention to economical questions. A full half of his
audience in the Conservatoire des Arts et Métiers consisted of
foreigners—English, Russians, Poles, Germans, Spaniards, Portu-
guese, and Greeks. The Crown Prince of Denmark got private
lessons from him.

LXXXII.

BROMESBERROW PLACE, LEDBURY, *Dec.* 16, 1822.

MY DEAR MALTHUS,

A long time has elapsed since there has been any
connection between us, and I take an early opportunity
after my arrival in England to address a few lines to you
principally with a view of having some account of yourself
and family, from your own pen. I have been actively employed since we last met, for not only have I wandered
about Switzerland but I have been as far as Florence. In
my way to Florence I deviated from the direct road to see
Venice, and on my return from it I did the same thing in
order to visit Genoa. Our journey has been an uncommonly prosperous one, for we have all enjoyed perfect
health and have met with few or no difficulties. My com-
panions as well as myself have very much enjoyed this
tour. When I was at Geneva I saw a good deal of our
friend Dumont, who accompanied us to Chamouny and
returned with us to Geneva. At Coppet [1] I met M. Sis-

---

[1] Necker's asylum in 1790 and the scene of his death in 1804, the
refuge also of his daughter Madame de Stael, when driven from Paris by
Napoleon. Madame de Stael died here in 1817, and her last book, 'Considérations sur les principaux événements de la Revolution Française,' was
brought out in 1818 by her son the Baron de Stael and the Duc de Broglie
jointly. Sismondi had long been a familiar friend of the house, and it was
probably he who had introduced Ricardo. The 'Nouveaux Principes d'écon.
polit.' (Sismondi's chief economical work) had appeared in 1819.

mondi. He, the Duke of Broglie, and I had a long conversation on the points of difference between us : the Duke took my side, but after a long battle we each of us I believe remained in the same opinion that we commenced the discussion in. M. Sismondi has left a pleasing impression on my mind. Madame de Broglie had a great deal of patience and forbearance. She is, I think, a very agreeable lady. I stayed in Paris three weeks just previous to my return to England. M. de Broglie and the Baron de Stael arrived there after me. I had the pleasure of seeing them two or three times. I was very much pleased with M. Gallois[1], who made me acquainted with M. Destutt [de] Tracy[2], a very agreeable old gentleman, whose works I had read with pleasure. I do not entirely agree with him in his political economy; he is one of Say's school; there are, nevertheless, some points of difference between them. I saw Say several times, but our conversation did not turn much on subjects connected with political economy; he never led to those subjects, and I always fancied he did not much like to talk upon them. His brother, Louis Say[3], has published a thick volume of remarks upon Adam Smith's, his brother's, your, and my opinions. He is not satisfied with any of us. His principal object is to show that wealth consists in the abundance of enjoyable commodities ; he accuses us all of wishing to keep up what we call valuable commodities, without any regard to quantity, about which only the political economist should be anxious. I do not believe that any of us will plead guilty to this charge. I feel

[1] The publicist. See ' Malthus and his Work,' p. 416.

[2] See Ricardo, Works, p. 171 ; De Tracy agreed with Say's definitions of ' value,' ' riches,' and ' utility.' He was at this time 68, and his chequered life (of war, politics, and authorship) did not end till 1836. His economics are properly a branch of his philosophy.

[3] Louis had been, like his brother, in the Cotton manufacture, but left it for Sugar Refining. His ' Considérations sur l'industrie et la législation,' etc., published in 1822, is the book to which Ricardo refers.

fully assured that I do not merit it should be made against me.

M. Garnier[1] is dead; but previous to his death he had prepared an additional volume of notes for a new edition of his translation of the 'Wealth of Nations,' and which [*sic*] has lately been published. I had an opportunity of looking it over, and naturally turned to those places where he criticises me. He has bestowed a good deal of space on his remarks upon my work, but they do appear to me quite irrelevant. Neither he nor M. Say have (*sic*) succeeded in at all understanding what my opinions are. Your name often occurs in this last volume. I believe he differed from you also, but I had not time to read the whole of his book.

I hope you have been very industrious in my absence, and that we shall soon see the new edition of your last work[2]. I am anxious to know how you deal with the difficult question of value. I shall read you with great interest and attention.

I am sorry to find the agricultural distress continue. I was in hopes that it would have subsided before this time. I suppose we shall hear much on this subject next session of Parliament, and that I shall be a mark for all the country gentlemen. There is not an opinion I have given on the subject which I desire to recall. I only regret that my adversaries do not do me justice, and that they put sentiments in my mouth which I never uttered. Dr. Copplestone in his article in the Quarterly Review[3] charges me with maintaining the absurd doctrine that the price of gold bullion is a sure test of the value of bullion and

---

[1] Germain Garnier, author of 'L'Histoire de la Monnaie' and translator not only of 'The Wealth of Nations' but of 'Caleb Williams,' etc., had died 4th Oct., 1821.

[2] The 'Political Economy.' The 2nd ed. did not appear till 1836, after its author's death.

[3] April 1822, pp. 239 seq. on the State of the Currency. This is the article closely criticised by Tooke in 'High and Low Prices,' Part i. pp. 19 seq.

currency. A Mr. Paget has addressed a (printed) letter [1] to me, in which I am accused of holding the same opinion, and everybody knows how pertinaciously Cobbet[t] persists in saying that I have always done so. I must fight my cause as well as I can; I know it is an honest one (in spite of Mr. Western's [2] insinuations), and, if it be also founded in truth and on correct views, justice will be finally done to me.

I arrived in London the beginning of last week; I saw Tooke for a few minutes, and was glad to hear from him that he had been writing and was nearly ready for the press. I have a very good opinion of his judgment and of the soundness of his views; he will, I think, from his practical knowledge, throw much light on the question of the influence of an over-supply or of an increased demand, without a corresponding supply, on price [3].

I am now on a visit to my son. On the 27th I shall go to Gatcomb for a week. From the 3rd to the 17th January I shall be with Mrs. Austin at Bradley, Wottonunderedge, and from the 17th to the 2nd February with Mrs. Clutterbuck, Widcomb, Bath. Where shall you pass your holidays? Is there any probability of my seeing you at Bath? I should be glad to meet you there.

I read in the papers with much concern of the renewal of disturbances amongst the young men at the college. I know how distressing to you such insubordination is, and greatly regretted that you should have been again exposed to it. I hope that order was quickly restored.

I saw Mr. Whishaw in London for a few minutes. I am

---

[1] 'A Letter to David Ricardo, Esq., M.P., on the true principle of estimating the extent of the late Depreciation in the Currency and on the effects of Mr. Peel's Bill for the Resumption of Cash Payments by the Bank,' by Thomas Paget, Esq., 1822 (July). It contains more rhetoric than logic.

[2] One of his chief Parliamentary opponents, in the agricultural interest.

[3] 'Thoughts and Details on High and Low Prices' was published early in 1823. Tooke was for thirty years a Russia merchant.

not without hopes of seeing him at Mrs. Smith's at Easton Grey, where I mean to pass two nights on my way to Bradley. . .

Believe me,

Ever truly yours,

DAVID RICARDO.

LXXXIII.

MY DEAR MALTHUS,　　　　　　LONDON, 29 *April*, 1823.

After the most attentive consideration which I can give to your book [1], I cannot agree with you in considering labour, in the sense in which you use it, as a good measure of value. Neither can I discover exactly what connexion the constant labour necessary to produce the wages and profits on a commodity has with its value. If it be a good measure for one commodity, it must be for all commodities; and, as well as valuing wheat by the constant quantity of labour necessary to produce the particular quantity given to the workman, together with the profit of the farmer on that particular quantity, I might value cloth or any other thing by the same rule.

I know, indeed, that I might make out a table [2] precisely such as yours, in which the only alteration would be the word cloth instead of the word wheat, and you would probably then ask me whether your principle were not of universal application. I should answer that it contains in it that radical objection which you make against the proposed measure of your opponents. You may, if you please, arbitrarily select labour as a measure of value, and explain all the science of political economy by it, in the same way as any other man might select gold or any other com-

---

[1] 'The Measure of Value Stated and Illustrated, with an Application of it to the Alterations in the Value of the English Currency since 1790,' London, 1823.

[2] See note to this letter.

modity; but you can no more connect it with a principle
or show its invariability than he could. Let me suppose
that cloth could not be made in less than two years; the
first line of my table must be altered, and the figures would
stand in the following order:—

150, 100, 25 per cent. 7½, 2½, 10, 10, 15.

They would do so because ten pieces of cloth would, with
the accumulation of profit for two years, be of the same
value as a commodity, the result of the same quantity of
labour, which could be produced in two years. I do not
know how you will treat this objection, but in my opinion
it is fatal to your whole theory.

I have the same objection to your measure, which I have
always professed; you choose[1] a variable measure for an
invariable standard. Who can say that a plague which
should take off half our people would not alter the value of
labour? We might, indeed, agree to transfer the variation to
the commodities, and to say that they had fallen and not that
labour had risen, but I can see no advantage in the change.

We might again discover modes by which the necessaries
of the labourer might be produced with uncommon facility;
and, in consequence of the stimulus which the good situation of the labourers might give to population, the reward
of the labour in necessaries might be no higher than before;
would it be right in this case, in which nothing had really
altered but necessaries and labour, to say that they only
had remained steadily at the same value, and, because a
given quantity of corn or of labour will exchange only for
(perhaps) ¾ of the former quantity of linen, cloth, or
money, to declare that it was the linen, cloth, or money
which had risen in value, not labour and corn which
had fallen?

Two countries are equally skilful and industrious; but
in one the people live on the cheap food of potatoes, in the

---

[1] Here as elsewhere written 'chuse.'

other on the dear food, wheat. You will allow that profits
will be higher in the one country than the other. You
will allow, too, that money may be nearly of the same value
in both, if we choose anything else as a measure of value
but labour. You will further agree that there might be an
extensive trade between such countries. If a man sent a
pipe of wine from the potato [1] country, which cost £100
and which might be sold at £110 in the wheat country,
you would say that the wine was at a higher value in the
country from which it was exported, merely because, in
that country, it could command more labour. You would
say this although the wine would not only exchange for
more money but for more of every other commodity in the
wheat country. I contend that this is a novelty which
cannot be considered an improvement; it would confound
all our usual notions, and would impose upon us the necessity of learning a new language. All mankind would say
that wine was dearer in the wheat than in the potato
country, and that labour was of less value in the latter.
In page 31 there is a long passage on the reason for
choosing labour as a standard, with which I am not
satisfied. A piece of cloth is 120 yards in length and
is to be divided between *A* and *B*; it is obvious that in
proportion as much is given to *A* less will be given to *B*
and vice versa. This will be true, although the value of
the whole 120 yards be £100, £50, or £5. Is it not then
a begging of the question to assume the constant value
because the quantity is constant, and because it is always
to be divided between two persons?

Allowing you your premises, I see very few instances in
which I can quarrel with your conclusions. I agree with
all you say concerning the glut of commodities; allow
to you your measure, and it is impossible to differ in the
result.

[1] Written here as elsewhere ' potatoe.'

I hope soon to see you. I have hardly been able to find time to write this letter, I am so busily engaged. I am serving on a committee.

Ever yours,

DAVID RICARDO.

NOTE.—The table referred to in this letter is the following:—

Table illustrating the invariable Value of Labour and its Results.

	2	3	4	5	6	7	8	9
	Quarters of corn produced by 10 men or varying fertility of the soil.	Yearly corn wages to each labourer, determined by the demand and supply.	Advances in corn wages, or variable produce commanding the labour of 10 men.	Rate of profits under the foregoing circumstances.	Quantity of labour required to produce the wages of 10 men under the foregoing circumstances.	Quantity of profits on the advances of labour.	Invariable value of the wages of a given number of men.	Value of 100 qrs. of corn under the varying circumstances supposed.	Value of the produce of 10 men under the circumstances supposed.
	150 qrs.	12 qrs.	120 qrs.	25 p. c.	8	2	10	8·33	12·5
	150	13	130	15·38	8·66	1·34	10	7·7	11·53
	150	10	100	50	6·6	3·4	10	10	15
	140	12	120	16·66	8·6	1·4	10	7·14	11·6
	140	11	110	27·2	7·85	2·15	10	9·09	12·7
	130	12	120	8·3	9·23	0·77	10	8·33	10·8
	130	10	100	30	7·7	2·3	10	10	13
	120	11	110	9	9·17	0·83	10	9·09	10·9
	120	10	100	20	·8·33	1·67	10	10	12
	110	10	100	10	9·09	·91	10	10	11
	110	9	90	22·2	8·18	1·82	10	11·1	12·2
	100	9	90	11·1	9	1	10	11·1	11·1
	100	8	80	25	8	2	10	12·5	12·5
	90	8	80	12·5	8·88	1·12	10	12·5	11·25

('Measure of Value,' p. 38.)

Columns 5 to 9 contain the debateable matter.

LXXXIV.

MY DEAR MALTHUS,   LONDON, 28 *May*, 1823.

I will, to the best of my power, state my objections
to your arguments respecting the measure of value. You
have yourself stated, as an objection to my view on this
subject, that a commodity produced with labour and capital
united, cannot be a measure of value for any other commodities than such as are produced precisely under the
same circumstances, and in this I have agreed that you
are substantially correct. If all commodities were produced in one day and by labour only without the assistance of capital, they would vary in proportion as the
quantity of labour employed on their production increased
or diminished. If the same quantity of labour was constantly employed on the production of money, money
would be an accurate measure of absolute value, and, if
shrimps or nuts or any other thing. rose or fell in such
money, it would only be because more or less labour was
employed in procuring them. Under such circumstances
every commodity which was the produce of a day's labour
would naturally command a day's labour, and therefore
the value of a commodity would be in proportion to the
quantity of labour which it would command. But, though
such a money would measure accurately the value of every.
commodity produced under circumstances exactly similar,
it would not be an accurate measure of the value of other
commodities produced with a large quantity of capital,
employed for a length of time. In the case just supposed
a quantity of shrimps would be as accurate a measure of
value as a quantity of money produced by the same
quantity of labour ; but, when capital is employed and
cloth is the product of labour and capital, you justly say

that cloth is not a correct measure of the value of shrimps
and of silver, picked up by labour alone, on the sea shore ;
and yet with singular inconsistency, as I cannot help
thinking, you contend that the shrimps and the silver,
picked up by labour alone on the sea shore, are accurate
measures of the value of cloth. If you are right, then
must cloth be also an accurate measure of value, because
the thing measured must be as good a measure as the thing
with which you measure. When I say that £4 and a
quarter of wheat are of the same value, I can measure
other values by the quarter of wheat as well as by the £4.
You say: 'It is conceded that, when labour alone is concerned in the production of commodities, and there is no
question of time, both the absolute and exchangeable
values of such commodities may be accurately measured
by the quantity of labour employed upon them.' Nothing
can, I think, be more correct, and it is perfectly accordant
with what I have been saying. Your mistake appears to
me to be this: you show us that under certain conditions
a certain commodity would be a measure of absolute value,
and then you apply it to cases where the conditions are not
complied with, and suppose it to be a measure of absolute
value in those cases also. You appear to me, too, to deceive
yourself when you think you prove your proposition,
because your proof only amounts to this, that your
measure is a good measure of exchangeable value but
not of absolute value. You say: 'If the accumulated and
immediate labour worked up in a commodity be of any
assumed value, £100 for instance, and the profits of the
value of £20, including the compound profits upon the
labour worked up in the materials, the whole will be of the
value of £120. Of this value $\frac{1}{6}$ only belongs to profits,
the rest or $\frac{5}{6}$ may be considered as the product of pure
labour.' This is quite true, whether we value the commodity by the quantity of labour actually employed upon

it, by the quantity which it will command when brought to market, or by the quantity of money, or any other commodity, for which it is exchanged; $\frac{5}{6}$, in all cases, will belong to the workmen and $\frac{1}{6}$ to the master. 'Consequently the value of $\frac{5}{6}$ of the produce is determined by the quantity of labour employed on the whole; and the value of the whole produce by the quantity of labour employed upon it with the addition of $\frac{1}{5}$ of that quantity.' This is really saying no more than that, when profits are one sixth of the value of the whole commodity (in which no rent enters), the other $\frac{5}{6}$ go to reward the labourers, and that the portion so going to the labourers may itself be resolved into labour and profits in the same proportion of 5 and 1. Five men produce six pieces of cloth, of which 5 are paid to them, the men; if profits fall one half, the men will receive $5\frac{1}{2}$ pieces, and then you say the cloth is of less value; but in what medium? In labour, you answer. You appear to me to advance a proposition that cloth is of less value when it will exchange for less labour, and to prove it by showing the fact, merely, that it actually does exchange for less labour.

You say: 'But, when labour is concerned, it follows from what has been conceded that the value of the produce is determined by the quantity of labour employed upon it.' By value here you mean absolute value; and then you immediately apply this measure of absolute value, which is only conceded in a particular case, to a general proposition, and say 'consequently;' consequently on what? On this particular case; 'consequently the value of $\frac{5}{6}$ of the produce is determined by the quantity of labour employed on the whole,' that is to say 'consequently the quantity of labour which $\frac{5}{6}$ of the produce will command is determined by the quantity of labour employed on the whole;' the same is true, in the same sense, of $\frac{4}{6}$, $\frac{5}{7}$, $\frac{4}{5}$, $\frac{4}{9}$ or of any other proportions in which the whole may be divided. My only object has been to show, and, if I am not mistaken, I have succeeded in showing, that a measure of value, which is only allowed to be accurate in a particular case where no capital is employed, is arbitrarily applied by you to cases where capital and time necessarily enter into the consideration.

I fear I have been guilty of many repetitions. I shall not regret it, however, if I have made myself understood.

[The last sheet is wanting. The fragment on page 105 does not match this fragment.]

NOTE.—On 12th June, 1822, in one of Ricardo's most important speeches on Resumption (afterwards published as a pamphlet), he speaks of those who propose to make Corn, on a ten years' average, the standard of value instead of money. To prove gold more variable than corn, they and their authorities, Locke and Adam Smith are (he says) obliged to begin by supposing gold invariable. ' Unless the medium in which the price of corn is estimated could be asserted to be invariable in its value, how could corn be said not to have varied in relative value? If they must admit the medium to be variable—and who could deny it?—then what became of the argument?' Nothing is more difficult than to ascertain the variations in the value of money: ' To do so with any accuracy we should have an invariable measure of value; but such a measure we never had nor ever can have.' (Cf. Pol. Econ. and Tax. ch. i. § 7, Works, p. 28.) But we can speak with accuracy of depreciation; we can see to it that the standard is always the same standard, and that our currency conforms to it, even if the standard itself may vary in value. (See Note to Letter XXXI.)

LXXXV.

MY DEAR MALTHUS,   LONDON, 13 *July*, 1823.

McCulloch and I did not settle the question of value before we parted,—it is too difficult a one to settle in a conversation; I heard everything he had to urge in favour of his view, and promised, during my holiday, to bestow a good deal of consideration on it. He means exactly what you say;—he does not contend that commodities exchange for each other according to the quantity of labour actually worked up in them, but he constitutes a commodity the general measure, by which he estimates the value of all others. A pipe of wine kept for three years has no more labour worked up in it than a pipe of wine kept for a day, but he says the additional value on account of time must be estimated by the accumulations which a like amount of capital actively employed in the support of labour would make in the same time. An oak-tree which has been growing for 200 years has very little labour actually worked up in it, but its value is to be estimated by the accumulated capital which the original labour employed would give in the same time. He and you in fact differ as to your original measure. I think he could not give any other good reason for choosing a medium which requires labour and capital to produce it, rather than one which requires labour only, excepting that commodities in general require the combination of the two, and that a measure, to have any claim to be even an approximation to an accurate one, should itself be produced under circumstances somewhat similar to the commodities which it is to measure. If all things required precisely the same quantities of capital and labour, and for the same length of time, to produce them, any one of them would be an accurate measure of the rest; but this is not the case; the conditions admit of infinite variety, and therefore whichever we choose it can only be an approximation to truth, and we are bound to give good reasons for preferring it.

I should, indeed, be wanting in candour if I refused to admit that my money measure would not measure the quantity of labour worked up in commodities. I have admitted it over and over again. I am also ready to admit that your money measure will measure exactly the

quantity of labour and profits together of which commodities are composed, but so will my money measure.
Neither of them will measure the quantity of labour alone
worked up in commodities, but they will both measure the
quantity of labour and profits together of which commodities are composed. Suppose gold always to require
the same quantity of labour, for one year, before it can be
brought to market, will you say that all variations in
wages and profits may not be estimated in this medium?
You would indeed say that many of those variations would
be ascribable to the variations in the value of the medium,
and not to any alteration in the value of the thing
measured, because you do not think that it is any proof
of invariability in a commodity that it requires always the
same quantity of labour, and the same duration of time to
produce it. If I allow the justice of your objection, I am
at liberty to apply the same to your medium. The same
quantity of labour applied for a day will always produce the
same given quantity of gold; gold is therefore an invariable
measure, you say. I find this gold vary in relation to
another commodity which always requires the same
quantity of labour and capital to produce it; you say it
is never the gold but it is always the commodity which
varies, and, when you are asked why, you answer because
labour never varies. Double the quantity of labour in a
country or diminish it one half, always leaving the funds
which are to employ it at precisely the same amount, and
you tell us, notwithstanding the condition of the labourer
is in the one case a very distressed one, in the other a very
prosperous one, that the value of his labour has not varied.
I cannot subscribe to the justness of this language. The
question is whether you are right, not whether I am wrong.
Suppose that a man in India could pick up in a day
precisely the same quantity of gold as in England, and that
all trade in provisions were forbid between the two

countries. The small quantity of rice and clothing in India which are necessary for the support of a labourer would be of precisely the same value as the quantity of wheat and clothing necessary for a labourer in England. But this would not long continue. All manufactured commodities would be of a high comparative money value in India, and consequently we should export manufactured commodities and import gold; the reward of a labourer in England would come to be a much larger quantity of gold than he could actually pick up here. No gold would be then obtained in England but by means of importation. Under these circumstances you would say that money was of a low value in England, and you would be correct if all men agreed to constitute labour the measure of value; but in this they do not agree, and, as we should find that at the very moment that gold was low, relatively to labour, in England, it was high relatively to manufactured commodities of every description, with which in fact gold would be purchased from India, if we took these commodities for the measure, we should be bound to say that gold was cheap in England and dear in India. You must remember that the point in dispute is whether labour be the correct measure of value; you must not then take the fact for granted, and then offer it as a proof of your correct conclusion.

We leave London for Gatcomb early to-morrow morning. . . We shall have one bed disengaged if you and Mrs. Malthus will come over to us. I am sorry I cannot ask all your party.

Ever truly yours,

DAVID RICARDO.

LXXXVI [1].

[MINCHINHAMPTON, *Aug.* 3, 1823.]
MY DEAR MALTHUS,

The value of almost all commodities is made up of labour and profits, but in choosing a measure of value it is not necessary that it should possess the property of determining what proportion of the value of the commodity measured belongs to wages, and what proportion belongs to profits. You make it a reproach on my proposed measure that it will not do this, and prefer your own because it will. Now, as I do not think this quality essential to a measure of value, I shall not defend mine for not possessing this quality. This consideration appears to me wholly foreign to the question under discussion.

We agree, I believe, that nothing can be a measure of value which does not itself possess value. We agree too, I believe, that a measure of value to be a good one should itself be invariable, and further that in selecting one thing as a measure of value rather than another we are bound to show some good reason for such selection, for, if a good reason be not given, the choice is altogether arbitrary. Now the measure proposed by you has value, and therefore [is] not to be objected against on account of any deficiency of that quality; but I do not think it is invariable, and by the concession which you make in your last letter you appear to give up your measure, for you say that 'you expressed yourself without sufficient care, when you intimated that, if any number of labourers were imported or exported, the value of labour would remain the same.' This is a large concession indeed, and I think entirely subverts your measure, because, if it be true of labourers exported or imported, it must be true also of labourers born or dying in the country. If by poor laws imprudent marriages are

---

[1] Franked by himself. Date and address only on cover.

encouraged and population becomes excessive, the effect on
the value of labour will be precisely the same as if labourers
had been imported ; and, if an epidemic disorder break out
and many labourers die, it will be the same as if they were
exported. Nay more, if the people be well educated and
be taught caution and foresight with regard to the increase
of their numbers, who shall say that the effect on the value
of labour will not be the same as an exportation of
labourers? You have, I think, been imprudent, which
is much at variance with your usual practice, in conceding
this point, and you allow us to enter into your fortress and
spike all your guns. You add indeed : ' This will only be
true after the supply comes to be affected by the increased
or diminished number of labourers.' When will the supply
not be affected by the increased or diminished number?
What follows will not assist you, for you say: ' If the corn
obtained by twenty men be divided among ten, then the
value of the wages of ten men will be less than the quantity
of labour employed to produce them with the addition of
profits, and vice versa.' What profits? They might have
been 50 per cent., and may from the circumstance mentioned be reduced to 5 per cent. You speak of profits in
this place as if they were a fixed amount, and forget that
they fall when wages rise. Besides, I will not admit the
extravagant supposition that the corn obtained by the
labour of twenty men is bestowed as wages on ten men;
but I will suppose that the corn obtained by twenty men
had been sufficient to command the labour of thirty men,
but that owing to a diminished supply of labour this same
quantity of corn obtained by the same number of men is
bestowed as wages on twenty-two men. In this case I ask
you whether corn has fallen in value in the proportion of
thirty to twenty-two? If you say Yes, then you do not
admit that labour may rise in value in consequence of
exporting labourers; and, if you say No, there is an end of

your measure, because you then acknowledge that commodities do not vary according to the quantity of labour they can command. I do not see how you are to extricate yourself from this dilemma. I cannot discover what the value of the precious metals in different countries can have to do with this question. A piece of cloth or a piece of muslin can command more labour in India than in England; on this we are agreed, but we are not agreed in our explanation of this fact. You say the piece of cloth or muslin is more valuable in India than in England, and your proof is that it can command more labour in India. You would say so, although both cloth and muslin were exported from India to England, from the country where they are dear to the country where they are cheap. I, on the contrary, say that it is not the cloth and muslin which are dear in India and cheap in England, but it is labour which is cheap in India and dear in England, and that cloth and muslin would come to England from India although there were no such commodities as gold and silver on the face of the earth. I say further that you are bound to admit this by the concession which you have made, for you must admit that labour might be rendered cheap as effectually in England by prevailing on English labourers to be satisfied with the modest remuneration of food paid in India, as by the importation of labourers ; and, if you do not admit it, I beg to ask why you refuse to do so. I beg you to point out the distinction between a supply of labourers from abroad, with a consequently reduced remuneration of food, and a supply of labourers from the principle of population, and a consequent reduction in the remuneration paid in food. Can you be said to have given a good reason for the selection which you have made of a measure of value when it will not bear close examination? You have repeatedly said that a commodity, on which a quantity of labour has been bestowed, will always exchange for a like quantity, together with an additional quantity which will constitute the profits on the advances. Now this I consider to be your main proposition, and on its truth must depend according to your own view the correctness of your measure. Is it true then that every commodity exchanges for two quantities of labour, one equal to the quantity actually worked up in it, another equal to the quantity which the profits will command? I say it is not. This year corn is cheap, and I must give a certain quantity of it to procure the labour of ten men to be worked up in the commodity which I manufacture ; but next year, when I take my commodity to market, corn is dear and wages high, and therefore to procure a certain quantity of labour I must give more of my finished commodity than I should have given if corn had been plenty [*sic*] and wages low. If corn had been cheap and wages low, my profits would have been high ; as it is, they are low. I want to know in these two cases whether the commodity does really exchange for the two specific quantities of labour mentioned above. You answer my question by saying that you always make a reserve of the first quantity, and all above it you call profits. But I contend that labour of one value has been expended on the commodity, and, when it comes to market, it is exchanged for labour of another value, and that is the sole reason why the balance, over and above the labour expended on it, is small. Why is it small but because the value of labour is high ? No such thing, you say ; labour never varies ; and yet you cannot but confess that, if corn had been abundant and if wages had remained the same, the manufactured commodity would have exchanged for a great deal more labour. You say : ' How comes it about that labour should remain of the same value in the progress of society, when it is known that it must require more labour to produce it ?' You must mean 'to produce the remuneration paid for it ;' and you add : ' The answer to this question is that, as profits depend upon the *proportion* of the whole produce which goes to labour, it must necessarily happen that the increase of value occasioned by the additional quantity of labour will be exactly counterbalanced by the diminution in the amount of profits, leaving the value of labour the same.' I confess I cannot understand this answer. We are inquiring about the meaning which should be attached to the words ' increase of value,' ' diminution of value.' You tell me that increase of value means an increased power of commanding labour. I deny that this definition is a correct one, because I deny the invariability of the standard measure you have chosen ; and to prove its invariability you speak of the proportion in which the whole produce is divided, and that, if wages have more, profits have less ;—all which is true, but what connection do you prove between this proposition and the invariability in your measure of value ? In your answer you use the words 'increase of value ;' that is to explain the meaning of the words required to be understood by the use of the words themselves. You mistake McCulloch's and my objection to your doctrine if you suppose it to be on account of its making the same quantity of labour of the same value, while the condition of the labourer is very different ; we do not object to it on that account, because, as you justly observe, our own doctrines require the same admission ; but we object to your saying that, from whatever cause it may arise that the labourer's condition is deteriorated, he is always receiving the same value as wages. When *our* labourers are badly off, although (we say) they have wages of the same value, profits must necessarily be very low; according to you wages would be of the same value whether profits were 2 per cent. or 50 per cent.

I think I have shown you that your long letter was acceptable by doing that which is really a difficult task to me, writing a longer one myself. I am, however, only labouring in my vocation and trying to understand the most difficult question in political economy. All I have hitherto done is to convince myself more and more of the extreme difficulty of finding an unobjectionable measure of value. As far as I have yet been [able] to reflect upon McCulloch's and Mill's suggestion, I am not satisfied with it. They make the best defence for my measure[1], but they do not really get rid of all the objections. I believe however that, though not without fault, it is the best.

I am sorry you could not spare a few days for a visit to us; if you will come to Gatcomb before we go to town, I shall be very glad to see you.

I have been writing a few pages in favour of my project of a National Bank[2], with a view to prove that the nation would lose nothing in profits by abolishing the Bank of England, and that the sole effect of the change would be to transfer a part of the profits of the bank to the national treasury. . .

Yours ever,
DAVID RICARDO.

NOTE.—Arguments very similar to those of this letter have been used against Malthus by Julius Pierstorff, in his book on 'Die Lehre vom Unternehmergewinn' (Berlin, 1875), where the views of Malthus and Ricardo are compared with one another. There is, however, shrewder criticism of Ricardo's whole doctrine in Böhm Bawerk's 'Geschichte und Kritik der Kapital-Zins-Theorien,' Innsbrück, 1884. A neat *reductio ad absurdum* of the view, held more or less explicitly by MacCulloch and others, that cost is enough to explain value, is given by Böhm Bawerk in his 'Grundzüge der Theorie des wirthschaftlichen Güterwerths' (Jena, 1886, p. 72), in a passage of which this is the conclusion: 'To explain the value of a commodity by its cost is to explain it by the value of the means of its production. But how have the latter their value?

---

[1] Gold, with many reservations. See Wks., pp. 29 to 33. But compare p. 231 below.

[2] Published in 1824 by his family, and reprinted in Wks., ed. MacC., pp. 499 seq.

Logically we must answer from *their* cost, in other words from the means of production a degree farther back, and so on backwards. Now, clearly, if we pursue this regress, we either arrive at commodities which are not themselves ' produced,' e. g. land and labour, and our explanation of all value by cost has failed us ; or else we explain even these sophistically as being in a sense ' products,' and owing their value to their cost, e. g. the labour as owing its value to the cost of the labourer's subsistence, and in this case we are bound to go farther back and explain the value of the means of subsistence by *their* cost, i.e. the labour that produced them ; and we reason endlessly in a circle.'

LXXXVII [1].

GATCOMB PARK, MINCHINHAMPTON,
15*th Aug.*, 1823.

MY DEAR MALTHUS,

It is a prudent step in you to withdraw your concession, for I am sure that your theory could not stand with it. You find fault with my measure of value, you say, because it varies with the varying profits of other commodities. This is, I acknowledge, an imperfection in it when used to measure other commodities in which there enters more or less of profits than enters into my measure ; but you do not appear to see that against your measure the same objection holds good, for your measure contains no profits at all, and therefore never can be an accurate measure of value for commodities which do contain profits. If I had no other arguments to offer against your measure, this which I am going to mention *when used to you* would be fatal to it. You say that my measure cannot measure commodities produced by labour alone. Granted ; but, if it be true, how can your measure measure commodities produced with labour and profits united ? You might just as well say that three times two are six and that twice three are not six, or that a foot measure was a good mea-

---

[1] Franked by himself.

sure for a yard but a yard was not a good measure for a foot. If your measure will measure my commodity accurately, mine must do the same by yours. These are identical propositions, and I confess I see no answer that can be made to me. The fact really is that no accurate measure of absolute value can be found. No one doubts the desirableness of having one; but all we can ever hope to get is one tolerably well calculated to measure the greatest number of commodities, and therefore I should have no hesitation in admitting your measure to be the best, under all circumstances, if you could show that the greatest number of commodities were produced by labour alone without the intervention of capital. On the other hand, if a greater number of commodities are produced under the circumstances which I suppose to attend the production of the commodity which I choose for my measure, then mine would be the best measure. You will understand that in either case I suppose a degree of arbitrariness in the selection, and I only contend that it would be best employed in selecting mine.

When you say that my great mistake is in considering commodities made up of labour alone and not of labour and profits, I think the error is yours, not mine, for that is precisely what you do; you measure commodities by labour alone, which have both labour and profits in them. You surely will not say that my money, produced by labour and capital, and by which I propose to measure other things, omits profits. Yours does; what profits are there in shrimps or in gold picked up by daily labour, on account of the labourer, on the sea-shore? How much more justly then might this accusation be brought against you!

You object to me that I am inconsistent in wishing to leave the consideration of the value of money here and in India out of the question, when speaking of the value of labour and of commodities in this country and in India.

I, you say, to leave out the consideration of the value of the precious metals, who have proposed a measure formed of them! There is nothing inconsistent in this. In examining your proposition which rejects my measure and adopts another, I must try it by your doctrines and not by mine which you reject. A conclusion founded on my premises might be a just one, but, if you dispute my premises and substitute others, the conclusion may no longer be the same; and in examining your doctrines I must attend only to the conclusions to which your premises would lead me. You ask: 'Would you really say that cloth and muslin were not dear in India where they cost four or five times as much labour as in England?' You know I would not, because I estimate value by the quantity of labour worked up in a commodity; but by the cost in labour of cloth and muslin in India you do not mean the quantity of labour actually employed on their production, but the quantity which the finished commodity can command in exchange. The difference between us is this; you say a commodity is dear because it will command a great quantity of labour, I say it is only dear when a great quantity has been bestowed on its production. In India a commodity may be produced with twenty days' labour, and may command thirty days' labour. In England it may be produced by twenty-five days' labour and command only twenty-nine. According to you this commodity is dearer in India, according to me it is dearer in England.

Now here is my objection against your measure as a general measure of value, that, notwithstanding more labour may be bestowed on a commodity, it may fall in value estimated in your measure; it may exchange for a less quantity of labour. This is impossible when you apply your measure legitimately to those objects only which it is calculated to measure. Would it be possible, for example, to apply more labour to the production of shrimps or to pick up grains of gold on the sea-shore, and yet to sell those commodities for less labour than before? Certainly not; but it would be quite possible to bestow more labour on the making of a piece of cloth, and yet for cloth to exchange for a less quantity of labour than before. This is another argument in my mind conclusive against the expediency of adopting your measure.

I repeat once more that the same trade precisely would go on between India and Europe, as far as regards commodities, if no such thing as money made of gold and silver existed in the world. All commodities would in that case as well as now command a much larger quantity of labour in India than in England; and, if we wanted to know how much more, either of those commodities, as well as money, would enable us to ascertain. The same thing which makes money of a low value in England makes many other commodities of a low value there; and the political economist in accounting for the low value of one accounts at the same time for the low value of the others. I do not object to accounting for the low value of gold in particular countries; but I say it is not material to an enquiry into a general measure of value, particularly if it be itself objected to as forming any element in that measure.

Suppose a farmer to have a certain quantity of cattle and implements and a hundred quarters of wheat,—that he expends this wheat in supporting a certain quantity of labour, and that the result is 110 quarters of wheat and an increase of one-tenth also in his cattle and implements; would not his profits be 10 per cent. whatever might be the price of labour the following year? If the 110 quarters could command no more labour than the 100 quarters could command before, he would, according to you, have made no profits; and you are right if we admit that yours is a correct measure of value; he would have a profit in kind but no profit in value. If wheat was the measure of value, he would have a profit in kind, and the same profit in value. If money was the correct measure of value and he commenced with £100, he would have 10 per cent. profit if the value of his produce was £110. All these results leave the question of a measure of value undecided, and prove nothing but the convenience, in your estimation, of adopting one in preference to another. The labourer, however, who lived by his labour would find it difficult to be persuaded that his labour was of the same value at two periods, in one of which he had abundance of food and clothing, and in another he was absolutely starving for want. What he might think would certainly not affect the philosophy of the question ; but it would be at least as good a reason against the measure you propose as that of the farmer in favour of it, when he found that he had no profits because he had no greater command of labour, although he might have more corn or more money. You call every increase of value nominal which is not an increase in the measure you propose. I do not object to your doing so ; but those who do not agree with you in the propriety of adopting this measure may argue very consistently in saying they are possessed of more value when they have £110 than when they had £100, although the larger sum may not when it is realized command so much labour as the smaller sum did before, because they not only admit but contend that labour may rise and fall in value, and therefore in respect to labour he may be poorer, although he possesses a greater value.

I have said that the value of most commodities is made up of labour and profits. If this be so, you observe, ' it is as clear as the sun that the variable wages which command the same quantity of labour must be of the same value, *because* they will always cost in their production the same quantity of labour with the addition of the profits upon that labour.' I confess that I cannot see the connection of this conclusion with the premises. Whether you divide a commodity in eight, seven, or six divisions, it will always be divided into two portions, variable portions, but always two. If the division be in eight, the portions may be six and two, five and three, four and four, seven and one. If seven, they may be six and one, five and two, four and three, and so on. Now this is my admission. What we want to know is what the number of those divisions are, or what the value of the commodity is, whether eight, seven, or six? And have I come a bit nearer to this knowledge by admitting that whatever the value may be it will be divided between two persons? Whatever you give to the labourer is made up of labour and profits, and therefore the value of labour is constant! This is your proposition. To me it wants every quality of clearness. I find that at one time I give a man ten bushels of wheat for the same quantity of his labour for which at another time I give him eight bushels. Wheat, according to you, falls in the proportion of ten to eight. I ask why? And your answer is, because ' as the positive value of the labour worked up in the wages increases, the positive value of the profits (the other component part of their whole value) diminishes exactly in the same degree.' Now does this positive value refer to the same quantity of wheat? Certainly not, but to two different quantities, to ten bushels at one time, to eight at another. You add : ' If these two propositions['] (namely the one I have just mentioned and the invariability of labour as a measure of value) ' can properly be considered as having no connection with each other, I must have quite lost myself on these subjects, and can hardly hope to show the connection by anything which I can say further[']. I hope you do not suspect me of shutting my eyes against conviction ; but, if this proposition is so very clear as it is to you, I cannot account for my want of power to understand it. I still think that the invariability of your measure is the *definition* with which you set out, and not the *conclusion* to which you arrive by any legitimate argument. My complaint against you is that you claim to have given us an accurate measure of value, and I object to your claim, not that I have succeeded and you have failed, but that we have both failed, that there is not and cannot be an accurate measure of value, and that the [most th]at any man can do is to find out a measure of value applicable in a great many cases, and not very far deviating from accuracy in many others. This is all I have pretended to do, or now pretend to have done; and, if you advanced no higher claims, I would be more humble ; but I cannot allow that you have succeeded in the great object you aimed at. In answering you I am really using those weapons by which alone you say you can be defeated, and which are I confess equally applicable to your measure and to mine, I mean the argument of the non-existence of any measure of absolute value. There is no such thing ; your measure as well as mine will measure variations arising from more or less labour being required to produce commodities, but the difficulty is respecting the varying proportions which go to labour and profits. The alteration in these proportions alters the relative value of things in the degree that more or less of labour or profit enters into them; and for these variations there has never been, and I think never will be, any perfect measure of value.

I have lost no time in answering your letter, for I am just now warm in the subject, and cannot do better than disburthen myself on paper.

Ever, my dear Malthus,

Truly yours,

DAVID RICARDO.

LXXXVIII[1].

My dear Malthus,   Gatcomb Park, 31 *Aug.*, 1823.

I have only a few words more to say on the subject of value, and I have done. You cannot avail yourself of the argument that a foot may measure the variable height of a man, although the variable height of a man cannot truly measure the foot, because you have agreed that under certain circumstances the man's height is not variable, and it is to those circumstances that I always refer. You say of my measure, and say truly, that if all commodities were produced under the same circumstances of time, etc., as itself, it would be a perfect measure, and you say further that it is now a perfect measure for all commodities produced under such circumstances. If then under certain circumstances mine is a perfect measure, and yours is always a perfect one, under those circumstances certain commodities ought to vary in these two measures just in the same degree. Do they so? Certainly not, then one of the measures must be imperfect. If they are both perfect mine ought to measure yours as well as yours mine.

There is no impropriety in your saying with Adam Smith[2] that 'labour will measure not only that part of the whole value of the commodity which resolves itself into labour, but also that which resolves itself into profit,' because it is the fact. But is not this true also of any variable measure you could fix on? Is it not true of iron, copper, lead, cloth, corn, etc., etc.? The question is about an invariable measure of value, and your proof of invariability is that it will measure profits as well as labour, which every variable measure will also do.

I have acknowledged that my measure is inaccurate, you

---

[1] Franked by himself.   [2] W. of N., I. vi. 23, 1.

say, I have so; but not because it would not do everything
which you assert your's will do, but because I am not secure
of its invariability.   Shrimps are worth £10 in my money;
—it becomes necessary, we will suppose, in order to improve
the shrimps to keep them one year when profits are 10 per
cent.; shrimps at the end of that time will be worth £11.
They have gained a value of £1.   Now where is the difference whether you value them in labour and say that at
the first period they are worth ten days' labour and subsequently eleven, or say that at the first period they are
worth £10, subsequently £11?

I am not sure that your language is accurate when you
say that 'labour is the real advance in kind, and profits
may be correctly estimated upon the advances whatever
they may be.'   A farmer's capital consists of raw produce,
and his real advances in kind are raw produce.   His
advances are worth and can command a certain quantity of labour undoubtedly, and his profits are nothing
unless the produce he obtains will command more if he
estimates both advances and profits in labour, but so it is
in any other commodity in which he may value his advances and returns.   Does it signify whether it be labour
or any other thing, provided there be no reason to suspect
that it has altered in value?   I know that you will say
that provided his produce is sure to command a certain
quantity of labour he is sure of being able to reproduce,
not so if he estimates in any other thing, because that
thing and labour may have undergone a great relative
alteration.   But may not the real alteration be in the value
of labour, and, if he act on the presumption of its remaining
at its then rate, may he not be wofully mistaken, and be
a loser instead of a gainer?   Your argument always supposes labour to be of an uniform value, and if we yielded
that point to you there would be no question between us.
A manufacturer who uniformly used no other measure of

value than that which you recommend would be as infallibly liable to great disappointments as he is now exposed to in the vulgar variable medium in which he is accustomed to estimate value.

And now, my dear Malthus, I have done.   Like other disputants, after much discussion we each retain our own opinions.   These discussions, however, never influence our friendship; I should not like you more than I do if you agreed in opinion with me.

Pray give Mrs. Ricardo's and my kind regards to Mrs. Malthus.

Yours truly,

DAVID RICARDO.

NOTE.—Ricardo died at Gatcomb on 11th Sept., 1823, of an abscess in the head, which caused great suffering. He was buried in the vault of a church at Huish, near Chippenham, Wilts; and his friend Joseph Hume was among the mourners. As he was only fifty-one years of age, his death was a great shock to his friends and caused something like dismay among his disciples. ' I never loved anybody out of my own family so much.   Our interchange of opinions was so unreserved, and the object after which we were both enquiring was so entirely the truth and nothing else, that I cannot but think we sooner or later must have agreed.' So said Malthus, in Empson's hearing[1].

James Mill[2], albeit unused to the melting mood, was overwhelmed with grief, and in a letter to MacCulloch, 19th Sept., 1823, writes of the closing scenes with much tenderness of feeling.

---

[1] Edin. Rev., Jan. 1837, p. 499.   [2] Life, pp. 209-213.

CHRONICLE.

1809. Ricardo's letters in 'Morning Chronicle' ('High Price of Bullion'). Quarterly Review founded. Corunna (Jan.), Talavera, Wagram, Walcheren. Continuance of Orders in Council and Berlin Decrees. Perceval, Premier. King's Jubilee. O. P. riots. Bad harvest. Rise in wheat. Fall in other articles.

1810. Letters I (25th Feb.) to V (Aug.).—Lines of Torres Vedras, Busaco. Bullion Committee (report, 8th June). Burdett and Parliamentary privilege. Fair harvest. Commercial and Agricultural Depression. Many failures. South American market overstocked. Trade with United States re-opened.

1811. Letters VI to X (Dec.).—Ricardo's 'Reply to Bosanquet,' Malthus' article on 'Depreciation.' 'Curse of Kehama.' Fuentes Onoro, Albuera. Napoleon's estrangement from Russia. Virtual close of George III's reign. Questions of Regency. Castlereagh and Sidmouth in the Government. Poor harvest and high prices of wheat. Lord King's letter to his tenants. Currency debates in Parliament. Government loan to Merchants. Slight revival of trade. Stoppage of trade with United States.

1812. Letters XI and XII (Dec.).—'Childe Harold,' I and II. Ciudad Rodrigo, Badajoz, Salamanca. Moscow Campaign. Repeal of Orders in Council (June). War with United States. Catholic Association. Murder of Perceval (May). Liverpool, Premier. Williams' murders in Ratcliff Highway. Depression of trade. Luddite outbreaks. Cold and wet summer. High price of corn.

1813. Letter XIII (Dec.).—Malthus' 'Letter to Lord Grenville.' Southey, Laureate. Vittoria, S. Sebastian. Lützen, Katzbach, Dresden, Leipzig. Affairs of Princess Charlotte. Joanna Southcote. Prosecutions for seditious libel. Removal of Company's monopoly of East India trade. Good harvest. Rise in Colonial produce.

1814. Letters XIV to XXI (Dec.).—Malthus' 'Observations on the Corn Laws.' 'Waverley.' 'The Excursion.' Treaty of Chaumont. Abdication of Napoleon (April). First Treaty of Paris. Congress at Vienna. Capture of Washington. Peace of Ghent (Dec.). Trial of Cochrane. Burning of Custom House (Feb.). Introduction of Corn Bill. Repeal of Corn Bounty. Relapse in prices of Colonial produce. Indifferent harvest. Medium prices of corn.

1815. Letters XXII to ·XL (Dec.).—Ricardo's ' Influence of Low Price of Corn.' Malthus' ' Grounds for an Opinion,' and ' Rent.' Napoleon in France (March). Treaty of Vienna. Waterloo. Second Treaty of Paris (Nov.). Bad Season. New Corn Law. Luddite outbreaks. Low Corn prices. Low general prices.

1816. Letters XLI to LI (Oct.)—Ricardo's ' Economical and Secure Currency.' Bombardment of Algiers. War taxation kept up. Adoption of Gold standard by Act of Parliament. Income-tax rejected. Agitation about Civil List. Cobbett's cheap ' Political Register.' Spa Fields. Luddite outbreaks. Petition of London Corporation. Continued fall of general prices. Bad harvest. Rise in Corn.

1817. Letters LII to LXIV (Dec.).—Ricardo's ' Political Economy and Taxation.' Malthus' ' Statements respecting the East-India College.' Malthus' visit to Ireland. Ricardo's to Flanders, Germany, and France. Death of Horner (8th Feb.). ' Biographia Literaria,' ' Revolt of Islam,' ' Lalla Rookh.' Committee on Sinecures. Suspension of Habeas Corpus. Derby Insurrection. Blanketeers. Attack on Regent. Death of Princess Charlotte. Hone's Trials. Fair Harvest. Rise in general prices.

1818. Letters LXV to LXVIII (Aug.).—Mackintosh at Hailey-bury. Ricardo Sheriff of Gloucestershire. Death of Romilly. ' Childe Harold,' III, IV. Congress of Aix-la-Chapelle. Secret Committees on disaffection. Act of Indemnity. Poor Law Bill. Scotch Borough Reform. Debates on Resumption of Cash payments. Royal Marriages. Renewal of Alien Act. General Election (June, July). Manchester strike. Fair harvest. Increased general imports and fall of general prices.

1819. Letters LXIX and LXX (Nov.).—Malthus F.R.S. Ricardo M.P. for Portarlington. Act for Resumption of Cash payments. The 'Radicals.' Factory Act. Poor Law Amendment. Penal Law Amendment. Peterloo massacre. The Six Acts. Fall in Cotton. Trade healthier. Fair harvest.

1820. Letters LXXI to LXXV (Nov.).—Malthus' 'Political Economy.' Malthus' visit to France. Ricardo's 'Funding System.' 'The Cenci.' Death of George III. Insurrection in Spain. Congress of Troppau. General Election. Queen Caroline. Cato Street Conspiracy. Political trials. Reform movement. Popular Education. Penal law amendment. Good harvest. Low prices of corn. Agricultural distress.

1821. Letters LXXVI to LXXXI (Nov.).—Foundation of Political Economy Club. Death of Keats. King's Coronation, and Visit to Ireland. *De facto* Resumption of cash payments. Interference with the Press. 'Bridge Street Gang.' Coalition of Liverpool ministry with the Grenvilles. Retirement of Sidmouth. Insurrection in Greece. Death of Napoleon. Large harvest, poor in quality. Fall in wheat. Low general prices.

1822. Letter LXXXII (Dec.).—Ricardo's 'Protection to Agriculture.' Ricardo's visit to Italy and Switzerland. Death of Shelley. New Marriage Act. New Corn Law. Wellesley in Ireland. Suicide of Castlereagh. Canning at the Foreign Office. Wellington at Verona. Ashantee War. Dispute with United States about Oregon territory. Habeas Corpus suspended in Ireland. Good harvest. Low corn prices. Large importations of wheat from Ireland. General prosperity. Agricultural distress.

1823. Letters LXXXIII to LXXXVIII (31st Aug.).—Malthus' 'Measure of Value,' and article on Tooke. Malthus Associate of Royal Society of Literature. Ricardo's 'National Bank' (written). Death of Ricardo, 11th Sept. Essays of Elia. Byron in Greece. Burmese War. French invasion of Spain. Recognition of South American Independence. Huskisson at Board of Trade. Amendment of Navigation Laws. Canning's Jamaica circular. Catholic Association. Poor harvest, but medium prices of corn. Low general prices. Increased general imports.

INDEX.

THE END.

July, 1887.

Clarendon Press, Oxford

A SELECTION OF

BOOKS

PUBLISHED FOR THE UNIVERSITY BY

HENRY FROWDE,

AT THE OXFORD UNIVERSITY PRESS WAREHOUSE,

AMEN CORNER, LONDON.

ALSO TO BE HAD AT THE

CLARENDON PRESS DEPOSITORY, OXFORD.

[*Every book is bound in cloth, unless otherwise described.*]

LEXICONS, GRAMMARS, ORIENTAL WORKS, &c.

ANGLO-SAXON.—*An Anglo-Saxon Dictionary*, based on the MS. Collections of the late Joseph Bosworth, D.D., Professor of Anglo-Saxon, Oxford. Edited and enlarged by Prof. T. N. Toller, M.A. (To be completed in four parts.) Parts I and II. A—HWISTLIAN. 4to. 15*s.* each.

CHINESE.—*A Handbook of the Chinese Language.* By James Summers. 1863. 8vo. half bound, 1*l.* 8*s.*

—— *A Record of Buddhistic Kingdoms,* by the Chinese Monk FÂ-HIEN. Translated and annotated by James Legge, M.A., LL.D. Crown 4to. cloth back, 10*s.* 6*d.*

ENGLISH.—*A New English Dictionary, on Historical Principles:* founded mainly on the materials collected by the Philological Society. Edited by James A. H. Murray, LL.D., with the assistance of many Scholars and men of Science. Part I. A—ANT. Part II. ANT—BATTEN. Part III. BATTER—BOZ. Imperial 4to. 12*s.* 6*d.* each.

—— *An Etymological Dictionary of the English Language.* By W. W. Skeat, Litt.D. *Second Edition.* 1884. 4to. 2*l.* 4*s.*

——Supplement to the First Edition of the above. 4to. 2*s.* 6*d.*

—— *A Concise Etymological Dictionary of the English Language.* By W. W. Skeat, Litt.D. *Second Edition.* 1885. Crown 8vo. 5*s.* 6*d.*

[9]　　　　　B

GREEK.—*A Greek-English Lexicon*, by Henry George
Liddell, D.D., and Robert Scott, D.D. Seventh Edition, Revised and Augmented throughout. 1883. 4to. 1*l.* 16*s.*

—— *A Greek-English Lexicon*, abridged from Liddell and
Scott's 4to. edition, chiefly for the use of Schools. Twenty-first Edition.
1884. Square 12mo. 7*s.* 6*d.*

—— *A copious Greek-English Vocabulary*, compiled from
the best authorities. 1850. 24mo. 3*s.*

—— *A Practical Introduction to Greek Accentuation*, by H.
W. Chandler, M.A. Second Edition. 1881. 8vo. 10*s.* 6*d.*

HEBREW.—*The Book of Hebrew Roots*, by Abu 'l-Walîd
Marwân ibn Janâh, otherwise called Rabbî Yônâh. Now first edited, with an
Appendix, by Ad. Neubauer. 1875. 4to. 2*l.* 7*s.* 6*d.*

—— *A Treatise on the use of the Tenses in Hebrew.* By
S. R. Driver, D.D. Second Edition. 1881. Extra fcap. 8vo. 7*s.* 6*d.*

—— *Hebrew Accentuation of Psalms, Proverbs, and Job.*
By William Wickes, D.D. 1881. Demy 8vo. stiff covers, 5*s.*

—— *A Treatise on the Accentuation of the twenty-one so-called
Prose Books of the Old Testament.* By William Wickes, D.D. 1887. Demy
8vo. 10*s.* 6*d.*

ICELANDIC.—*An Icelandic-English Dictionary*, based on the
MS. collections of the late Richard Cleasby. Enlarged and completed by
G. Vigfússon, M.A. With an Introduction, and Life of Richard Cleasby, by
G. Webbe Dasent, D.C.L. 1874. 4to. 3*l.* 7*s.*

—— *A List of English Words the Etymology of which is
illustrated by comparison with Icelandic.* Prepared in the form of an
APPENDIX to the above. By W. W. Skeat, Litt.D. 1876. stitched, 2*s.*

—— *An Icelandic Primer*, with Grammar, Notes, and
Glossary. By Henry Sweet, M.A. Extra fcap. 8vo. 3*s.* 6*d.*

—— *An Icelandic Prose Reader*, with Notes, Grammar and
Glossary, by Dr. Gudbrand Vigfússon and F. York Powell, M.A. 1879.
Extra fcap. 8vo. 10*s.* 6*d.*

LATIN.—*A Latin Dictionary*, founded on Andrews' edition
of Freund's Latin Dictionary, revised, enlarged, and in great part rewritten
by Charlton T. Lewis, Ph.D., and Charles Short, LL.D. 1879. 4to. 1*l.* 5*s.*

MELANESIAN.—*The Melanesian Languages.* By R. H.
Codrington, D.D., of the Melanesian Mission. 8vo. 18*s.*

SANSKRIT.—*A Practical Grammar of the Sanskrit Language*,
arranged with reference to the Classical Languages of Europe, for the use of
English Students, by Sir M. Monier-Williams, M.A. Fourth Edition. 8vo. 15*s.*

—— *A Sanskrit-English Dictionary*, Etymologically and
Philologically arranged, with special reference to Greek, Latin, German, Anglo-
Saxon, English, and other cognate Indo-European Languages. By Sir M.
Monier-Williams, M.A. 1872. 4to. 4*l.* 14*s.* 6*d.*

SANSKRIT.—*Nalopákhyánam.* Story of Nala, an Episode of
the Mahá-Bhárata: the Sanskrit text, with a copious Vocabulary, and an
improved version of Dean Milman's Translation, by Sir M. Monier-Williams,
M.A. Second Edition, Revised and Improved. 1879. 8vo. 15*s.*

—— *Sakuntalá.* A Sanskrit Drama, in Seven Acts. Edited
by Sir M. Monier-Williams, M.A. Second Edition, 1876. 8vo. 21*s.*

SYRIAC.—*Thesaurus Syriacus:* collegerunt Quatremère, Bern-
stein, Lorsbach, Arnoldi, Agrell, Field, Roediger: edidit R. Payne Smith,
S.T.P. Fasc. I-VI. 1868-83. sm. fol. each, 1*l.* 1*s.* Fasc. VII. 1*l.* 11*s.* 6*d.*

Vol. I, containing Fasc. I-V, sm. fol. 5*l.* 5*s.*

—— *The Book of Kalilah and Dimnah.* Translated from Arabic
into Syriac. Edited by W. Wright, LL.D. 1884. 8vo. 21*s.*

GREEK CLASSICS, &c.

Aristophanes: A Complete Concordance to the Comedies
and Fragments. By Henry Dunbar, M.D. 4to. 1*l.* 1*s.* .

Aristotle: The Politics, with Introduction, Notes, etc., by
W. L. Newman, M.A., Fellow of Balliol College, Oxford. Vols. I. and II.
Nearly ready.

Aristotle: The Politics, translated into English, with Introduction, Marginal Analysis, Notes, and Indices, by B. Jowett, M.A. Medium
8vo. 2 vols. 21*s.*

Catalogus Codicum Graecorum Sinaiticorum. Scripsit V.
Gardthausen Lipsiensis. With six pages of Facsimiles. 8vo. *linen,* 25*s.*

Heracliti Ephesii Reliquiae. Recensuit I. Bywater, M.A.
Appendicis loco additae sunt Diogenis Laertii Vita Heracliti, Particulae Hip-
pocratei De Diaeta Libri Primi, Epistolae Heracliteae. 1877. 8vo. 6*s.*

Herculanensium Voluminum Partes II. 1824. 8vo. 10*s.*

Fragmenta Herculanensia. A Descriptive Catalogue of the
Oxford copies of the Herculanean Rolls, together with the texts of several
papyri, accompanied by facsimiles. Edited by Walter Scott, M.A., Fellow
of Merton College, Oxford. Royal 8vo. *cloth,* 21*s.*

Homer: A Complete Concordance to the Odyssey and
Hymns of Homer; to which is added a Concordance to the Parallel Passages
in the Iliad, Odyssey, and Hymus. By Henry Dunbar, M.D. 1880. 4to. 1*l.* 1*s.*

—— *Scholia Graeca in Iliadem.* Edited by Professor W.
Dindorf, after a new collation of the Venetian MSS. by D. B. Monro, M.A.,
Provost of Oriel College. 4 vols. 8vo. 2*l.* 10*s.* Vols. V and VI. *In the Press.*

—— *Scholia Graeca in Odysseam.* Edidit Guil. Dindorfius.
Tomi II. 1855. 8vo. 15*s.* 6*d.*

Plato : Apology, with a revised Text and English Notes, and
a Digest of Platonic Idioms, by James Riddell, M.A. 1878. 8vo. 8*s*. 6*d*.

—— *Philebus*, with a revised Text and English Notes, by
Edward Poste, M.A. 1860. 8vo. 7*s*. 6*d*.

—— *Sophistes and Politicus*, with a revised Text and English
Notes, by L. Campbell, M.A. 1867. 8vo. 18*s*.

—— *Theaetetus*, with a revised Text and English Notes,
by L. Campbell, M.A. Second Edition. 8vo. 10*s*. 6*d*.

—— *The Dialogues*, translated into English, with Analyses
and Introductions, by B. Jowett, M.A. A new Edition in 5 volumes, medium
8vo. 1875. 3*l*. 10*s*.

—— *The Republic*, translated into English, with an Analysis
and Introduction, by B. Jowett, M.A. Medium 8vo. 12*s*. 6*d*.

Thucydides : Translated into English, with Introduction,
Marginal Analysis, Notes, and Indices. By B. Jowett, M.A. 2 vols. 1881.
Medium 8vo. 1*l*. 12*s*.

THE HOLY SCRIPTURES, &c.

STUDIA BIBLICA.—Essays in Biblical Archæology and Criticism, and kindred subjects. By Members of the University of Oxford. 8vo.
10*s*. 6*d*.

———————

ENGLISH.—*The Holy Bible in the earliest English Versions*,
made from the Latin Vulgate by John Wycliffe and his followers: edited by
the Rev. J. Forshall and Sir F. Madden. 4 vols. 1850. Royal 4to. 3*l*. 3*s*.

[Also reprinted from the above, with Introduction and Glossary
by W. W. Skeat, M.A.

—— *The Books of Job, Psalms, Proverbs, Ecclesiastes, and the
Song of Solomon :* according to the Wycliffite Version made by Nicholas
de Hereford, about A.D. 1381, and Revised by John Purvey, about A.D. 1388.
Extra fcap. 8vo. 3*s*. 6*d*.

—— *The New Testament in English*, according to the Version
by John Wycliffe, about A.D. 1380, and Revised by John Purvey, about A.D.
1388. Extra fcap. 8vo. 6*s*.]

———————

ENGLISH.—*The Holy Bible:* an exact reprint, page for page, of the Authorised Version published in the year 1611. Demy 4to. half bound, 1*l.* 1*s.*

—— *The Psalter, or Psalms of David, and certain Canticles,* with a Translation and Exposition in English, by Richard Rolle of Hampole. Edited by H. R. Bramley, M.A., Fellow of S. M. Magdalen College, Oxford. With an Introduction and Glossary. Demy 8vo. 1*l.* 1*s.*

—— *Lectures on Ecclesiastes.* Delivered in Westminster Abbey by the Very Rev. George Granville Bradley, D.D., Dean of Westminster. Crown 8vo. 4*s.* 6*d.*

GOTHIC.—*The Gospel of St. Mark in Gothic,* according to the translation made by Wulfila in the Fourth Century. Edited with a Grammatical Introduction and Glossarial Index by W. W. Skeat, M.A. Extra fcap. 8vo. 4*s.*

GREEK.—*Vetus Testamentum* ex Versione Septuaginta Interpretum secundum exemplar Vaticanum Romae editum. Accedit potior varietas Codicis Alexandrini. Tomi III. Editio Altera. 18mo. 18*s.*

—— *Origenis Hexaplorum* quae supersunt; sive, Veterum Interpretum Graecorum in totum Vetus Testamentum Fragmenta. Edidit Fridericus Field, A.M. 2 vols. 1875. 4to. 5*l.* 5*s.*

—— *The Book of Wisdom:* the Greek Text, the Latin Vulgate, and the Authorised English Version; with an Introduction, Critical Apparatus, and a Commentary. By William J. Deane, M.A. Small 4to. 12*s.* 6*d.*

—— *Novum Testamentum Graece.* Antiquissimorum Codicum Textus in ordine parallelo dispositi. Accedit collatio Codicis Sinaitici. Edidit E. H. Hansell, S.T.B. Tomi III. 1864. 8vo. half morocco. Price reduced to 24*s.*

—— *Novum Testamentum Graece.* Accedunt parallela S. Scripturae loca, etc. Edidit Carolus Lloyd, S.T.P.R. 18mo. 3*s.*

On writing paper, with wide margin, 10*s.*

—— *Novum Testamentum Graece* juxta Exemplar Millianum. 18mo. 2*s.* 6*d.* On writing paper, with wide margin, 9*s.*

—— *Evangelia Sacra Graece.* Fcap. 8vo. limp, 1*s.* 6*d.*

—— *The Greek Testament,* with the Readings adopted by the Revisers of the Authorised Version:—

(1) Pica type, with Marginal References. Demy 8vo. 10*s.* 6*d.*

(2) Long Primer type. Fcap. 8vo. 4*s.* 6*d.*.

(3) The same, on writing paper, with wide margin, 15*s.*

—— *The Parallel New Testament,* Greek and English; being the Authorised Version, 1611; the Revised Version, 1881; and the Greek Text followed in the Revised Version. 8vo. 12*s.* 6*d.*

The Revised Version is the joint property of the Universities of Oxford and Cambridge.

GREEK.—*Canon Muratorianus:* the earliest Catalogue of the
Books of the New Testament. Edited with Notes and a Facsimile of the
MS. in the Ambrosian Library at Milan, by S. P. Tregelles, LL.D. 1867.
4to. 10s. 6d.

—— *Outlines of Textual Criticism applied to the New Testament.* By C. E. Hammond, M.A. Fourth Edition. Extra fcap. 8vo. 3s. 6d.

HEBREW, etc.—*The Psalms in Hebrew without points.* 1879.
Crown 8vo. Price reduced to 2s., in stiff cover.

—— *A Commentary on the Book of Proverbs.* Attributed
to Abraham Ibn Ezra. Edited from a MS. in the Bodleian Library by
S. R. Driver, M.A. Crown 8vo. paper covers, 3s. 6d.

—— *The Book of Tobit.* A Chaldee Text, from a unique
MS. in the Bodleian Library; with other Rabbinical Texts, English Translations, and the Itala. Edited by Ad. Neubauer, M.A. 1878. Crown 8vo. 6s.

—— *Horae Hebraicae et Talmudicae,* a J. Lightfoot. A new
Edition, by R. Gandell, M.A. 4 vols. 1859. 8vo. 1l. 1s.

LATIN.—*Libri Psalmorum* Versio antiqua Latina, cum Para-
phrasi Anglo-Saxonica. Edidit B. Thorpe, F.A.S. 1835. 8vo. 10s. 6d.

—— *Old-Latin Biblical Texts: No. I.* The Gospel according
to St. Matthew from the St. Germain MS. (g₁). Edited with Introduction
and Appendices by John Wordsworth, D.D. Small 4to., stiff covers, 6s.

—— *Old-Latin Biblical Texts: No. II.* Portions of the Gospels
according to St. Mark and St. Matthew, from the Bobbio MS. (k), &c.
Edited by John Wordsworth, D.D., W. Sanday, M.A., D.D., and H. J. White,
M.A. Small 4to., stiff covers, 21s.

OLD-FRENCH.—*Libri Psalmorum* Versio antiqua Gallica e
Cod. MS. in Bibl. Bodleiana adservato, una cum Versione Metrica aliisque
Monumentis pervetustis. Nunc primum descripsit et edidit Franciscus Michel,
Phil. Doc. 1860. 8vo. 10s. 6d.

FATHERS OF THE CHURCH, &c.

St. Athanasius: Historical Writings, according to the Bene-
dictine Text. With an Introduction by William Bright. D.D. 1881. Crown
8vo. 10s. 6d.

—— *Orations against the Arians.* With an Account of his
Life by William Bright, D.D. 1873. Crown 8vo. 9s.

St. Augustine: Select Anti-Pelagian Treatises, and the Acts
of the Second Council of Orange. With an Introduction by William Bright,
D.D. Crown 8vo. 9s.

Canons of the First Four General Councils of Nicaea, Constantinople, Ephesus, and Chalcedon. 1877. Crown 8vo. 2s. 6d.

—— *Notes on the Canons of the First Four General Councils.* By William Bright, D.D. 1882. Crown 8vo. 5s. 6d.

Cyrilli Archiepiscopi Alexandrini in XII Prophetas. Edidit P. E. Pusey, A.M. Tomi II. 1868. 8vo. cloth. 2l. 2s.

—— *in D. Joannis Evangelium.* Accedunt Fragmenta varia necnon Tractatus ad Tiberium Diaconum duo. Edidit post Aubertum P. E. Pusey, A.M. Tomi III. 1872. 8vo. 2l. 5s.

—— *Commentarii in Lucae Evangelium* quae supersunt Syriace. E MSS. apud Mus. Britan. edidit R. Payne Smith, A.M. 1858. 4to. 1l. 2s.

—— Translated by R. Payne Smith, M.A. 2 vols. 1859. 8vo. 14s.

Ephraemi Syri, Rabulae Episcopi Edesseni, Balaei, aliorumque Opera Selecta. E Codd. Syriacis MSS. in Museo Britannico et Bibliotheca Bodleiana asservatis primus edidit J. J. Overbeck. 1865. 8vo. 1l. 1s.

Eusebius' Ecclesiastical History, according to the text of Burton, with an Introduction by William Bright, D.D. 1881. Crown 8vo. 8s. 6d.

Irenaeus: The Third Book of St. Irenaeus, Bishop of Lyons, against Heresies. With short Notes and a Glossary by H. Deane, B.D. 1874. Crown 8vo. 5s. 6d.

Patrum Apostolicorum, S. Clementis Romani, S. Ignatii, S. Polycarpi, quae supersunt. Edidit Guil. Jacobson, S.T.P.R. Tomi II. Fourth Edition, 1863. 8vo. 1l. 1s.

Socrates' Ecclesiastical History, according to the Text of Hussey, with an Introduction by William Bright, D.D. 1878. Crown 8vo. 7s. 6d.

ECCLESIASTICAL HISTORY, BIOGRAPHY, &c.

Ancient Liturgy of the Church of England, according to the uses of Sarum, York, Hereford, and Bangor, and the Roman Liturgy arranged in parallel columns, with preface and notes. By William Maskell, M.A. Third Edition. 1882. 8vo. 15s.

Baedae Historia Ecclesiastica. Edited, with English Notes, by G. H. Moberly, M.A. 1881. Crown 8vo. 10s. 6d.

Bright (W.). Chapters of Early English Church History.
1878. 8vo. 12s.

Burnet's History of the Reformation of the Church of England.
A new Edition. Carefully revised, and the Records collated with the originals,
by N. Pocock, M.A. 7 vols. 1865. 8vo. *Price reduced to 1l. 10s.*

Councils and Ecclesiastical Documents relating to Great Britain
and Ireland. Edited, after Spelman and Wilkins, by A. W. Haddan, B.D.,
and W. Stubbs, M.A. Vols. I. and III. 1869-71. Medium 8vo. each 1l. 1s.

> Vol. II. Part I. 1873. Medium 8vo. 10s. 6d.

> Vol. II. Part II. 1878. Church of Ireland; Memorials of St. Patrick.
> Stiff covers, 3s. 6d.

Hamilton (John, Archbishop of St. Andrews), The Catechism
of. Edited, with Introduction and Glossary, by Thomas Graves Law. With
a Preface by the Right Hon. W. E. Gladstone. 8vo. 12s. 6d.

Hammond (C. E.). Liturgies, Eastern and Western. Edited,
with Introduction, Notes, and Liturgical Glossary. 1878. Crown 8vo. 10s. 6d.

An Appendix to the above. 1879. Crown 8vo. paper covers, 1s. 6d.

John, Bishop of Ephesus. The Third Part of his Eccle-
siastical History. [In Syriac.] Now first edited by William Cureton, M.A.
1853. 4to. 1l. 12s.

—— Translated by R. Payne Smith, M.A. 1860. 8vo. 10s.

Leofric Missal, The, as used in the Cathedral of Exeter
during the Episcopate of its first Bishop, A.D. 1050-1072; together with some
Account of the Red Book of Derby, the Missal of Robert of Jumièges, and a
few other early MS. Service Books of the English Church. Edited, with Introduction and Notes, by F. E. Warren, B.D. 4to. half morocco, 35s.

Monumenta Ritualia Ecclesiae Anglicanae. The occasional
Offices of the Church of England according to the old use of Salisbury, the
Prymer in English, and other prayers and forms, with dissertations and notes.
By William Maskell, M.A. Second Edition. 1882. 3 vols. 8vo. 2l. 10s.

Records of the Reformation. The Divorce, 1527-1533. Mostly
now for the first time printed from MSS. in the British Museum and other libra-
ries. Collected and arranged by N. Pocock, M.A. 1870. 2 vols. 8vo. 1l. 16s.

Shirley (W. W.). Some Account of the Church in the Apostolic
Age. Second Edition, 1874. Fcap. 8vo. 3s. 6d.

Stubbs (W.). Registrum Sacrum Anglicanum. An attempt
to exhibit the course of Episcopal Succession in England. 1858. Small 4to.
8s. 6d.

Warren (F. E.). Liturgy and Ritual of the Celtic Church.
1881. 8vo. 14s.

ENGLISH THEOLOGY.

Bampton Lectures, 1886. *The Christian Platonists of Alexandria.* By Charles Bigg, D.D. 8vo. 10s. 6d.

Butler's Works, with an Index to the Analogy. 2 vols. 1874. 8vo. 11s.

Also separately,

Sermons, 5s. 6d. *Analogy of Religion*, 5s. 6d

Greswell's Harmonia Evangelica. Fifth Edition. 8vo. 1855. 9s. 6d.

Heurtley's Harmonia Symbolica: Creeds of the Western Church. 1858. 8vo. 6s. 6d.

Homilies appointed to be read in Churches. Edited by J. Griffiths, M.A. 1859. 8vo. 7s. 6d.

Hooker's Works, with his life by Walton, arranged by John Keble, M.A. Sixth Edition, 1874. 3 vols. 8vo. 1l. 11s. 6d.

—— the text as arranged by John Keble, M.A. 2 vols. 1875. 8vo. 11s.

Jewel's Works. Edited by R. W. Jelf, D.D. 8 vols. 1848. 8vo. 1l. 10s.

Pearson's Exposition of the Creed. Revised and corrected by E. Burton, D.D. Sixth Edition, 1877. 8vo. 10s. 6d.

Waterland's Review of the Doctrine of the Eucharist, with a Preface by the late Bishop of London. Crown 8vo. 6s. 6d.

—— *Works*, with Life, by Bp. Van Mildert. A new Edition, with copious Indexes. 6 vols. 1856. 8vo. 2l. 11s.

Wheatly's Illustration of the Book of Common Prayer. A new Edition, 1846. 8vo. 5s.

Wyclif. A Catalogue of the Original Works of John Wyclif, by W. W. Shirley, D.D. 1865. 8vo. 3s. 6d.

—— *Select English Works.* By T. Arnold, M.A. 3 vols. 1869–1871. 8vo. 1l. 1s.

—— *Trialogus.* With the Supplement now first edited. By Gotthard Lechler. 1869. 8vo. 7s.

HISTORICAL AND DOCUMENTARY WORKS.

British Barrows, a Record of the Examination of Sepulchral
Mounds in various parts of England. By William Greenwell, M.A., F.S.A.
Together with Description of Figures of Skulls, General Remarks on Pre-
historic Crania, and an Appendix by George Rolleston, M.D., F.R.S. 1877.
Medium 8vo. 25*s.*

Clarendon's History of the Rebellion and Civil Wars in
England. 7 vols. 1839. 18mo. 1*l.* 1*s.*

Clarendon's History of the Rebellion and Civil Wars in
England. Also his Life, written by himself, in which is included a Con-
tinuation of his History of the Grand Rebellion. With copious Indexes.
In one volume, royal 8vo. 1842. 1*l.* 2*s.*

Clinton's Epitome of the Fasti Hellenici. 1851. 8vo. 6*s.* 6*d.*

—— *Epitome of the Fasti Romani.* 1854. 8vo. 7*s.*

Corpvs Poeticvm Boreale. The Poetry of the Old Northern
Tongue, from the Earliest Times to the Thirteenth Century. Edited, clas-
·sified, and translated, with Introduction, Excursus, and Notes, by Gudbrand
Vigfússon, M.A., and F. York Powell, M.A. 2 vols. 1883. 8vo. 42*s.*

Freeman (E. A.). *History of the Norman Conquest of England;* its Causes and Results. In Six Volumes. 8vo. 5*l.* 9*s.* 6*d.*

—— *The Reign of William Rufus and the Accession of*
Henry the First. 2 vols. 8vo. 1*l.* 16*s.*

Gascoigne's Theological Dictionary ("Liber Veritatum"):
Selected Passages, illustrating the condition of Church and State, 1403-1458.
With an Introduction by James E. Thorold Rogers, M.A. Small 4to.
10*s.* 6*d.*

Johnson (Samuel, LL.D.), Boswell's Life of; including
Boswell's Journal of a Tour to the Hebrides, and Johnson's Diary of a
Journey into North Wales. Edited by G. Birkbeck Hill, D.C.L. In six
volumes, medium 8vo. With Portraits and Facsimiles of Handwriting.
Half bound, 3*l.* 3*s.* *Just Published.*

Magna Carta, a careful Reprint. Edited by W. Stubbs, D.D.
1879. 4to. stitched, 1*s.*

Passio et Miracula Beati Olaui. Edited from a Twelfth-
Century MS. in the Library of Corpus Christi College, Oxford, with an
Introduction and Notes, by Frederick Metcalfe, M.A. Small 4to. stiff
covers, 6*s.*

Protests of the Lords, including those which have been expunged, from 1624 to 1874; with Historical Introductions. Edited by James E. Thorold Rogers, M.A. 1875. 3 vols. 8vo. 2*l.* 2*s.*

Rogers (J. E. T.). History of Agriculture and Prices in England, A.D. 1259–1793.

> Vols. I and II (1259–1400). 1866. 8vo. 2*l.* 2*s.*
>
> Vols. III and IV (1401–1582). 1882. 8vo. 2*l.* 10*s.*

Saxon Chronicles (Two of the) parallel, with Supplementary Extracts from the Others. Edited, with Introduction, Notes, and a Glossarial Index, by J. Earle, M.A. 1865. 8vo. 16*s.*

Stubbs (W., D.D.). Seventeen Lectures on the Study of Medieval and Modern History, &c., delivered at Oxford 1867–1884. Demy 8vo. half-bound, 10*s.* 6*d.*

Sturlunga Saga, including the Islendinga Saga of Lawman Sturla Thordsson and other works. Edited by Dr. Gudbrand Vigfússon. In 2 vols. 1878. 8vo. 2*l.* 2*s.*

York Plays. The Plays performed by the Crafts or Mysteries of York on the day of Corpus Christi in the 14th, 15th, and 16th centuries. Now first printed from the unique MS. in the Library of Lord Ashburnham. Edited with Introduction and Glossary by Lucy Toulmin Smith. 8vo. 21*s.*

Statutes made for the University of Oxford, and for the Colleges and Halls therein, by the University of Oxford Commissioners. 1882. 8vo. 12*s.* 6*d.*

Statuta Universitatis Oxoniensis. 1886. 8vo. 5*s.*

The Examination Statutes for the Degrees of B.A., B. Mus., B.C.L., and B.M. Revised to Trinity Term, 1887. 8vo. sewed, 1*s.*

The Student's Handbook to the University and Colleges of Oxford. Extra fcap. 8vo. 2*s.* 6*d.*

The Oxford University Calendar for the year 1887. Crown 8vo. 4*s.* 6*d.*

The present Edition includes all Class Lists and other University distinctions for the seven years ending with 1886.

Also, supplementary to the above, price 5s. (pp. 606),

The Honours Register of the University of Oxford. A complete Record of University Honours, Officers, Distinctions, and Class Lists; of the Heads of Colleges, &c., &c., from the Thirteenth Century to 1883.

· MATHEMATICS, PHYSICAL SCIENCE, &c.

Acland (H. W., M.D., F.R.S.). Synopsis of the Pathological
Series in the Oxford Museum. 1867. 8vo. 2s. 6d.

De Bary (Dr. A.). Comparative Anatomy of the Vegetative
Organs of the Phanerogams and Ferns. Translated and Annotated by F. O.
Bower, M.A., F.L.S., and D. H. Scott, M.A., Ph.D., F.L.S. With 241
woodcuts and an Index. Royal 8vo., half morocco, 1l. 2s. 6d.

Goebel (Dr. K.). Outlines of Classification and Special Mor-
phology of Plants. A New Edition of Sachs' Text-Book of Botany, Book II.
English Translation by H. E. F. Garnsey, M.A. Revised by I. Bayley Balfour,
M.A., M.D., F.R.S. With 407 Woodcuts. Royal 8vo. half morocco, 21s.

Sachs (Julius von). Lectures on the Physiology of Plants.
Translated by H. Marshall Ward, M.A. With 445 Woodcuts. Royal 8vo.
half morocco, 1l. 11s. 6d. *Just Published.*

De Bary (Dr. A). Comparative Morphology and Biology of
the Fungi, Mycetozoa and Bacteria. Authorised English Translation by
Henry E. F. Garnsey, M.A. Revised by Isaac Bayley Balfour, M.A., M.D.,
F.R.S. With 198 Woodcuts. Royal 8vo., half morocco, 1l. 2s. 6d.

Müller (J.). On certain Variations in the Vocal Organs of
the Passeres that have hitherto escaped notice. Translated by F. J. Bell, B.A.,
and edited, with an Appendix, by A. H. Garrod. M.A., F.R.S. With Plates.
1878. 4to. paper covers, 7s. 6d.

Price (Bartholomew, M.A., F.R.S.). Treatise on Infinitesimal
Calculus.

Vol. I. Differential Calculus. Second Edition. 8vo. 14s. 6d.

Vol. II. Integral Calculus, Calculus of Variations, and Differential Equations.
Second Edition, 1865. 8vo. 18s.

Vol. III. Statics, including Attractions; Dynamics of a Material Particle.
Second Edition, 1868. 8vo. 16s.

Vol. IV. Dynamics of Material Systems; together with a chapter on Theoretical Dynamics, by W. F. Donkin, M.A., F.R.S. 1862. 8vo. 16s.

Pritchard (C., D.D., F.R.S.). Uranometria Nova Oxoniensis.
A Photometric determination of the magnitudes of all Stars visible to the naked
eye, from the Pole to ten degrees south of the Equator. 1885. Royal 8vo. 8s. 6d.

—— *Astronomical Observations* made at the University
Observatory, Oxford, under the direction of C. Pritchard, D.D. No. 1.
1878. Royal 8vo. paper covers, 3s. 6d.

Rigaud's Correspondence of Scientific Men of the 17th *Century*,
with Table of Contents by A. de Morgan, and Index by the Rev. J. Rigaud,
M.A. 2 vols. 1841–1862. 8vo. 18s. 6d.

*Rolleston (George, M.D., F.R.S.). Scientific Papers and Ad-
dresses.* Arranged and Edited by William Turner, M.B., F.R.S. With a
Biographical Sketch by Edward Tylor, F.R.S. With Portrait, Plates, and
Woodcuts. 2 vols. 8vo. 1l. 4s.

*Westwood (J. O., M.A., F.R.S.). Thesaurus Entomologicus
Hopeianus,* or a Description of the rarest Insects in the Collection given to
the University by the Rev. William Hope. With 40 Plates. 1874. Small
folio, half morocco, 7l. 10s.

The Sacred Books of the East.

TRANSLATED BY VARIOUS ORIENTAL SCHOLARS, AND EDITED BY
F. MAX MÜLLER.

[Demy 8vo. cloth.]

Vol. I. The Upanishads. Translated by F. Max Müller.
Part I. The *Kh*ândogya-upanishad, The Talavakâra-upanishad, The Aitareya-
âra*n*yaka, The Kaushîtaki-brâhma*n*a-upanishad, and The Vâ*g*asaneyi-sa*m*hitâ-
upanishad. 10s. 6d.

Vol. II. The Sacred Laws of the Âryas, as taught in the
Schools of Âpastamba, Gautama, Vâsish*th*a, and Baudhâyana. Translated by
Prof. Georg Bühler. Part I. Âpastamba and Gautama. 10s. 6d.

Vol. III. The Sacred Books of China. The Texts of Con-
fucianism. Translated by James Legge. Part I. The Shû King, The Reli-
gious portions of the Shih King, and The Hsiâo King. 12s. 6d.

Vol. IV. The Zend-Avesta. Translated by James Darme-
steter. Part I. The Vendîdâd. 10s. 6d.

Vol. V. The Pahlavi Texts. Translated by E. W. West.
Part I. The Bundahi*s*, Bahman Ya*s*t, and Shâyast lâ-shâyast. 12s. 6d.

Vols. VI and IX. The Qur'ân. Parts I and II. Translated
by E. H. Palmer. 21s.

Vol. VII. The Institutes of Vish*n*u. Translated by Julius
Jolly. 10s. 6d.

Vol. VIII. The Bhagavadgîtâ, with The Sanatsugâtîya, and
The Anugîtâ. Translated by Kâshinâth Trimbak Telang. 10s. 6d.

Vol. X. The Dhammapada, translated from Pâli by F. Max
Müller; and The Sutta-Nipâta, translated from Pâli by V. Fausböll; being
Canonical Books of the Buddhists. 10s. 6d.

Vol. XI. Buddhist Suttas. Translated from Pâli by T. W.
Rhys Davids. 1. The Mahâparinibbâna Suttanta ; 2. The Dhamma-kakka-
ppavattana Sutta ; 3. The Tevigga Suttanta; 4. The Akankheyya Sutta ;
5. The Ketokhila Sutta ; 6. The Mahâ-sudassana Suttanta'; 7. The Sabbâsava
Sutta. 10s. 6d.

Vol. XII. The Satapatha-Brâhmana, according to the Text
of the Mâdhyandina School. Translated by Julius Eggeling. Part I.
Books I and II. 12s. 6d.

Vol. XIII. Vinaya Texts. Translated from the Pâli by
T. W. Rhys Davids and Hermann Oldenberg. Part I. The Pâtimokkha.
The Mahâvagga, I–IV. 10s. 6d.

Vol. XIV. The Sacred Laws of the Âryas, as taught in the
Schools of Apastamba, Gautama, Vâsishtha and Baudhâyana. Translated
by Georg Bühler. Part II. Vâsishtha and Baudhâyana. 10s. 6d.

Vol. XV. The Upanishads. Translated by F. Max Müller.
Part II. The Katha-upanishad, The Mundaka-upanishad, The Taittirîyaka-
upanishad, The Brihadâranyaka-upanishad, The Svetasvatara-upanishad, The
Prasna-upanishad, and The Maitrâyana-Brâhmana-upanishad. 10s. 6d.

Vol. XVI. The Sacred Books of China. The Texts of Confucianism. Translated by James Legge. Part II. The Yî King. 10s. 6d.

Vol. XVII. Vinaya Texts. Translated from the Pâli by
T. W. Rhys Davids and Hermann Oldenberg. Part II. The Mahâvagga,
V–X. The Kullavagga, I–III. 10s. 6d.

Vol. XVIII. Pahlavi Texts. Translated by E. W. West.
Part II. The Dâdistân-î Dînîk and The Epistles of Mânûskîhar. 12s. 6d.

Vol. XIX. The Fo-sho-hing-tsan-king. A Life of Buddha
by Asvaghosha Bodhisattva, translated from Sanskrit into Chinese by Dhar-
maraksha, A.D. 420, and from Chinese into English by Samuel Beal. 10s. 6d.

Vol. XX. Vinaya Texts. Translated from the Pâli by T. W.
Rhys Davids and Hermann Oldenberg. Part III. The Kullavagga, IV–XII.
10s. 6d.

Vol. XXI. The Saddharma-pu*nd*arîka; or, the Lotus of the
True Law. Translated by H. Kern. 12*s*. 6*d*.

Vol. XXII. *G*aina-Sûtras. Translated from Prâkrit by Hermann Jacobi. Part I. The Â*k*ârâṅga-Sûtra. The Kalpa-Sûtra. 10*s*. 6*d*.

Vol. XXIII. The Zend-Avesta. Translated by James Dar-
mesteter. Part II. The Sîrôzahs, Ya*s*ts, and Nyâyi*s*. 10*s*. 6*d*.

Vol. XXIV. Pahlavi Texts. Translated by E. W. West.
Part III. Dînâ-î Maînôg-î Khirad, *S*îkand-gûmânîk, and Sad-Dar. 10*s*. 6*d*.

Second Series.

Vol. XXV. Manu. Translated by Georg Bühler. 21*s*.

Vol. XXVI. The *S*atapatha-Brâhma*n*a. Translated by
Julius Eggeling. Part II. 12*s*. 6*d*.

Vols. XXVII and XXVIII. The Sacred Books of China.
The Texts of Confucianism. Translated by James Legge. Parts III and IV.
The Lî *K*î, or Collection of Treatises on the Rules of Propriety, or Ceremonial
Usages. 25*s*.

Vols. XXIX and XXX. The G*r*ihya-Sûtras, Rules of Vedic
Domestic Ceremonies. Translated by Hermann Oldenberg.

Part I (Vol. XXIX), 12*s*. 6*d*. *Just Published.*

Part II (Vol. XXX). *In the Press.*

Vol. XXXI. The Zend-Avesta. Part III. The Yasna,
Visparad, Âfrînagân, and Gâhs. Translated by L. H. Mills. 12*s*. 6*d*.

The following Volumes are in the Press:—

Vol. XXXII. Vedic Hymns. Translated by F. Max Müller.
Part I.

Vol. XXXIII. Nârada, and some Minor Law-books.
Translated by Julius Jolly. [*Preparing.*]

Vol. XXXIV. The Vedânta-Sûtras, with *S*aṅkara's Commentary. Translated by G. Thibaut. [*Preparing.*]

*** *The Second Series will consist of Twenty-Four Volumes.*

𝕮𝖑𝖆𝖗𝖊𝖓𝖉𝖔𝖓 𝕻𝖗𝖊𝖘𝖘 𝕾𝖾𝖗𝖎𝖊𝖘

I. ENGLISH, &c.

A First Reading Book. By Marie Eichens of Berlin ; and
edited by Anne J. Clough. Extra fcap. 8vo. stiff covers, 4*d.*

Oxford Reading Book, Part I. For Little Children. Extra
fcap. 8vo. stiff covers, 6*d.*

Oxford Reading Book, Part II. For Junior Classes. Extra
fcap. 8vo. stiff covers, 6*d.*

An Elementary English Grammar and Exercise Book. By
O. W. Tancock, M.A. Second Edition. Extra fcap. 8vo. 1*s.* 6*d.*

An English Grammar and Reading Book, for Lower Forms
in Classical Schools. By O. W. Tancock, M.A. Fourth Edition. Extra
fcap. 8vo. 3*s.* 6*d.*

Typical Selections from the best English Writers, with Introductory Notices. Second Edition. In 2 vols. Extra fcap. 8vo. 3*s.* 6*d.* each.
  Vol. I. Latimer to Berkeley.   Vol. II. Pope to Macaulay.

Shairp (J. C., LL.D.). Aspects of Poetry; being Lectures
delivered at Oxford. Crown 8vo. 10*s.* 6*d.*

A Book for the Beginner in Anglo-Saxon. By John Earle,
M.A. Third Edition. Extra fcap. 8vo. 2*s.* 6*d.*

An Anglo-Saxon Reader. In Prose and Verse. With Grammatical Introduction, Notes, and Glossary. By Henry Sweet. M.A. Fourth
Edition, Revised and Enlarged. Extra fcap. 8vo. 8*s.* 6*d.*

A Second Anglo-Saxon Reader. By the same Author. Extra
fcap. 8vo. *Nearly ready.*

An Anglo-Saxon Primer, with Grammar, Notes, and Glossary.
By the same Author. Second Edition. Extra fcap. 8vo. 2*s.* 6*d.*

Old English Reading Primers; edited by Henry Sweet, M.A.
  I. Selected Homilies of Ælfric. Extra fcap. 8vo., stiff covers, 1*s.* 6*d.*
  II. Extracts from Alfred's Orosius. Extra fcap. 8vo., stiff covers, 1*s.* 6*d.*

First Middle English Primer, with Grammar and Glossary.
By the same Author. Extra fcap. 8vo. 2*s.*

Second Middle English Primer. Extracts from Chaucer,
with Grammar and Glossary. By the same Author. Extra fcap. 8vo. 2*s.*

Principles of English Etymology. First Series. *The Native
Element.* By W. W. Skeat, Litt.D. Crown 8vo. 9*s.* *Just Published.*

The Philology of the English Tongue. By J. Earle, M.A.
Third Edition. Extra fcap. 8vo. 7s. 6d.

An Icelandic Primer, with Grammar, Notes, and Glossary.
By the same Author. Extra fcap. 8vo. 3s. 6d.

An Icelandic Prose Reader, with Notes, Grammar, and Glossary.
By G. Vigfússon, M.A., and F. York Powell, M.A. Ext. fcap. 8vo. 10s. 6d.

A Handbook of Phonetics, including a Popular Exposition of
the Principles of Spelling Reform. By H. Sweet, M.A. Extra fcap. 8vo. 4s. 6d.

Elementarbuch des Gesprochenen Englisch. Grammatik,
Texte und Glossar. Von Henry Sweet. Extra fcap. 8vo., stiff covers, 2s. 6d.

The Ormulum; with the Notes and Glossary of Dr. R. M.
White. Edited by R. Holt, M.A. 1878. 2 vols. Extra fcap. 8vo. 21s.

Specimens of Early English. A New and Revised Edition.
With Introduction, Notes, and Glossarial Index. By R. Morris, LL.D., and
W. W. Skeat, Litt.D.

    Part I. From Old English Homilies to King Horn (A.D. 1150 to A.D. 1300).
    Second Edition. Extra fcap. 8vo. 9s.

    Part II. From Robert of Gloucester to Gower (A.D. 1298 to A.D. 1393).
    Second Edition. Extra fcap. 8vo. 7s. 6d.

Specimens of English Literature, from the 'Ploughmans
Crede' to the 'Shepheardes Calender' (A.D. 1394 to A.D. 1579). With Introduction, Notes, and Glossarial Index. By W. W. Skeat, Litt.D. Extra fcap.
8vo. 7s. 6d.

The Vision of William concerning Piers the Plowman, in three
Parallel Texts; together with *Richard the Redeless.* By William Langland
.(about 1362–1399 A.D.). Edited from numerous Manuscripts, with Preface,
Notes, and a Glossary, by W. W. Skeat, Litt.D. 2 vols. 8vo. 31s. 6d.

The Vision of William concerning Piers the Plowman, by
William Langland. Edited, with Notes, by W. W. Skeat, Litt.D. Third
Edition. Extra fcap. 8vo. 4s. 6d.

Chaucer. I. *The Prologue to the Canterbury Tales;* the
Knightes Tale; The Nonne Prestes Tale. Edited by R. Morris, Editor of
Specimens of Early English, &c., &c. Extra fcap. 8vo. 2s. 6d.

—— II. *The Prioresses Tale; Sir Thopas;* The Monkes
Tale; The Clerkes Tale; The Squieres Tale, &c. Edited by W. W. Skeat,
Litt.D. Third Edition. Extra fcap. 8vo. 4s. 6d.

—— III. *The Tale of the Man of Lawe;* The Pardoneres
Tale; The Second Nonnes Tale; The Chanouns Yemannes Tale. By the
same Editor. Second Edition. Extra fcap. 8vo. 4s. 6d.

Gamelyn, The Tale of. Edited with Notes, Glossary, &c., by
W. W. Skeat, Litt.D. Extra fcap. 8vo. Stiff covers, 1s. 6d.

Minot (Laurence). Poems. Edited, with Introduction and
Notes, by Joseph Hall, M.A., Head Master of the Hulme Grammar School,
Manchester. Extra fcap. 8vo. 4s. 6d. *Just Published.*

c

Spenser's Faery Queene. Books I and II. Designed chiefly
for the use of Schools. With Introduction, Notes, and Glossary. By G. W.
Kitchin, D.D. Extra fcap. 8vo. 2*s.* 6*d.* each.

Hooker. Ecclesiastical Polity, Book I. Edited by R. W.
Church, M.A. Second Edition. Extra fcap. 8vo. 2*s.*

OLD ENGLISH DRAMA.

The Pilgrimage to Parnassus with *The Two Parts of the
Return from Parnassus.* Three Comedies performed in St. John's College,
Cambridge, A.D. MDXCVII–MDCI. Edited from MSS. by the Rev. W. D.
Macray, M.A., F.S.A. Medium 8vo. Bevelled Boards, Gilt top, 8*s.* 6*d.*

*Marlowe and Greene. Marlowe's Tragical History of Dr.
Faustus,* and *Greene's Honourable History of Friar Bacon and Friar Bungay.*
Edited by A. W. Ward, M.A. *New and Enlarged Edition.* Extra fcap.
8vo. 6*s.* 6*d.*

Marlowe. Edward II. With Introduction, Notes, &c. By
O. W. Tancock, M.A. Extra fcap. 8vo. 3*s.*

SHAKESPEARE.

Shakespeare. Select Plays. Edited by W. G. Clark, M.A.,
and W. Aldis Wright, M.A. Extra fcap. 8vo. stiff covers.

The Merchant of Venice. 1*s.*	Macbeth. 1*s.* 6*d.*
Richard the Second. 1*s.* 6*d.*	Hamlet. 2*s.*

Edited by W. Aldis Wright, M.A.

The Tempest. 1*s.* 6*d.*	Midsummer Night's Dream. 1*s.* 6*d.*
As You Like It. 1*s.* 6*d.*	Coriolanus. 2*s.* 6*d.*
Julius Cæsar. 2*s.*	Henry the Fifth. 2*s.*
Richard the Third. 2*s.* 6*d.*	Twelfth Night. 1*s.* 6*d.*
King Lear. 1*s.* 6*d.*	King John. 1*s.* 6*d.*

Shakespeare as a Dramatic Artist; a popular Illustration of
the Principles of Scientific Criticism. By R. G. Moulton, M.A. Crown 8vo. 5*s.*

Bacon. I. *Advancement of Learning.* Edited by W. Aldis
Wright, M.A. Second Edition. Extra fcap. 8vo. 4*s.* 6*d.*

—— II. *The Essays.* With Introduction and Notes. By
S. H. Reynolds, M.A., late Fellow of Brasenose College. *In Preparation.*

Milton. I. *Areopagitica.* With Introduction and Notes. By
John W. Hales, M.A. Third Edition. Extra fcap. 8vo. 3*s.*

—— II. *Poems.* Edited by R. C. Browne, M.A. 2 vols.
Fifth Edition. Extra fcap. 8vo. 6*s.* 6*d.* Sold separately, Vol. I. 4*s.*; Vol. II. 3*s.*

In paper covers:—

Lycidas, 3*d.*   L'Allegro, 3*d.*   Il Penseroso, 4*d.*   Comus, 6*d.*
Samson Agonistes, 6*d.*

—— III. *Samson Agonistes.* Edited with Introduction and
Notes by John Churton Collins. Extra fcap. 8vo. stiff covers, 1*s.*

Bunyan. I. *The Pilgrim's Progress, Grace Abounding, Rela-*
tion of the Imprisonment of Mr. John Bunyan. Edited, with Biographical
Introduction and Notes, by E. Venables, M.A. 1879. Extra fcap. 8vo. 5s.
In ornamental Parchment, 6s.

—— **II.** *Holy War,* &c. Edited by E. Venables, M.A.
In the Press.

Clarendon. *History of the Rebellion. Book VI.* Edited
by T. Arnold, M.A. Extra fcap. 8vo. 4s. 6d.

Dryden. *Select Poems.* Stanzas on the Death of Oliver
Cromwell; Astræa Redux; Annus Mirabilis; Absalom and Achitophel;
Religio Laici; The Hind and the Panther. Edited by W. D. Christie, M.A.
Second Edition. Extra fcap. 8vo. 3s. 6d.

Locke's *Conduct of the Understanding.* Edited, with Introduction, Notes, &c., by T. Fowler, D.D. Second Edition. Extra fcap. 8vo. 2s.

Addison. *Selections from Papers in the Spectator.* With Notes.
By T. Arnold, M.A. Extra fcap. 8vo. 4s. 6d. In ornamental Parchment, 6s.

Steele. *Selections from the Tatler, Spectator, and Guardian.*
Edited by Austin Dobson. Extra fcap. 8vo. 4s. 6d. In white Parchment, 7s. 6d.

Pope. With Introduction and Notes. By Mark Pattison, B.D.

—— **I.** *Essay on Man.* Extra fcap. 8vo. 1s. 6d.

—— **II.** *Satires and Epistles.* Extra fcap. 8vo. 2s.

Parnell. *The Hermit.* Paper covers, 2d.

Gray. *Selected Poems.* Edited by Edmund Gosse. Extra
fcap. 8vo. Stiff covers, 1s. 6d. In white Parchment, 3s.

—— *Elegy and Ode on Eton College.* Paper covers, 2d.

Goldsmith. *The Deserted Village.* Paper covers, 2d.

Johnson. I. *Rasselas; Lives of Dryden and Pope.* Edited
by Alfred Milnes, M.A. (London). Extra fcap. 8vo. 4s. 6d., or *Lives of*
Dryden and Pope only, stiff covers, 2s. 6d.

—— **II.** *Vanity of Human Wishes.* With Notes, by E. J.
Payne, M.A. Paper covers, 4d.

Boswell's *Life of Johnson. With the Journal of a Tour to*
the Hebrides. Edited, with copious Notes, Appendices, and Index, by G.
Birkbeck Hill, D.C.L., Pembroke College. With Portraits and Facsimiles.
6 vols. Medium 8vo. *Half bound, 3l. 3s. Just Published.*

Cowper. Edited, with Life, Introductions, and Notes, by
H. T. Griffith, B.A.

—— **I.** *The Didactic Poems of* 1782, with Selections from the
Minor Pieces, A.D. 1779–1783. Extra fcap. 8vo. 3s.

—— **II.** *The Task, with Tirocinium,* and Selections from the
Minor Poems, A.D. 1784–1799. Second Edition. Extra fcap. 8vo. 3s.

Burke. Select Works. Edited, with Introduction and Notes, by E. J. Payne, M.A.

—— I. *Thoughts on the Present Discontents; the two Speeches on America* Second Edition. Extra fcap. 8vo. 4*s. 6d.*

—— II. *Reflections on the French Revolution.* Second Edition. Extra fcap. 8vo. 5*s.*

—— III. *Four Letters on the Proposals for Peace with the* Regicide Directory of France. Second Edition. Extra fcap. 8vo. 5*s.*

Keats. Hyperion, Book I. With Notes by W. T. Arnold, B.A. Paper covers, 4*d.*

Byron. Childe Harold. Edited, with Introduction and Notes, by H. F. Tozer, M.A. Extra fcap. 8vo. 3*s. 6d.* In white Parchment, 5*s.*

Scott. Lay of the Last Minstrel. Edited with Preface and Notes by W. Minto. M.A. With Map. Extra fcap. 8vo. Stiff covers, 2*s.* Ornamental Parchment, 3*s. 6d.*

—— *Lay of the Last Minstrel.* Introduction and Canto I, with Preface and Notes, by the same Editor. 6*d.*

II. LATIN.

Rudimenta Latina. Comprising Accidence, and Exercises of a very Elementary Character, for the use of Beginners. By John Barrow Allen, M.A. Extra fcap. 8vo. 2*s.*

An Elementary Latin Grammar. By the same Author. Forty-second Thousand. Extra fcap. 8vo. 2*s. 6d.*

A First Latin Exercise Book. By the same Author. Fourth Edition. Extra fcap. 8vo. 2*s. 6d.*

A Second Latin Exercise Book. By the same Author. Extra fcap. 8vo. 3*s. 6d.*

Reddenda Minora, or Easy Passages, Latin and Greek, for Unseen Translation. For the use of Lower Forms. Composed and selected by C. S. Jerram, M.A. Extra fcap. 8vo. 1*s. 6d.*

Anglice Reddenda, or Easy Extracts, Latin and Greek, for Unseen Translation. By C. S. Jerram, M.A. Third Edition, Revised and Enlarged. Extra fcap. 8vo. 2*s. 6d.*

Anglice Reddenda. Second Series. By the same Author. Extra fcap. 8vo. 3*s. Just Published.*

Passages for Translation into Latin. For the use of Passmen and others. Selected by J. Y. Sargent, M.A. Sixth Edition. Extra fcap. 8vo. 2*s. 6d.*

Exercises in Latin Prose Composition; with Introduction, Notes, and Passages of Graduated Difficulty for Translation into Latin. By G. G. Ramsay, M.A., LL.D. Second Edition. Extra fcap. 8vo. 4*s. 6d.*

Hints and Helps for Latin Elegiacs. By H. Lee-Warner, M.A.
Extra fcap. 8vo. 3s. 6d.

First Latin Reader. By T. J. Nunns, M.A. Third Edition.
Extra fcap. 8vo. 2s.

Caesar. The Commentaries (for Schools). With Notes and
Maps. By Charles E. Moberly, M.A.

> Part I. *The Gallic War.* Second Edition. Extra fcap. 8vo. 4s. 6d.
> Part II. *The Civil War.* Extra fcap. 8vo. 3s. 6d.
> *The Civil War.* Book I. Second Edition. Extra fcap. 8vo. 2s.

Cicero. Speeches against Catilina. By E. A. Upcott, M.A.,
Assistant Master in Wellington College. *In the Press.*

Cicero. Selection of interesting and descriptive passages. With
Notes. By Henry Walford, M.A. In three Parts. Extra fcap. 8vo. 4s. 6d.

> Each Part separately, limp, 1s. 6d.

> Part I. Anecdotes from Grecian and Roman History. Third Edition.
> Part II. Omens and Dreams: Beauties of Nature. Third Edition.
> Part III. Rome's Rule of her Provinces. Third Edition.

Cicero. De Senectute. Edited, with Introduction and Notes,
by L. Huxley, M.A. In one or two Parts. Extra fcap. 8vo. 2s.

Cicero. Selected Letters (for Schools). With Notes. By the
late C. E. Prichard, M.A., and E. R. Bernard, M.A. Second Edition.
Extra fcap. 8vo. 3s.

Cicero. Select Orations (for Schools). In Verrem I. De
Imperio Gn. Pompeii. Pro Archia. Philippica IX. With Introduction and
Notes by J. R. King, M.A. Second Edition. Extra fcap. 8vo. 2s. 6d.

Cornelius Nepos. With Notes. By Oscar Browning, M.A.
Second Edition. Extra fcap. 8vo. 2s. 6d.

Horace. Selected Odes. With Notes for the use of a Fifth
Form. By E. C. Wickham, M.A. In one or two Parts. Extra fcap. 8vo.
cloth, 2s.

Livy. Selections (for Schools). With Notes and Maps. By
H. Lee-Warner, M.A. Extra fcap. 8vo. In Parts, limp, each 1s. 6d.

> Part I. The Caudine Disaster. Part II. Hannibal's Campaign
> in Italy. Part III. The Macedonian War.

Livy. Books V–VII. With Introduction and Notes. By
A. R. Cluer, B.A. Second Edition. Revised by P. E. Matheson, M.A.
(In one or two vols.) Extra fcap. 8vo. 5s.

Livy. Books XXI, XXII, and XXIII. With Introduction
and Notes. By M. T. Tatham, M.A. Extra fcap. 8vo. 4s. 6d.

Ovid. Selections for the use of Schools. With Introductions
and Notes, and an Appendix on the Roman Calendar. By W. Ramsay, M.A.
Edited by G. G. Ramsay, M.A. Third Edition. Extra fcap. 8vo. 5s. 6d.

Ovid. Tristia. Book I. The Text revised, with an Introduction and Notes. By S. G. Owen, B.A. Extra fcap. 8vo. 3*s.* 6*d.*

Plautus. Captivi. Edited by W. M. Lindsay, M.A. Extra
fcap. 8vo. (In one or two Parts). 2*s.* 6*d. Just Published.*

Plautus. The Trinummus. With Notes and Introductions.
(Intended for the Higher Forms of Public Schools.) By C. E. Freeman, M.A.,
and A. Sloman, M.A. Extra fcap. 8vo. 3*s.*

Pliny. Selected Letters (for Schools). With Notes. By the
late C. E. Prichard, M.A., and E. R. Bernard, M.A. Extra fcap. 8vo. 3*s.*

Sallust. With Introduction and Notes. By W. W. Capes,
M.A. Extra fcap. 8vo. 4*s.* 6*d.*

Tacitus. The Annals. Books I–IV. Edited, with Introduc-
tion and Notes (for the use of Schools and Junior Students), by H. Furneaux,
M.A. Extra fcap. 8vo. 5*s.*

Terence. Andria. With Notes and Introductions. By C.
E. Freeman, M.A., and A. Sloman, M.A. Extra fcap. 8vo. 3*s.*

—— *Adelphi.* With Notes and Introductions. (Intended for
the Higher Forms of Public Schools.) By A. Sloman, M.A. Extra fcap.
8vo. 3*s.*

Tibullus and Propertius. Selections. Edited by G. G. Ramsay,
M.A. Extra fcap. 8vo. (In one or two vols.) 6*s.*

Virgil. With Introduction and Notes. By T. L. Papillon,
M.A. Two vols. Crown 8vo. 10*s.* 6*d.* The Text separately, 4*s.* 6*d.*

Virgil. The Eclogues. Edited by C. S. Jerram, M.A. In
two Parts. Crown 8vo. *Nearly ready.*

Avianus, The Fables of. Edited, with Prolegomena, Critical
Apparatus, Commentary, etc. By Robinson Ellis, M.A., LL.D. Demy 8vo.
8*s.* 6*d.*

Catulli Veronensis Liber. Iterum recognovit, apparatum cri-
ticum prolegomena appendices addidit, Robinson Ellis, A.M. 1878. Demy
8vo. 16*s.*

—— *A Commentary on Catullus.* By Robinson Ellis, M.A.
1876. Demy 8vo. 16*s.*

Catulli Veronensis Carmina Selecta, secundum recognitionem
Robinson Ellis, A.M. Extra fcap. 8vo. 3*s.* 6*d.*

Cicero de Oratore. With Introduction and Notes. By A. S.
Wilkins, M.A.
Book I. 1879. 8vo. 6*s.*   Book II. 1881. 8vo. 5*s.*

—— *Philippic Orations.* With Notes. By J. R. King, M.A.
Second Edition. 1879. 8vo. 10*s.* 6*d.*

Cicero. Select Letters. With English Introductions, Notes, and Appendices. By Albert Watson, M.A. Third Edition. Demy 8vo. 18*s*.

—— *Select Letters.* Text. By the same Editor. Second Edition. Extra fcap. 8vo. 4*s*.

—— *pro Cluentio.* With Introduction and Notes. By W. Ramsay, M.A. Edited by G. G. Ramsay, M.A. 2nd Ed. Ext. fcap. 8vo. 3*s*. 6*d*.

Horace. With a Commentary. Volume I. The Odes, Carmen Seculare, and Epodes. By Edward C. Wickham, M.A. Second Edition. 1877. Demy 8vo. 12*s*.

—— A reprint of the above, in a size suitable for the use of Schools. In one or two Parts. Extra fcap. 8vo. 6*s*.

Livy, Book I. With Introduction, Historical Examination, and Notes. By J. R. Seeley, M.A. Second Edition. 1881. 8vo. 6*s*.

Ovid. P. Ovidii Nasonis Ibis. Ex Novis Codicibus edidit, Scholia Vetera Commentarium cum Prolegomenis Appendice Indice addidit, R. Ellis, A.M. 8vo. 10*s*. 6*d*.

Persius. The Satires. With a Translation and Commentary. By John Conington, M.A. Edited by Henry Nettleship, M.A. Second Edition. 1874. 8vo. 7*s*. 6*d*.

Juvenal. XIII Satires. Edited, with Introduction and Notes, by C. H. Pearson, M.A., and Herbert A. Strong, M.A., LL.D., Professor of Latin in Liverpool University College, Victoria University. In two Parts. Crown 8vo. Complete, 6*s*.

Also separately, Part I. Introduction, Text, etc., 3*s*. Part II. Notes, 3*s*. 6*d*.

Tacitus. The Annals. Books I-VI. Edited, with Introduction and Notes, by H. Furneaux, M.A. 8vo. 18*s*.

Nettleship (H., M.A.). Lectures and Essays on Subjects connected with Latin Scholarship and Literature. Crown 8vo. 7*s*. 6*d*.

—— *The Roman Satura:* its original form in connection with its literary development. 8vo. sewed, 1*s*.

—— *Ancient Lives of Vergil.* With an Essay on the Poems of Vergil, in connection with his Life and Times. 8vo. sewed, 2*s*.

Papillon (T. L., M.A.). A Manual of Comparative Philology. Third Edition, Revised and Corrected. 1882. Crown 8vo. 6*s*.

Pinder (North, M.A.). Selections from the less known Latin Poets. 1869. 8vo. 15*s*.

Sellar (W. Y., M.A.). Roman Poets of the Augustan Age. VIRGIL. New Edition. 1883. Crown 8vo. 9*s*.

—— *Roman Poets of the Republic.* New Edition, Revised and Enlarged. 1881. 8vo. 14*s*.

Wordsworth (J., M.A.). Fragments and Specimens of Early Latin. With Introductions and Notes. 1874. 8vo. 18*s*.

III. GREEK.

A Greek Primer, for the use of beginners in that Language. By the Right Rev. Charles Wordsworth, D.C.L. Seventh Edition. Extra fcap. 8vo. 1s. 6d.

Easy Greek Reader. By Evelyn Abbott, M.A. In one or two Parts. Extra fcap. 8vo. 3s.

Graecae Grammaticae Rudimenta in usum Scholarum. Auctore Carolo Wordsworth, D.C.L. Nineteenth Edition, 1882. 12mo. 4s.

A Greek-English Lexicon, abridged from Liddell and Scott's 4to. edition, chiefly for the use of Schools. Twenty-first Edition. 1886. Square 12mo. 7s. 6d.

Greek Verbs, Irregular and Defective; their forms, meaning, and quantity; embracing all the Tenses used by Greek writers, with references to the passages in which they are found. By W. Veitch. Fourth Edition. Crown 8vo. 10s. 6d.

The Elements of Greek Accentuation (for Schools): abridged from his larger work by H. W. Chandler, M.A. Extra fcap. 8vo. 2s. 6d.

A SERIES OF GRADUATED GREEK READERS:—

First Greek Reader. By W. G. Rushbrooke, M.L. Second Edition. Extra fcap. 8vo. 2s. 6d.

Second Greek Reader. By A. M. Bell, M.A. Extra fcap. 8vo. 3s. 6d.

Fourth Greek Reader; being Specimens of Greek Dialects. With Introductions, etc. By W. W. Merry, D.D. Extra fcap. 8vo. 4s. 6d.

Fifth Greek Reader. Selections from Greek Epic and Dramatic Poetry, with Introductions and Notes. By Evelyn Abbott, M.A. Extra fcap. 8vo. 4s. 6d.

The Golden Treasury of Ancient Greek Poetry: being a Collection of the finest passages in the Greek Classic Poets, with Introductory Notices and Notes. By R. S. Wright. M.A. Extra fcap. 8vo. 8s. 6d.

A Golden Treasury of Greek Prose, being a Collection of the finest passages in the principal Greek Prose Writers, with Introductory Notices and Notes. By R. S. Wright, M.A., and J. E. L. Shadwell, M.A. Extra fcap. 8vo. 4s. 6d.

Aeschylus. Prometheus Bound (for Schools). With Introduction and Notes, by A. O. Prickard, M.A. Second Edition. Extra fcap. 8vo. 2s.

—— *Agamemnon.* With Introduction and Notes, by Arthur Sidgwick, M.A. Second Edition. Extra fcap. 8vo. 3s.

—— *Choephoroi.* With Introduction and Notes by the same Editor. Extra fcap. 8vo. 3s.

Aristophanes. In Single Plays. Edited, with English Notes,
Introductions, &c., by W. W. Merry, M.A. Extra fcap. 8vo.

I. The Clouds, Second Edition, 2*s*.

II. The Acharnians, Third Edition. In one or two parts, 3*s*.

III. The Frogs, Second Edition. In one or two parts, 3*s*.

Cebes. Tabula. With Introduction and Notes. By C. S.
Jerram, M.A. Extra fcap. 8vo. 2*s*. 6*d*.

Demosthenes. Olynthiacs and Philippics. Edited by Evelyn
Abbott, M.A. Extra fcap. 8vo. In two Parts. *In the Press.*

Euripides. Alcestis (for Schools). By C. S. Jerram, M.A.
Extra fcap. 8vo. 2*s*. 6*d*.

—— *Helena.* Edited, with Introduction, Notes, etc., for
Upper and Middle Forms. By C. S. Jerram, M.A. Extra fcap. 8vo. 3*s*.

—— *Iphigenia in Tauris.* Edited, with Introduction, Notes,
etc., for Upper and Middle Forms. By C. S. Jerram, M.A. Extra fcap. 8vo.
cloth, 3*s*.

—— *Medea.* By C. B. Heberden, M.A. In one or two Parts.
Extra fcap. 8vo. 2*s*.

Herodotus, Selections from. Edited, with Introduction, Notes,
and a Map, by W. W. Merry, D.D. Extra fcap. 8vo. 2*s*. 6*d*.

Homer. Odyssey, Books I–XII (for Schools). By W. W.
Merry, D.D. Thirty-second Thousand. Extra fcap. 8vo. 4*s*. 6*d*.

Book II, separately, 1*s*. 6*d*.

—— *Odyssey,* Books XIII–XXIV (for Schools). By the
same Editor. Second Edition. Extra fcap. 8vo. 5*s*.

—— *Iliad,* Book I (for Schools). By D. B. Monro, M.A.
Second Edition. Extra fcap. 8vo. 2*s*.

—— *Iliad,* Books I–XII (for Schools). With an Introduction,
a brief Homeric Grammar, and Notes. By D. B. Monro, M.A. Second
Edition. Extra fcap. 8vo. 6*s*.

—— *Iliad,* Books VI and XXI. With Introduction and
Notes. By Herbert Hailstone, M.A. Extra fcap. 8vo. 1*s*. 6*d*. each.

Lucian. Vera Historia (for Schools). By C. S. Jerram,
M.A. Second Edition. Extra fcap. 8vo. 1*s*. 6*d*.

Plato. Meno. With Introduction and Notes. By St. George
Stock, M.A., Pembroke College. Extra fcap. 8vo. (In one or two Parts.)
2*s*. 6*d*. *Just Published.*

Plato. Selections from the Dialogues [including the whole of
the *Apology* and *Crito*]. With Introduction and Notes by John Purves, M.A.,
and a Preface by the Rev. B. Jowett, M.A. Extra fcap. 8vo. 6*s*. 6*d*.

C 3

Sophocles. For the use of Schools. Edited with Introductions and English Notes By Lewis Campbell, M.A., and Evelyn Abbott, M.A. *New and Revised Edition.* 2 Vols. Extra fcap. 8vo. 10s. 6d.

    Sold separately, Vol. I, Text, 4s. 6d.; Vol. II, Explanatory Notes, 6s.

Sophocles. In Single Plays, with English Notes, &c. By Lewis Campbell, M.A., and Evelyn Abbott, M.A. Extra fcap. 8vo. limp.

    Oedipus Tyrannus, Philoctetes. New and Revised Edition, 2s. each.

    Oedipus Coloneus,   Antigone, 1s. 9d. each.

    Ajax,   Electra,   Trachiniae, 2s. each.

—— *Oedipus Rex:* Dindorf's Text, with Notes by the present Bishop of St. David's. Extra fcap. 8vo. limp, 1s. 6d.

Theocritus (for Schools). With Notes. By H. Kynaston, D.D. (late Snow). Third Edition. Extra fcap. 8vo. 4s. 6d.

Xenophon. Easy Selections (for Junior Classes). With a Vocabulary, Notes, and Map. By J. S. Phillpotts, B.C.L., and C. S. Jerram, M.A. Third Edition. Extra fcap. 8vo. 3s. 6d.

—— *Selections* (for Schools). With Notes and Maps. By J. S. Phillpotts. B.C.L. Fourth Edition. Extra fcap. 8vo. 3s. 6d.

—— *Anabasis,* Book I. Edited for the use of Junior Classes and Private Students. With Introduction, Notes, etc. By J. Marshall, M.A., Rector of the Royal High School, Edinburgh. Extra fcap. 8vo. 2s. 6d.

—— *Anabasis,* Book II. With Notes and Map. By C. S. Jerram, M.A. Extra fcap. 8vo. 2s.

—— *Cyropaedia,* Books IV and V. With Introduction and Notes by C. Bigg, D.D. Extra fcap. 8vo. 2s. 6d.

Aristotle's Politics. By W. L. Newman, M.A. [*In the Press.*]

Aristotelian Studies. I. On the Structure of the Seventh Book of the Nicomachean Ethics. By J.C. Wilson, M.A. 8vo. stiff, 5s.

Aristotelis Ethica Nicomachea, ex recensione Immanuelis Bekkeri. Crown 8vo. 5s.

Demosthenes and Aeschines. The Orations of Demosthenes and Æschines on the Crown. With Introductory Essays and Notes. By G. A. Simcox, M.A., and W. H. Simcox, M.A. 1872. 8vo. 12s.

Head (Barclay V.). Historia Numorum: A Manual of Greek Numismatics. Royal 8vo. half-bound. 2l. 2s.

Hicks (E. L., M.A.). A Manual of Greek Historical Inscriptions. Demy 8vo. 10s. 6d.

Homer. *Odyssey,* Books I–XII. Edited with English Notes, Appendices, etc. By W. W. Merry, D.D., and the late James Riddell, M.A. 1886. Second Edition. Demy 8vo. 16s.

Homer. *A Grammar of the Homeric Dialect.* By D. B. Monro, M.A. Demy 8vo. 10s. 6d.

Sophocles. The Plays and Fragments. With English Notes and Introductions, by Lewis Campbell, M.A. 2 vols.

Vol. I. Oedipus Tyrannus. Oedipus Coloneus. Antigone. 8vo. 16s.

Vol. II. Ajax. Electra. Trachiniae. Philoctetes. Fragments. 8vo. 16s.

IV. FRENCH AND ITALIAN.

Brachet's Etymological Dictionary of the French Language, with a Preface on the Principles of French Etymology. Translated into English by G. W. Kitchin, D.D. Third Edition. Crown 8vo. 7s. 6d.

—— *Historical Grammar of the French Language.* Translated into English by G. W. Kitchin, D.D. Fourth Edition. Extra fcap. 8vo. 3s. 6d.

Works by GEORGE SAINTSBURY, M.A.

Primer of French Literature. Extra fcap. 8vo. 2s.

Short History of French Literature. Crown 8vo. 10s. 6d.

Specimens of French Literature, from Villon to Hugo. Crown 8vo. 9s.

MASTERPIECES OF THE FRENCH DRAMA.

Corneille's Horace. Edited, with Introduction and Notes, by George Saintsbury, M.A. Extra fcap. 8vo. 2s. 6d.

Molière's Les Précieuses Ridicules. Edited, with Introduction and Notes, by Andrew Lang, M.A. Extra fcap. 8vo. 1s. 6d.

Racine's Esther. Edited, with Introduction and Notes, by George Saintsbury, M.A. Extra fcap. 8vo. 2s.

Beaumarchais' Le Barbier de Séville. Edited, with Introduction and Notes, by Austin Dobson. Extra fcap. 8vo. 2s. 6d.

Voltaire's Mérope. Edited, with Introduction and Notes, by George Saintsbury. Extra fcap. 8vo. cloth, 2s.

Musset's On ne badine pas avec l'Amour, and *Fantasio.* Edited, with Prolegomena, Notes, etc., by Walter Herries Pollock. Extra fcap. 8vo. 2s.

The above six Plays may be had in ornamental case, and bound in Imitation Parchment, price 12s. 6d.

Sainte-Beuve. Selections from the Causeries du Lundi. Edited
by George Saintsbury. Extra fcap. 8vo. 2s.

Quinet's Lettres à sa Mère. Selected and edited by George
Saintsbury. Extra fcap. 8vo. 2s.

Gautier, Théophile. Scenes of Travel. Selected and Edited
by George Saintsbury. Extra fcap. 8vo. 2s.

L'Éloquence de la Chaire et de la Tribune Françaises. Edited
by Paul Blouët, B.A. (Univ. Gallic.). Vol. I. French Sacred Oratory.
Extra fcap. 8vo. 2s. 6d.

Edited by GUSTAVE MASSON, B.A.

Corneille's Cinna. With Notes, Glossary, etc. Extra fcap. 8vo.
cloth, 2s. Stiff covers, 1s. 6d.

Louis XIV, and his Contemporaries; as described in Extracts
from the best Memoirs of the Seventeenth Century. With English Notes,
Genealogical Tables, &c. Extra fcap. 8vo. 2s. 6d.

Maistre, Xavier de. Voyage autour de ma Chambre. Ourika,
by *Madame de Duras;* Le Vieux Tailleur, by *MM. Erckmann-Chatrian;*
La Veillée de Vincennes, by *Alfred de Vigny;* Les Jumeaux de l'Hôtel
Corneille, by *Edmond About;* Mésaventures d'un Écolier, by *Rodolphe Töpffer.*
Third Edition, Revised and Corrected. Extra fcap. 8vo. 2s. 6d.

Molière's Les Fourberies de Scapin, and *Racine's Athalie.*
With Voltaire's Life of Molière. Extra fcap. 8vo. 2s. 6d.

Molière's Les Fourberies de Scapin. With Voltaire's Life of
Molière. Extra fcap. 8vo. stiff covers, 1s. 6d.

Molière's Les Femmes Savantes. With Notes, Glossary, etc.
Extra fcap. 8vo. *cloth,* 2s. Stiff covers, 1s. 6d.

Racine's Andromaque, and *Corneille's Le Menteur.* With
Louis Racine's Life of his Father. Extra fcap. 8vo. 2s. 6d.

Regnard's Le Joueur, and *Brueys and Palaprat's Le Grondeur.*
Extra fcap. 8vo. 2s. 6d.

*Sévigné, Madame de, and her chief Contemporaries, Selections
from the Correspondence of.* Intended more especially for Girls' Schools.
Extra fcap. 8vo. 3s.

_____

Dante. Selections from the Inferno. With Introduction and
Notes. By H. B. Cotterill, B.A. Extra fcap. 8vo. 4s. 6d.

Tasso. La Gerusalemme Liberata. Cantos i, ii. With Introduction and Notes. By the same Editor. Extra fcap. 8vo. 2s. 6d.

V. GERMAN.

Scherer (*W.*). *A History of German Literature.* Translated
from the Third German Edition by Mrs. F. Conybeare. Edited by F. Max
Müller. 2 vols. 8vo. 21*s.*

Max Müller. The German Classics, from the Fourth to the
Nineteenth Century. With Biographical Notices, Translations into Modern
German, and Notes. By F. Max Müller, M.A. A New Edition, Revised,
Enlarged, and Adapted to Wilhelm Scherer's 'History of German Literature,'
by F. Lichtenstein. 2 vols. crown 8vo. 21*s.*

GERMAN COURSE. By HERMANN LANGE.

The Germans at Home; a Practical Introduction to German
Conversation, with an Appendix containing the Essentials of German Grammar.
Third Edition. 8vo. 2*s.* 6*d.*

The German Manual; a German Grammar, Reading Book,
and a Handbook of German Conversation. 8vo. 7*s.* 6*d.*

Grammar of the German Language. 8vo. 3*s.* 6*d.*

German Composition; A Theoretical and Practical Guide to
the Art of Translating English Prose into German. 8vo. 4*s.* 6*d.*

German Spelling; A Synopsis of the Changes which it has
undergone through the Government Regulations of 1880. Paper covers, 6*d.*

Lessing's Laokoon. With Introduction, English Notes, etc.
By A. Hamann, Phil. Doc., M.A. Extra fcap. 8vo. 4*s.* 6*d.*

Schiller's Wilhelm Tell. Translated into English Verse by
E. Massie, M.A. Extra fcap. 8vo. 5*s.*

Also, Edited by C. A. BUCHHEIM, Phil. Doc.

Becker's Friedrich der Grosse. Extra fcap. 8vo. *In the Press.*

Goethe's Egmont. With a Life of Goethe, &c. Third Edition.
. Extra fcap. 8vo. 3*s.*

—— *Iphigenie auf Tauris.* A Drama. With a Critical Introduction and Notes. Second Edition. Extra fcap. 8vo. 3*s.*

Heine's Prosa, being Selections from his Prose Works. With
English Notes, etc. Extra fcap. 8vo. 4*s.* 6*d.*

Heine's Harzreise. With Life of Heine, Descriptive Sketch
of the Harz, and Index. Extra fcap. 8vo. paper covers, 1*s.* 6*d.*; cloth, 2*s.* 6*d.*

Lessing's Minna von Barnhelm. A Comedy. With a Life
of Lessing,. Critical Analysis, etc. Extra fcap. 8vo. 3*s.* 6*d.*

—— *Nathan der Weise.* With Introduction, Notes, etc.
Extra fcap. 8vo. 4*s.* 6*d.*

Schiller's Historische Skizzen; Egmont's Leben und Tod, and
Belagerung von Antwerpen. With a Map. Extra fcap. 8vo. 2s. 6d.

—— *Wilhelm Tell.* With a Life of Schiller; an his-
torical and critical Introduction, Arguments, and a complete Commentary,
and Map. Sixth Edition. Extra fcap. 8vo. 3s. 6d.

—— *Wilhelm Tell.* School Edition. With Map. 2s.

Modern German Reader. A Graduated Collection of Ex-
tracts in Prose and Poetry from Modern German writers:—
Part I. With English Notes, a Grammatical Appendix, and a complete
Vocabulary. Fourth Edition. Extra fcap. 8vo. 2s. 6d.
Part II. With English Notes and an Index. Extra fcap. 8vo. 2s. 6d.

Niebuhr's Griechische Heroen-Geschichten. Tales of Greek
Heroes. Edited with English Notes and a Vocabulary, by Emma S. Buchheim.
School Edition. Extra fcap. 8vo., *cloth,* 2s. *Stiff covers,* 1s. 6d.

VI. MATHEMATICS, PHYSICAL SCIENCE, &c.

By LEWIS HENSLEY, M.A.

Figures made Easy: a first Arithmetic Book. Crown 8vo. 6d.

Answers to the Examples in Figures made Easy, together
with two thousand additional Examples, with Answers. Crown 8vo. 1s.

The Scholar's Arithmetic. Crown 8vo. 2s. 6d.

Answers to the Examples in the Scholar's Arithmetic. Crown
8vo. 1s. 6d.

The Scholar's Algebra. Crown 8vo. 2s. 6d.

Aldis (W. S., M.A.). A Text-Book of Algebra. Crown 8vo.
Nearly ready.

Baynes (R. E., M.A.). Lessons on Thermodynamics. 1878.
Crown 8vo. 7s. 6d.

*Chambers (G. F., F.R.A.S.). A Handbook of Descriptive
Astronomy.* Third Edition. 1877. Demy 8vo. 28s.

Clarke (Col. A. R., C.B., R.E.). Geodesy. 1880. 8vo. 12s. 6d.

Cremona (Luigi). Elements of Projective Geometry. Translated by C. Leudesdorf, M.A. 8vo. 12s. 6d.

Donkin. Acoustics. Second Edition. Crown 8vo. 7s. 6d.

Euclid Revised. Containing the Essentials of the Elements
of Plane Geometry as given by Euclid in his first Six Books. Edited by
R. C. J. Nixon, M.A. Crown 8vo. 7s. 6d.

Sold separately as follows,

Books I–IV. 3s. 6d. Books I, II. 1s. 6d.
Book I. 1s.

Galton (Douglas, C.B., F.R.S.). The Construction of Healthy
Dwellings. Demy 8vo. 10s. 6d.

Hamilton (Sir R. G. C.), and J. Ball. Book-keeping. New
and enlarged Edition. Extra fcap. 8vo. limp cloth, 2s.
Ruled Exercise books adapted to the above may be had, price 2s.

Harcourt (A. G. Vernon, M.A.), and *H. G. Madan, M.A.*
Exercises in Practical Chemistry. Vol. I. Elementary Exercises. Fourth
Edition. Crown 8vo. 10s. 6d.

Maclaren (Archibald). A System of Physical Education :
Theoretical and Practical. Extra fcap. 8vo. 7s. 6d.

Madan (H. G., M.A.). Tables of Qualitative Analysis.
Large 4to. paper, 4s. 6d.

Maxwell (J. Clerk, M.A., F.R.S.). A Treatise on Electricity
and Magnetism. Second Edition. 2 vols. Demy 8vo. 1l. 11s. 6d.

—— *An Elementary Treatise on Electricity.* Edited by
William Garnett, M.A. Demy 8vo. 7s. 6d.

Minchin (G. M., M.A.). A Treatise on Statics with Applications to Physics. Third Edition, Corrected and Enlarged. Vol. I. *Equili-
brium of Coplanar Forces.* 8vo. 9s. Vol. II. *Statics.* 8vo. 16s.

—— *Uniplanar Kinematics of Solids and Fluids.* Crown
8vo. 7s. 6d.

Phillips (John, M.A., F.R.S.). Geology of Oxford and the
Valley of the Thames. 1871. 8vo. 21s.

—— *Vesuvius.* 1869. Crown 8vo. 10s. 6d.

Prestwich (Joseph, M.A., F.R.S.). Geology, Chemical, Physical,
and Stratigraphical. Vol. I. Chemical and Physical. Royal 8vo. 25s.

Roach (T., M.A.). Elementary Trigonometry. Crown 8vo.
4s. 6d. Just Published.

Rolleston's Forms of Animal Life. Illustrated by Descriptions
and Drawings of Dissections. New Edition. (*Nearly ready.*)

Smyth. A Cycle of Celestial Objects. Observed, Reduced,
and Discussed by Admiral W. H. Smyth, R.N. Revised, condensed, and
greatly enlarged by G. F. Chambers, F.R.A.S. 1881. 8vo. *Price reduced
to 12s.*

Stewart (Balfour, LL.D., F.R.S.). A Treatise on Heat, with
numerous Woodcuts and Diagrams. Fourth Edition. Extra fcap. 8vo.
7s. 6d.

Vernon-Harcourt (L. F., M.A.).   A Treatise on Rivers and
Canals, relating to the Control and Improvement of Rivers, and the Design,
Construction, and Development of Canals.   2 vols. (Vol. I, Text.   Vol. II,
Plates.) 8vo. 21s.

—— *Harbours and Docks;* their Physical Features, History,
Construction, Equipment, and Maintenance; with Statistics as to their Commercial Development.   2 vols. 8vo. 25s.

Watson (H. W., M.A.).   A Treatise on the Kinetic Theory
of Gases. 1876. 8vo. 3s. 6d.

Watson (H. W., D. Sc., F.R.S.), and S. H. Burbury, M.A.
I. *A Treatise on the Application of Generalised Coordinates to the Kinetics of*
a Material System. 1879. 8vo. 6s.
II. *The Mathematical Theory of Electricity and Magnetism.* Vol. I. Electro-
statics. 8vo. 10s. 6d.

Williamson (A. W., Phil. Doc., F.R.S.).   Chemistry for
Students. A new Edition, with Solutions. 1873. Extra fcap. 8vo. 8s. 6d.

VII. HISTORY.

Bluntschli (J. K.).   The Theory of the State.   By J. K.
Bluntschli, late Professor of Political Sciences in the University of Heidel-
berg.   Authorised English Translation from the Sixth German Edition.
Demy 8vo. half bound, 12s. 6d.

Finlay (George, LL.D.).   A History of Greece from its Conquest by the Romans to the present time, B.C. 146 to A.D. 1864.   A new
Edition, revised throughout, and in part re-written, with considerable additions, by the Author, and edited by H. F. Tozer, M.A. 7 vols. 8vo. 3l. 10s.

Fortescue (Sir John, Kt.).   The Governance of England:
otherwise called The Difference between an Absolute and a Limited Mon-
archy.   A Revised Text.   Edited, with Introduction, Notes, and Appendices,
by Charles Plummer, M.A. 8vo. half bound, 12s. 6d.

Freeman (E.A., D.C.L.).   A Short History of the Norman
Conquest of England.   Second Edition.   Extra fcap. 8vo. 2s. 6d.

George (H. B., M.A.). Genealogical Tables illustrative of Modern
History.   Third Edition, Revised and Enlarged.   Small 4to. 12s.

Hodgkin (T.).   Italy and her Invaders.   Illustrated with
Plates and Maps. Vols. I—IV., A.D. 376–553. 8vo. 3l. 8s.

Kitchin (G. W., D.D.).   A History of France.   With numerous
Maps, Plans, and Tables.   In Three Volumes.   *Second Edition.*   Crown 8vo.
each 10s. 6d.

    Vol. I. Down to the Year 1453.
    Vol. II. From 1453–1624.   Vol. III. From 1624–1793.

Payne (E. J., M.A.). A History of the United States of *America.* In the Press.

Ranke (L. von). A History of England, principally in the Seventeenth Century. Translated by Resident Members of the University of Oxford, under the superintendence of G. W. Kitchin, D.D., and C. W. Boase, M.A. 1875. 6 vols. 8vo. 3*l.* 3*s.*

Rawlinson (George, M.A.). A Manual of Ancient History. Second Edition. Demy 8vo. 14*s.*

Rogers (J. E. Thorold, M.A.). The First Nine Years of the *Bank of England.* 8vo. 8*s.* 6*d.*

Select Charters and other Illustrations of English Constitutional History, from the Earliest Times to the Reign of Edward I. Arranged and edited by W. Stubbs, D.D. Fifth Edition. 1883. Crown 8vo. 8*s.* 6*d.*

Stubbs (W., D.D.). The Constitutional History of England, in its Origin and Development. Library Edition. 3 vols. demy 8vo. 2*l.* 8*s.*

Also in 3 vols. crown 8vo. price 12*s.* each.

—— *Seventeen Lectures on the Study of Medieval and Modern History,* &c., delivered at Oxford 1867-1884. Demy 8vo. half-bound, 10*s.* 6*d.*

Wellesley. A Selection from the Despatches, Treaties, and other Papers of the Marquess Wellesley, K.G., during his Government of India. Edited by S. J. Owen, M.A. 1877. 8vo. 1*l.* 4*s.*

Wellington. A Selection from the Despatches, Treaties, and other Papers relating to India of Field-Marshal the Duke of Wellington, K.G. Edited by S. J. Owen, M.A. 1880. 8vo. 24*s.*

A History of British India. By S. J. Owen, M.A., Reader in Indian History in the University of Oxford. In preparation.

VIII. LAW.

Alberici Gentilis, I.C.D., I.C., De Iure Belli Libri Tres. Edidit T. E. Holland, I.C.D. 1877. Small 4to. half morocco, 21*s.*

Anson (Sir William R., Bart., D.C.L.). Principles of the *English Law of Contract, and of Agency in its Relation to Contract.* Fourth Edition. Demy 8vo. 10*s.* 6*d.*

—— *Law and Custom of the Constitution.* Part I. Parlia-. ment. Demy 8vo. 10*s.* 6*d.*

Bentham (Jeremy). An Introduction to the Principles of *Morals and Legislation.* Crown 8vo. 6*s.* 6*d.*

Digby (Kenelm E., M.A.). An Introduction to the History of *the Law of Real Property.* Third Edition. Demy 8vo. 10*s.* 6*d.*

Gaii Institutionum Juris Civilis Commentarii Quattuor; or, Elements of Roman Law by Gaius. With a Translation and Commentary by Edward Poste, M.A. Second Edition. 1875. 8vo. 18*s.*

Hall (*W. E., M.A.*). *International Law.* Second Ed. 8vo. 21*s.*

Holland (*T. E., D.C.L.*). *The Elements of Jurisprudence.* Third Edition. Demy 8vo. 10*s.* 6*d.*

—— *The European Concert in the Eastern Question*, a Collection of Treaties and other Public Acts. Edited, with Introductions and Notes, by Thomas Erskine Holland, D.C.L. 8vo. 12*s.* 6*d.*

Imperatoris Iustiniani Institutionum Libri Quattuor ; with Introductions, Commentary, Excursus and Translation. By J. B. Moyle, B.C.L., M.A. 2 vols. Demy 8vo. 21*s.*

Justinian, The Institutes of, edited as a recension of the Institutes of Gaius, by Thomas Erskine Holland, D.C.L. Second Edition, 1881. Extra fcap. 8vo. 5*s.*

Justinian, Select Titles from the Digest of. By T. E. Holland, D.C.L., and C. L. Shadwell, B.C.L. 8vo. 14*s.*

Also sold in Parts, in paper covers, as follows :—

Part I. Introductory Titles. 2*s.* 6*d.*   Part II. Family Law.   1*s.*
Part III. Property Law.   2*s.* 6*d.*   Part IV. Law of Obligations (No. 1).   3*s.* 6*d.*
Part IV. Law of Obligations (No. 2).   4*s.* 6*d.*

Lex Aquilia. The Roman Law of Damage to Property : being a Commentary on the Title of the Digest ' Ad Legem Aquiliam ' (ix. 2). With an Introduction to the Study of the Corpus Iuris Civilis. By Erwin Grueber, Dr. Jur., M.A. Demy 8vo. 10*s.* 6*d.*

Markby (*W., D.C.L.*). *Elements of Law* considered with reference to Principles of General Jurisprudence. Third Edition. Demy 8vo. 12*s.*6*d.*

Stokes (*Whitley, D.C.L.*). The Anglo-Indian Codes.
Vol. I. *Substantive Law.* 8vo. 30*s.* *Just Published.*
Vol. II. *Adjective Law.* In the Press.

Twiss (*Sir Travers, D.C.L.*). The Law of Nations considered as Independent Political Communities.
Part I. On the Rights and Duties of Nations in time of Peace. A new Edition, Revised and Enlarged. 1884. Demy 8vo. 15*s.*
Part II. On the Rights and Duties of Nations in Time of War. Second Edition, Revised. 1875. Demy 8vo. 21*s.*

IX. MENTAL AND MORAL PHILOSOPHY, &c.

Bacon's Novum Organum. Edited, with English Notes, by G. W. Kitchin, D.D. 1855. 8vo. 9*s.* 6*d.*

—— Translated by G. W. Kitchin, D.D. 1855. 8vo. 9*s.* 6*d.*

Berkeley. The Works of George Berkeley, D.D., formerly Bishop of Cloyne ; including many of his writings hitherto unpublished. With Prefaces, Annotations, and an Account of his Life and Philosophy, by Alexander Campbell Fraser, M.A. 4 vols. 1871. 8vo. 2*l.* 18*s.*
The Life, Letters, &c. 1 vol. 16*s.*

Berkeley. Selections from. With an Introduction and Notes.
For the use of Students in the Universities. By Alexander Campbell Fraser,
LL.D. Second Edition. Crown 8vo. 7*s.* 6*d.*

Fowler (T., D.D.). The Elements of Deductive Logic, designed
mainly for the use of Junior Students in the Universities. Eighth Edition,
with a Collection of Examples. Extra fcap. 8vo. 3*s.* 6*d.*

—— *The Elements of Inductive Logic,* designed mainly for
the use of Students in the Universities. Fourth Edition. Extra fcap. 8vo. 6*s.*

—— *and Wilson (J. M., B.D.). The Principles of Morals*
(Introductory Chapters). 8vo. *boards,* 3*s.* 6*d.*

—— *The Principles of Morals.* Part II. (Being the Body
of the Work.) 8vo. 10*s.* 6*d.*

Edited by T. FOWLER, D.D.

Bacon. Novum Organum. With Introduction, Notes, &c.
1878. 8vo. 14*s.*

Locke's Conduct of the Understanding. Second Edition.
Extra fcap. 8vo. 2*s.*

Danson (J. T.). The Wealth of Households. Crown 8vo. 5*s.*

Green (T. H., M.A.). Prolegomena to Ethics. Edited by
A. C. Bradley, M.A. Demy 8vo. 12*s.* 6*d.*

Hegel. The Logic of Hegel; translated from the Encyclo-
paedia of the Philosophical Sciences. With Prolegomena by William
Wallace, M.A. 1874. 8vo. 14*s.*

Lotze's Logic, in Three Books; of Thought, of Investigation,
and of Knowledge. English Translation; Edited by B. Bosanquet, M.A..
Fellow of University College, Oxford. 8vo. *cloth,* 12*s.* 6*d.*

—— *Metaphysic,* in Three Books; Ontology, Cosmology,
and Psychology. English Translation; Edited by B. Bosanquet, M.A.
8vo. *cloth,* 12*s.* 6*d.*

Martineau (James, D.D.). Types of Ethical Theory. Second
Edition. 2 vols. Crown 8vo. 15*s.*

Rogers (J. E. Thorold, M.A.). A Manual of Political Economy,
for the use of Schools. Third Edition. Extra fcap. 8vo. 4*s.* 6*d.*

Smith's Wealth of Nations. A new Edition, with Notes, by
J. E. Thorold Rogers, M.A. 2 vols. 8vo. 1880. 21*s.*

X. FINE ART.

Butler (A. J., M.A., F.S.A.)   The Ancient Coptic Churches of
Egypt. 2 vols. 8vo. 30s.

Head (Barclay V.). Historia Numorum. A Manual of Greek
Numismatics. Royal 8vo. *half morocco*, 42s.

Hullah (John). The Cultivation of the Speaking Voice.
Second Edition. Extra fcap. 8vo. 2s. 6d.

Jackson (T. G., M.A.). Dalmatia, the Quarnero and Istria;
with Cettigne in Montenegro and the Island of Grado. By T. G. Jackson,
M.A., Author of 'Modern Gothic Architecture.' In 3 vols. 8vo. With many
Plates and Illustrations. *Half bound*, 42s.

Ouseley (Sir F. A. Gore, Bart.).   A Treatise on Harmony.
Third Edition. 4to. 10s.

—— *A Treatise on Counterpoint, Canon, and Fugue*, based
upon that of Cherubini. Second Edition. 4to. 16s.

—— *A Treatise on Musical Form and General Composition.*
Second Edition. 4to. 10s.

Robinson (J. C., F.S.A.). A Critical Account of the Drawings
by Michel Angelo and Raffaello in the University Galleries, Oxford. 1870.
Crown 8vo. 4s.

Troutbeck (J., M.A.) and R. F. Dale, M.A.   A Music Primer
(for Schools). Second Edition. Crown 8vo. 1s. 6d.

Tyrwhitt (R. St. J., M.A.).   A Handbook of Pictorial Art.
With coloured Illustrations, Photographs, and a chapter on Perspective by
A. Macdonald. Second Edition. 1875. 8vo. half morocco, 18s.

Upcott (L. E., M.A.).   An Introduction to Greek Sculpture.
Crown 8vo. 4s. 6d.

—— + ——

LONDON: HENRY FROWDE,

Oxford University Press Warehouse, Amen Corner,

OXFORD: CLARENDON PRESS DEPOSITORY,
116 High Street.

☞ *The* Delegates of the Press *invite suggestions and advice from all persons
interested in education; and will be thankful for hints, &c. addressed to the*
Secretary to the Delegates, *Clarendon Press, Oxford.*

www.ingramcontent.com/pod-product-compliance
Lightning Source LLC
Chambersburg PA
CBHW020923120726
47905CB00008B/2354